Make the Dream Real

World-Building Performance by El Vez, The Mexican Elvis

Karen Jean Martinson

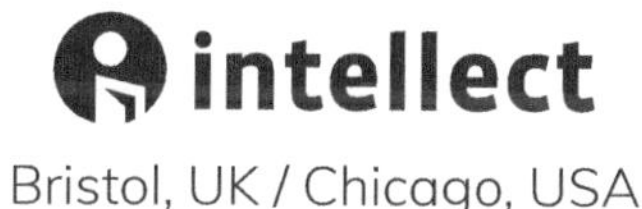

First published in the UK in 2025 by
Intellect, The Mill, Parnall Road, Fishponds, Bristol, BS16 3JG, UK

First published in the USA in 2025 by
Intellect, The University of Chicago Press, 1427 E. 60th Street,
Chicago, IL 60637, USA

A catalogue record for this book is available from the British Library.

Copy editor: MPS Limited
Cover designer: David Croy
Frontispiece image: : Lopez-as-El-Vez signs merch for a fan while wearing a shirt decorated to read 'I Hate El Vez,' *c*.2023.
Courtesy of Robert Lopez's collection.
Production manager: Sophia Munyengeterwa
Typesetter: MPS Limited

Hardback Print ISBN 978-1-83595-100-2
Paperback Print ISBN 978-1-83595-362-4
ePDF ISBN 978-1-83595-102-6
ePUB ISBN 978-1-83595-101-9

Printed and bound by Halstan

This is a peer-reviewed publication.

Make the Dream Real

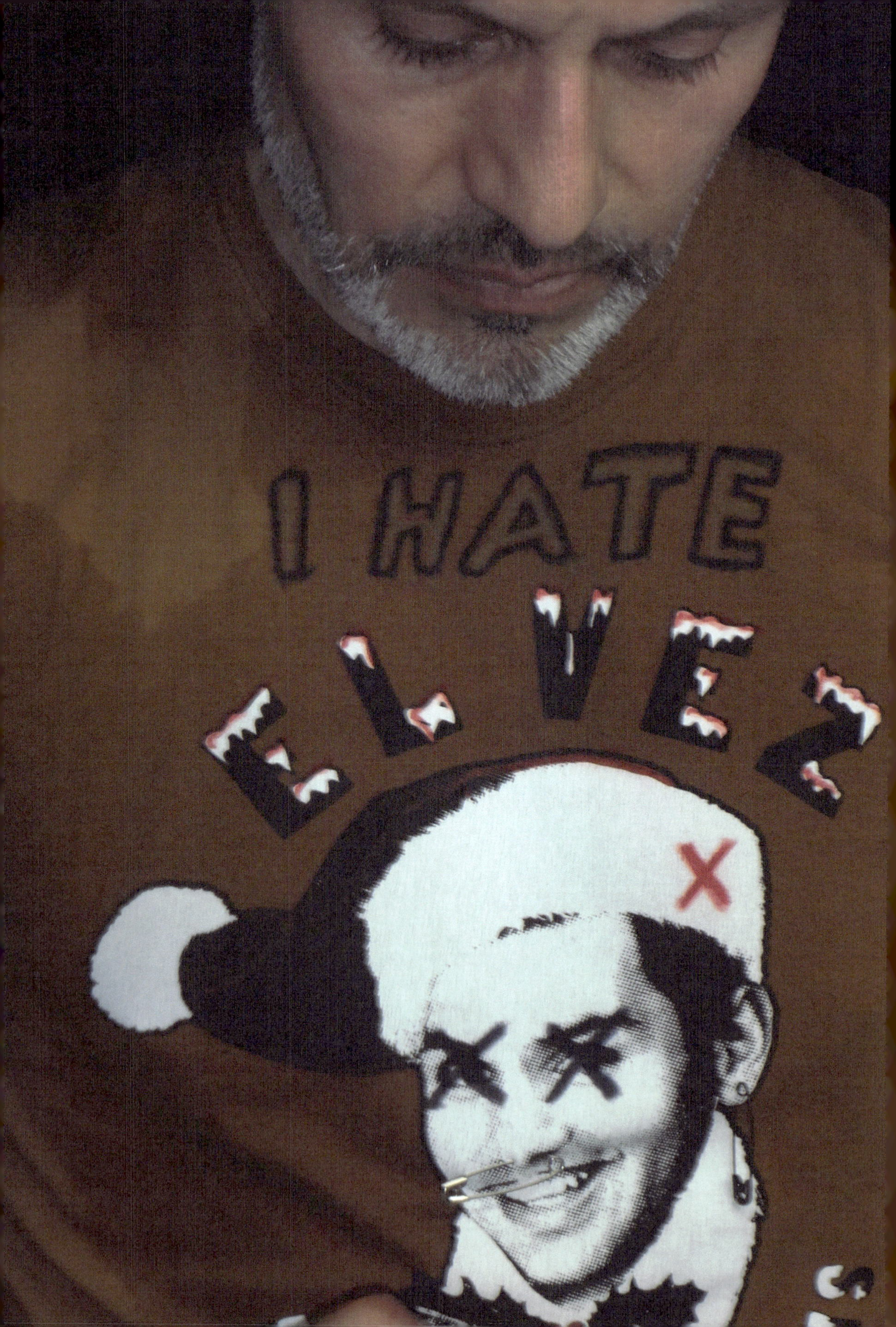
I HATE
ELVEZ

Contents

Figures

Acknowledgments

Robert always says, "you shouldn't have to read a book" to enjoy an El Vez show. But now you can!

This took a long time (like, a comically long time). Sure, there were legitimate reasons for that—job stuff, art stuff, life stuff—but it got to be a bit of a joke, especially because so many people, when they found out I was writing on El Vez, were excited about it. Really, it was embarrassing. "When's that book coming out?" "Umm ..." And now, here I am, literally writing these last few words before I send this off to production. It seems almost unreal. Because this book took so long, I have an immense list of people to thank. I will forget someone or ones, no doubt. I am sorry in advance.

I first saw El Vez as a graduate student, which means my grad student community is at the center of the ripple that became this book, and they occupy my inner circle of gratitude. I have to thank Fudge: Tom Lynch (and Raj Reddy), Richard (Rytch) Barber (and Michael Scott), and John Fletcher (and Alan Sikes); the other two parts of the Awesome Threesome (also known as Flocka): Megan Sanborn Jones (and Glen, Cohen, and Eden) and Lisa Arnold (and Hamlin Metzger); my bestie Kamesha Khan (and Mok, Kai, and Amir); and my whole Minnesota Mafia family. Shannon Walsh and Róisín O'Gorman were early writing partners; Joanne Zerdy got me my first book chapter; Wade Hollingshaus has invited me into his classes multiple times; and Scott Magelssen was always up to grab a coffee in Seattle. So many others shared parties, taco nights at Tracy's, frustration, and fun. Professors and mentors Michal Kobialka, Sonja Kuftinec, Tamara Underiner, Lou Bellamy, Margaret Werry, Mark Pedelty, and Jack Zipes all helped create an amazing community while teaching me to think with precision and encouraging me to embrace a dramaturgical mindset.

Much of this book first started at conferences, especially the American Society for Theatre Research (ASTR) and the Association for Theatre in Higher Education (ATHE). To all the people who sat on working groups and panels with me, or who came to my presentations and gave me feedback, I thank you. Way back when in 2015, ASTR honored me with the Grant for Researchers with Heavy Teaching Loads in support of this book project, and I am happy to have fulfilled the promise they saw in it and in me. And thank you to all my theatre conference friends and colleagues across the nation and world. You are awesome, and I love that we support each other.

At Chicago State University, I thank my friends and colleagues Christine List, Kamesha Khan (again!), and Kay Dawson for always supporting my research, and Gennifer Jackson and Letitia Leonard for their good vibes as well. The Center for Teaching and Research Excellence (CTRE) supported this work with multiple grants that helped fund travel to conferences and other research opportunities. Mercedes Byrd and Shawntia Grant assisted when El Vez visited campus, and all my students who attended his performance made a great audience.

All of my colleagues at Arizona State University contribute to making it a wonderful place to work, so I will limit my mentions to my closest friends, mentors, and artistic collaborators who helped develop this book and who hosted El Vez when he visited campus: Tamara Underiner (again!), Rachel Bowditch, Kristin Hunt, Mary McAvoy, Micha Espinosa, Guillermo Reyes, and Jeff McMahon. Heather Landes, Martin Schuring, Karen Schupp, and Sandy Stauffer have been pillars of knowledge and support as I make my way toward tenure. And my undergraduate and graduate students have been a joy, and have helped me better my teaching and push my thinking. This book was supported by subvention grants from the Herberger Institute of Design and the Arts Research Building Investment (HIRBI) and the Institute for Humanities Research (IHR) at Arizona State University. I also received a subvention award from the American Theatre and Drama Society (ATDS).

My Literary Managers and Dramaturgs of the Americas (LMDA) family has granted me another source of encouragement and community. Dan Smith has been my writing partner and general partner-in-crime for years now, and we get up to all kinds of good trouble. And all the other dramaturgs—way too many to name, but you know who you are—helped train me in research and creative practice, and helped me to articulate and refine the dramaturgical methodology at the heart of this book.

I thank Intellect, my editor Jess Lovett, my production editor Sophia Munyengeterwa, and the amazing peer reviewers who helped make this book so much better.

And my family, obviously. Mom, Dad, Mary, Rick, Linda, Jimmy, Susi, Brandon, Nicole, Sophia, Josh, and Cam. And all the cats on the family chat. And my chosen family, Krissy and Chris (and Sabrina and Evan), Lori and Mike, Curt and Kim (and Taylor), Josh and the rest of the Park Crew, Tom and Victoria Vickers, Jaedra and Andre, Lee and Maria, Chris and Kelly, Karen and Jay, James, Caleb, Bridget, and I know I am forgetting so many others. Heather and Josh Huntington (and Ethan and Lilly) deserve special recognition because they always graciously provide me with a place to stay when I randomly show up in L.A. on yet another El Vez trip, and they never complain when I roll in late after a show.

Huge thanks to the Lovely Elvettes, especially Crissy Guerrero, Pinky Turzo, Lysa Flores, and Tana the Tattooed Lady, and the Memphis Mariachis, especially Slim Evans, Kim Serene, Pierre Smith, Pat Beers, Lety Beers, Stephen Rey, Ashley Paul Ryu, and Declan Halloran, who, for the past twenty years, have allowed me to hang out backstage and take up space in the van and share drinks and food and stories, often while taking notes and asking annoying questions. And to others in the El Vez orbit, including Belinda Gordon, who gave her time for an interview, and Frank the Rat and Taggy Lee, who provided pictures.

And of course, Robert (duh). Thank you for you, and thank you for your art.

And my husband, Dave. I remember my Mom once asking if he liked El Vez—a question that had never occurred to me. She said, "Could you imagine if he didn't?" Thank goodness that never came up! He is there for my El Vez love, at the shows, in the car when I am blasting songs on repeat, late nights when I go down a YouTube rabbit hole, all the times I jet out of town to fun adventures, not to mention the countless days I have spent in front of the computer, doing nothing but thinking and writing about El Vez. On the upside, he's gotten to see some really great El Vez moments, including our own wedding, where we were declared husband and wife as El Vez ripped off his pants. Thank you, Dave, for all of your love and support. I'm not always an easy person to be married to. I love you, and I appreciate how much I can rely on you. Thanks, too, for the book cover. And just so everyone knows, Dave saw El Vez first, at the Blue Note in Columbia, Missouri—long before I ever even knew there was such a thing as a Mexican Elvis.

I hope, at least, with all this support, and all these years, you find this to be a good book to read. But I promise it will not be as much fun as seeing El Vez live. I hope you will do that, too.

The Forward: A Foreword

Robert Lopez

Wrong wrong wrong. The Doctor has gotten it all wrong. The Doctor has formulated her idea of El Vez and presented it to you in book form, complete with cross-references, quotes, and endnotes. To be read whilst keeping one eye looking backward, while the other looks forward. Years in the making and even more in the living. We have discussed, drank, debated, and argued over many theories regarding the values and intended ephemeral nature of theatrical performance, knowing in advance it was not answerable. Here in academic prose, she presents her options.

Way before I moved to Seattle (and before his house was torn down), I had read an article about Kurt Cobain. The interview took place in his soon-to-be last home. The writer noted on the upstairs of the long interior hallway of the house, it seems that Kurt had spray painted in giant red letters, "You will never know my full intent!" I always thought this very romantical. I imagined sunlight coming through the windows and accentuating the "no" in "know." What was the "artist" hiding? What was the artist's "secret"? Was there a "key" to the full understanding?

The best Art is done from memory. Where an incident, image, sensation, longing, shame, guilt, desire—a "something"—all age with time and become their memory impression. These aforementioned are then interpreted, romanticized, for better or worse, richer or poorer, till death do us part. We try to interpret that "something" which will always be "lost in translation."

As I look back on my catalog of music on Immigration (*Graciasland*) and Religion (*Boxing with God*), I see sadly/madly/gladly that "everything old is ..." now even older and ready for new interpretations. As of this writing, and with me now living in Mexico City, a former U.S. President is hawking a King James Version of the Bible, but re-imagined as An American Bible. The smile to me being the "King James Version," an admitted "interpretation"—in his case "interpreted" to best serve a "King." But not in an Elvis sense.

The Doctor here has interpreted my works in a manner that best serves her Interpretation. As I have in turn done with my original source materials.

I use many mediums. Music, images, ideas, and countless references. To me, The Performance is the Goal. That is the Art. Our Dear Doctor has chosen the Theatrical Presentation as her focus. But I believe that the whole process is The Performance: the sound check, the making of the costume, the writing of the song, the negotiation of the contract, the band, and the venue is the medium thus the message. (As a child I had misinterpreted the saying as "the Medium is the Massage" as in "Swedish Massage.") When you take the whole process and make it the Art, you can be more entertained. If you treat life as if walking into a Modern Art Gallery, and you think, "Is that just the fire extinguisher or is that the Art?," you are free to interpret the world. I have always heralded Marcel Duchamp, who is the Godfather of any Warholian ideas, in that the process is also the ART. Nobody knows that I have only eaten spaghetti noodles and butter for 100 days. Nobody knows I have slept in the same bed with the author and her husband both before they were married and also after I married them. And now you know. And that makes the whole process of where we are today more interesting. The Performance is The Art.

I have always been a fan of interpretation. It shows a mind at work. It can do so either correctly or incorrectly, but being free in its realm of "interpretation." I am an Interpretive Artist. An interpretation can shed a different light. A different take on an otherwise assumed standard of an older idea, or of one's own. And perhaps our interpretations change as we go through life, as we collect more information, or the again aforementioned images, sensations, longings, shames, guilts, desires ... which can all mellow or rot with time.

A while ago a new translation/interpretation of the fourteenth-century Italian tome Dante's *Inferno* was presented. One simple line from the new readings has always stuck with me: "Once, halfway through the journey of our life, I found myself inside a shadowy wood, Because the proper road had disappeared."

That is what our Dear Doctor has done here. In interpreting El Vez as Theatrical Study, she has lost her way, and in doing so gotten it wrong wrong wrong, but in turn she has gotten it so right. Right on! Write on! She will never know my true intent ... but therefore, neither will I.

Which one of me signs here?

The Kind People Have a Wonderful Dream: An Introduction

The kind people
Have a wonderful dream
George Bush on a Guillotine
Cause people like you
Make me feel so tired
When will you die?
When will you die?
When will you die?
When will you die?
When will you die?
And people like you
Make me feel so old inside
Please die
You kind people
Do not shelter this dream
Make it real
Make the dream real.

—El Vez's "George Bush on the Guillotine," an adaptation of Morrissey's "Margaret on the Guillotine"[1]

Four days before the 2004 election, El Vez, The Mexican Elvis, sweetly crooned his dream of the end of the Bush Administration from the stage of Cat's Cradle in Carrboro, North Carolina during his El Vez for Prez (also referred to as EV4P) tour (Figure 0.1). His "George Bush on the Guillotine" expresses exhaustion and exasperation at a presidency that, for many, was illegitimate. George W. Bush's Electoral College win in 2000, determined by the Supreme Court in a landmark 5–4 decision despite voting inconsistencies in Florida and Bush's failure to secure a majority of the popular vote, brought to power an Administration in which mass protests were diminished into "focus groups" to be ignored,[2] facts

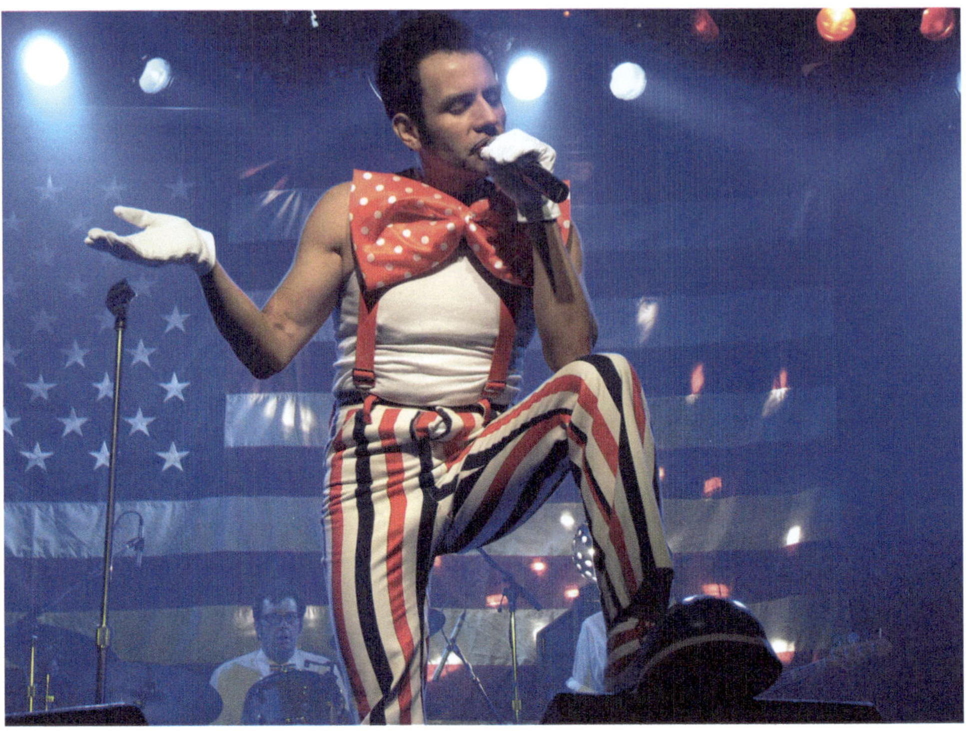

FIGURE 0.1: El Vez comments on the electoral process during the 2008 EV4P tour. Photograph by Megan Mayer.

were outweighed by instinct and faith, and "reality-based" communities were maligned because, according to a senior Bush advisor cited in *The New York Times Magazine*, "We're an empire now, and when we act, we create our own reality. And while you're studying that reality—judiciously, as you will—we'll act again, creating other new realities."[3] In fact, these imperial ambitions, such as the invasion of Afghanistan and Iraq—two of the United States' longest wars—and the declaration of the "War on Terror," were, until recently, ongoing; they were our shared, enduring reality, however judiciously some may study them to interpret their meaning. Other actions persist as well: the United States arguably is still recovering from the financial, social, educational, and cultural decisions made by the Bush Administration.[4] Indeed, the Bush Administration's partisan and at times populist rhetoric, its bellicose military actions, and its deregulatory economic policies that so disproportionately benefited the extremely wealthy laid a foundation that culminated in the 2016 election of President Donald J. Trump, who harnessed the frustration with neoliberalism that animates his base and linked it to racist and nativist ideologies—even as his administration ultimately reinforced and upheld neoliberal policy and ideology.[5] Despite Trump's defeat by President Joe Biden in 2020, this dangerous discourse continued to circulate throughout the 2024 election cycle, which first saw a Biden–Trump rematch, until the President stepped aside and Kamala Harris was nominated as the Democratic candidate.

In the live recording of the Cat's Cradle performance, released nine years later on El Vez's "Silver Jubilee" retrospective *God Save the King*, the crowd bursts into audible cheers and applause as El Vez sings for Bush's placement on the guillotine, and again as he repeats the question, "When will you die?" Clearly, among this audience, El Vez struck a chord. This is perhaps not surprising: Cat's Cradle, less than a mile from the University of North Carolina's Chapel Hill campus, bills itself as "the Triangle's premier live music venue for over 40 years."[6] A vibrant club in a college town, El Vez's audience seemingly was receptive to his message. Moreover, *God Save the King*'s 2013 CD release date occurred after the re-election of Barack Obama, which—if one leans left—further reinforces the sentiment of the song and the audience's approval of its message.

However, Robert Lopez, the man behind "the man, the myth, the mustache" that is El Vez, recalls that some fans were conflicted about how to interpret this song. He remembers that some "Latino Poli Sci" boys approached him after the show to question, "Are you asking us to kill the President?"[7] The question itself jars, marking a slippage wherein the performance is misread as the real. Interpreting the song lyrics literally, and assuming that the identity of the singer aligns directly with the character of the song, they expressed alarm, both at the request and with the jubilant response of the audience so willing to entertain a call for the public execution of the sitting president requested by a charismatic, benevolent-seeming figure.

When I initially drafted this introduction, well into the Trump Administration, the query also terrified me because it mirrored what seemed to be happening in our national discourse. Despite his background as a reality TV showman, Trump's words as President were not mere performance (though he clearly brought his own performative sensibility to the position)—they carried power. So when he refused to condemn the neo-Nazis and white nationalists whose Unite the Right Rally terrorized Charlottesville, or when he suggested that police should brutalize the suspects they arrest, or when he declared of immigrants "These aren't people, these are animals,"[8] or when he insisted the election was stolen and on January 6 prodded his supporters to attack the Capitol, telling them "if you don't fight like hell, you're not going to have a country anymore,"[9] insurrectionists and white supremacists who Trump had previously told to "stand back and stand by"[10] heard this as an endorsement of their beliefs and they acted on his discourse.[11] What is metaphoric in an El Vez show was all too real in Trump's America.

The misapprehension of Lopez's message by these young men also prompts questions about his style of rock performance: where is meaning found? In the lyrics? The sound? The banter? The performance around any one song? The concert as a whole? References outside of the performance event? The recording of the concert? The merch that is bought and sold? *Make the Dream Real: World-Building Performance by El Vez, The Mexican Elvis* strives to answer these sorts of dramaturgical questions. Indeed, one of the underlying aims of this book is to tease out the many ways that Lopez creates meaning on and off stage, and to theorize those meanings. Moreover, these questions can be broadened and applied to theatre and performance that seeks to promote progressive social change. By what mechanisms might change be effected through performance? What does that change look and feel like? How can that change be evaluated?

El Vez's performances present a powerful message of social justice and inclusion. *Make the Dream Real* interrogates how this message is activated through performance in what I am calling world-building, drawing on the work of Dorinne Kondo, by way of Diana Taylor: the use of a variety of theoretical, theatrical, and musical tactics that bring into being a progressive social space that refutes the current economic, political, social, and cultural configurations of the United States. World-building in an El Vez show actualizes the repeated refrain of "George Bush on the Guillotine"; it "makes the dream real" by imagining a society in which equal rights are guaranteed, inclusivity is fostered, difference is valued, and the violence of economic inequality is mitigated. But world-building through performance is not content to reside exclusively in the realm of the individual imagination or even the social imaginary; it goes on to temporarily create this new kind of social space in actual time and space. El Vez shows temporarily engender this world and allow an audience to experience what it would be like. This dream-made-real is linked to, yet different from, "The American Dream." Indeed, El Vez performances remake this as well (The Graciasland Dream?). They offer a vision of the United States where "we can go on together,"[12] and pledge "to make this land a better land than the world in which we live" by "help[ing] each man be a Mexican, with the knowledge that we give."[13] The performance of songs that express sentiments like these helps to imagine and construct a different social reality, one that resists essentialism, foregrounds collective action and inclusivity, and allows for an embodied celebration of diversity.

As I will discuss throughout the book, world-building happens through the imaginative work of the artist, augmented by his use of more tangible, sensorial elements. Specifically, I will track the world-building made possible through Lopez's use of irony and inauthenticity in shaping the persona of El Vez (Chapter 2); the dramaturgical structures, including costumes, stage banter, and musical selection, that undergird his performances (Chapters 3 and 4); and the music itself, which creates an audiotopia that audiences can enter into (Chapter 4). With its emphasis on performance, *Make the Dream Real* privileges the live. Still, my analysis makes use of both the archive—what Taylor refers to as the "supposedly enduring materials" by and about El Vez—and the repertoire—"the so-called ephemeral" embodied practices and knowledge transmitted through performance—in considering the world-building of El Vez.[14]

The notion of world-building takes as indisputable the fact that performance is at once an object of study and a way of knowing, for both performer and audience. As Taylor asserts in *The Archive and the Repertoire: Performing Cultural Memory in the Americas*, "Performances function as vital acts of transfer, transmitting social knowledge, memory, and a sense of identity [...] Embodied practice, along with and bound up with other cultural practices, offers a way of knowing."[15] That is, the act of performance both creates meaning and conveys it to others. It is a vital site for questioning, imagining new possibilities, and (temporarily) building new social spaces. In *Worldmaking: Race, Performance, and the Work of Creativity*, Kondo similarly stresses how performance harnesses the imagination, thus making it a site of potentiality. She writes, "Theater demonstrates that worlds are made, humanly imagined and fashioned, in collaboration with objects and technologies that are themselves replete with possibility."[16] Performance allows for world-building, and world-building is an act of knowledge production.

World-building in El Vez shows emerges in and through performance in part because of aesthetic choices Lopez makes, but it also requires the co-presence of the audience. Indeed, as Taylor posits about the embodied performance of the repertoire, "The repertoire requires presence: people participate in the production and reproduction of knowledge by 'being there,' being part of the transmission."[17] Kondo similarly notes, "Theater gathers bodies, both performers and audience, who share space and time, affecting and being affected by each other."[18] She refers to this as the performance's "fleshy messiness,"[19] referencing the physical, intellectual, and emotional ways that performance can impact audience members, along with its reciprocal nature. This helps to explain my emphasis on live performance; co-presence allows for the co-production of meaning. Of course, Philip Auslander, in his book *Liveness: Performance in a Mediatized Culture*, troubles the notion of "a rigorous conception of an ontology of liveness,"[20] noting that live performance, which is undeniably impacted by mediatization, does not exist in an oppositional relationship to other mediatized forms, nor does it retain some sort of special power and function that is lost in other media. While I do not disagree, I remain firmly partisan in my belief that the best way to experience El Vez is to see him live.

The world-building of El Vez performances exists against a backdrop of neoliberalism, with an awareness of how it has created our current conditions. As an economic and political ideology, neoliberalism lauds capitalist values and private enterprise, and suggests that the government's highest duty is to maintain an open, competitive, deregulated market that maximizes the amassing of capital. Extreme inequality, economic instability, and the hyper-commodification of all things are normalized under neoliberalism, as is corporate coziness with, and power over, government (even as the government is distrusted and made to take the blame for all things wrong in the world). Neoliberalism also functions as a social logic that impacts subject formation to reify privilege, often along the lines of race, gender identity and expression, sexual orientation, religious affiliation, and class. Under neoliberalism, everything, including human value, citizenship, and the polis, becomes financialized.

El Vez's performances stage a counterpoint to neoliberalism in both content and form to fight back against the continued, insidious creep of neoliberalism that has so transmogrified U.S. society, and indeed threatens to undo it.[21] By taking on our nation's most divisive issues, El Vez sings against the processes by which individuals are devalued and vilified. For example, in the 1990s, he critiqued California's controversial Proposition 187 and was outspoken in his critiques of immigration policy.[22] His more recent shows pointedly call out how U.S. domestic and foreign policy has brought harm to millions, at home and abroad, as when he addressed the War on Terror and its aftermath throughout the Bush and Obama Administrations, or when he identified the rise of white Christian nationalism under Trump and predicted the restriction of rights for women, the LGBTQ+ community, and BIPOC (Black, Indigenous, and people of color) individuals. He confronts large social problems head-on. And most importantly, he offers a counternarrative of mutual respect and support, all while creating an alternative social space. Lopez's artistic practice itself resists the containing mechanisms of neoliberalism, offering a model of subversion that can be harnessed by others who seek to promote radical social change. Finally, his form of engagement—a rock concert, in which communal revelry is the norm—short circuits the extreme partisanship rampant in our national discourse. *Make the Dream Real* interrogates how El Vez's playful engagements hold the United States to its egalitarian promises, voicing and enacting a just, expansive society through performance, one that allows its audience to not only imagine but also experience—however fleetingly—a collective social space that is ethically inclusive, and a hell of a lot of fun.

To the Legend I'm Adding On: A Brief Introduction to El Vez in Concert

El Vez, The Mexican Elvis is the fantastical creation of artist and musician Robert Lopez. From humble beginnings in 1988, when Lopez debuted El Vez during Memphis' Weep Week celebration, he has built an impressive act and has sustained himself as a working artist for over 30 years. Though he has collaborated with countless musicians who have performed with him over the course of his career, El Vez has always been exclusively under the artistic guidance (he sometimes jokes dictatorship) of Lopez. He has released several El Vez CDs, singles, music videos, and live DVDs. He is the subject of a documentary film, *El Rey de Rock 'n' Roll*, and has also appeared in other documentaries highlighting the cultural contributions of Latinx individuals to USAmerican culture. His gold lamé mariachi suit toured the country as part of *American Sabor: Latinos in U.S. Popular Music*, a traveling museum exhibit that was featured in several prominent locations, including at the Smithsonian. Countless fans have uploaded photos and bootleg performance videos of his shows to the internet, and he also maintains a YouTube channel and an active social media presence. He has toured extensively, both nationally and internationally, and has performed in a variety of venues, from dive bars to huge international music festivals to college campuses to venerated museum complexes to free concerts in public parks.

Though each tour is unique, all El Vez performances share common elements. They are genre-defying: though they function under the umbrella of rock performance, El Vez shows incorporate a distinctly theatrical sensibility. They are richly polysemous in text, image, and sound. More than just a collection of songs to be performed, they follow a loose dramaturgical arc and use stage banter and reworked lyrics to express key ideas; costumes, props, and spectacle to reinforce a storyline; and sound to create an anti-essentialist performance that builds a social space. Tours themselves are often titled and themed, whether grouped around holidays (Cinco de Mayo and Merry MeX-Mas), national politics (El Vez for Prez), or a specific topic of inquiry (The Gospel Show, which interrogated religion and religious intolerance; Rock & Revolution, which married Latinx culture to social revolution; or the Punk Rock Revue, which extolled the virtues and values of punk rock as a palliative to our current social conditions). Obviously, the themes help to create meaning and inform the dramaturgical structure of the show, and each tour allows Lopez to present to the audience his take on a given issue, via the persona of El Vez.

El Vez tours with his singers, the Lovely Elvettes, and his band, the Memphis Mariachis. Though Elvette and band membership has rotated throughout El Vez's performance history, the onstage relationship of the performers has remained largely consistent.[23] The Lovely Elvettes include Priscillita (whom El Vez will introduce by saying, "she's like a wife to me") and Lisa María ("she's like a daughter to me"), and at times Gladysita ("she's like a mother to me") and Qué Linda Thompson ("she's like a girlfriend to me"), each named after important women in Elvis's life, but with an El Vez twist. The Lovely Elvettes hold court next to El Vez throughout the show. Indeed, Lopez is quite clear that "their presentation seems to take apart the idea of the girl backup singer, and put it back together differently."[24] He notes that they stand even with him, in a line, stressing, "They are not backup singers. They are very strong, *up-front* singers. Some of the songs on the show deal with the power of women, and Latinas—like the 'Chicanisma' song—and that's where they are, I think."[25] They also are incredibly skilled singers and charismatic performers, and they hold their own against him. Similarly, the Memphis Mariachis are gifted musicians, as backing El Vez is an extremely demanding gig.[26]

The "script" of the performance, through which the persona of El Vez is revealed, includes both the stage banter and the rewritten lyrics of the songs. In putting together a tour, Lopez creates the set list and then maps out a "skeleton" of what he will say onstage, much like a *commedia dell'arte* scenario. He will "then improve it on the road,"[27] refining the wording of his monologues, tightening the timing of the jokes, making the many allusions embedded in the text clear and meaningful, and often layering in even more cultural and musical references. The result is a show that is finely honed but also dynamic, as Lopez very much improvises around the scenario and is especially adept at responding to audience members in the moment of performance. Written into the scenario are interactions with the Lovely Elvettes and the Memphis Mariachis.

Costume changes are necessarily set in advance and further support the meaning-making of the performances. A typical 90-minute show will include 5–15 costume changes by El Vez. These costume changes bring an element of camp to the performance, as they are over the top and spectacular. Some happen backstage, while others are featured front and center: El Vez might punctuate the line of a song by ripping off his tear-away pants with pure stripper bravado, or he might seductively strip down to his gold lamé hot pants to then perform a reverse strip tease and become an ancient pre-Columbian god. The Elvettes also change costumes, albeit not as often (or as publicly) as El Vez, to match his look and to mark the different sections of the show. The Mariachis are costumed as well, though theirs are more subdued than those of El Vez and the Elvettes, and they will only change for the encore, if at all. Some El Vez performances also make use of props and other specialty costume pieces.

And of course, there is the music. More than a showman or impressionist, Lopez is a virtuosic musician. Indeed, his skill as a rock performer is crucial to his project. It not only gets him gigs headlining in esteemed venues and opening for revered musical artists including David Bowie, Santana, and Bjork (to name only a few) but also ensures that he can keep a disparate audience engaged. Put simply, he has to be good, or people will leave, and if people leave, he will not get future bookings. First and foremost, Lopez offers his audience an accomplished and entertaining musical act; the political commentary and subversive content exist on top of a solid rock performance. He also capitalizes on the festive performance conventions of the rock concert, which favor partying, dancing, and singing along. His embrace of pleasure and entertainment aids Lopez's pointed interventions. He offers his audiences a tightly honed show that is hard to resist. From the moment the Mariachis take the stage, the music does not stop—the band vamps over costume changes and underscores the stage banter to keep the energy of the performance driving ahead.

Lopez's musical inventiveness adds further meaning to the content. In putting together his shows, he blends disparate musical styles and genres, reimagining popular songs and repurposing them for his own artistic message. He remakes Elvis songs, and those of other artists, to address a variety of social and political issues. Lopez intentionally mixes genres throughout his shows in the form of live musical sampling, placing next to each other soul, rap, glam, rock, punk, jazz, and Elvis. By effortlessly sliding between these genres during a single song and over the length of the show,[28] he actively resists essentialized understandings of sound and genre, adding further complexity to the message he crafts. In listening to El Vez, the audience experiences a new aural configuration—one that Lopez has carefully curated to be a space of inclusivity.

In short, El Vez shows pack an abundance of meaning into a highly energetic and engaging few hours. As I have already stated, I strongly believe that it is through live performance that El Vez is best experienced. As both a scholar and a fan (or an aca-fan, as I will touch on later in this introduction), I have spent the last two decades following his work, attending dozens of performances across the nation in a wide variety of venues and spending time with Lopez in both work and play. I have also logged countless hours poring over his archive: the CDs, posters, merch, music videos, interviews, concert footage, social media, TV coverage (now conveniently curated on the El Vez YouTube Channel), articles, and book chapters. In all of that labor, nothing has dulled for me. Quite the contrary, this extended study has only sharpened the experience of seeing him live, which is why I argue that nothing beats an El Vez show. They surpass categorization: they are deeply political, but are not as stridently message-driven as political theatre; they are theatrical, but use performative elements to make meaning differently from traditional theatre; they rock, but match musical abandon with intellectual engagement; they are money-making endeavors, but are refreshingly anti-corporate. The rich intertextuality of the performance, which features campy performativity and a sophisticated layering of references, allows Lopez to wrap a subversive message in a highly entertaining form, potentially reaching a diverse audience to craft a unique social space. Indeed, his subversiveness infused even his earliest work, and traces of his world-building are evident in the earliest scholarship about him, which I turn to next.

Just as Long as There Are Elvis Fans Who Are Paying, We'll Keep Playing: El Vez Scholarship at His Height, and After

Admittedly, I came to the El Vez game late, only catching the second part of Lopez's remarkable and ongoing career. I first saw El Vez in 2002, just past his most visible and prolific years. Throughout the 1990s, El Vez toured extensively, both nationally and internationally.[29] This was also the period when he recorded the bulk of his music, releasing two dozen singles, EPs, and full-length CDs. My work is indebted to the insights of scholars José David Saldívar and Michelle Habell-Pallán, who began analyzing his performances in the early part of his career. Their work provides a foundation to my own analyses, and to my conception of world-building. Both Salidívar and Habell-Pallán position El Vez as a subversive artist who uses popular culture to create a hybrid public discursive space that resists essentialist tropes as it allows for ambiguities and contradictions to emerge.

In his 1997 book *Border Matters: Remapping American Cultural Studies*, Saldívar establishes a borderlands approach to the field of cultural studies in the United States. Noting the prominence of the "frontier field-Imaginary"[30] within USAmerican culture, which looks to an ever-expanding frontier as a marker of progress and the promise of the future, Saldívar calls attention to the reality of displacement and disempowerment that such expansion causes. Moreover, he notes that the prospects of those in power indeed rely on the labor of the displaced and dispossessed—immigrants who alternate between invisibility and hypervisibility in the social imaginary. As a counter, Saldívar proposes adopting a "border discourse [that] not only produces power and reinforces it but also undermines it, makes it fragile, and allows one to map and perhaps thwart the cultures of U.S. empire."[31] His inquiry notes how artists such as Lopez, through engagements that marry popular culture to a subaltern perspective, allow for borderland contradictions to emerge.

Saldívar expands upon his analysis of El Vez in his 2002 article, "In Search of the 'Mexican Elvis': Border Matters, 'Americanicity,' and Post-State-Centric Thinking." In it, he notes how El Vez's performances bask in ambiguity and contradiction that allow for pleasure and engagement, an assertion that I further in my own analysis. By pulling "the discrepant American experiences together as a culture" that is then distilled through the figure of El Vez, Lopez practices "cross-ethnic translation and geopolitical displacement" that reveals how minoritized subjects "always negotiate between tradition and translation, convergences and displacement."[32] Defying a model of assimilation, El Vez instead offers transculturation to his audiences. Saldívar then broadens this, picking up on an El Vez catchphrase to consider how El Vez perhaps allows us to think beyond the nation-state. He notes:

> El Vez, The Mexican Elvis's translocal performance art thematizes a remarkable shift from acting and thinking at the state level to thinking and acting at the Elvisly (global) level. This shift, moreover, parallels a larger shift in the unit of analysis in US Latino/a studies—a new study of hemispheric and world cities, transnational studies, and a renewed focus on regions.[33]

Saldívar suggests that El Vez's performances offer a mode of thinking that could potentially restructure methodologies within the fields of American studies and cultural studies.

Habell-Pallán foregrounds how Lopez's art adopts an anti-essentialist stance, an idea that is crucial to my conceptualization of world-building. Habell-Pallán situates Lopez as part of a group of artists generationally distanced from first-wave Chicanx activism and animated instead by a punk sensibility of resistance. Such artists, including Lopez, create their art through the use of the popular because:

> In addition to constructing individual and collective identities, popular performance culture, as a hybrid form, often articulates social and historical conflicts and allows those who have little access to ways of intervening in the dominant modes of representation (film, television, print) to represent themselves in their own terms.[34]

Marginalized from power, they engage with popular culture specifically to disrupt it. In her 2005 book *Loca Motion: The Travels of Chicana and Latina Popular Culture*, Habell-Pallán foregrounds how Lopez serves as "a transculturator of popular culture" whose performances enable "multiple layers of cultural hybridity and [promote] complex instances of cross-cultural translation."[35] She highlights how El Vez's performances layer meaning on top of the Elvis image to create a public discursive space, a space that I posit as a site of world-building.

In addition to providing deep textual analyses of the lyrics of several El Vez hits, Habell-Pallán also documents the way that El Vez, steeped in a Southern Californian specificity, travels transnationally to strike resonances abroad. Recounting crowd reactions gleaned during the height of his touring, Habell-Pallán dissects how Turkish immigrants (and their children, born in Germany yet disallowed German citizenship) connected to El Vez songs such as "Immigration Time" and "Taking Care of Business." These songs, sung from the position of the devalued immigrant, offer a view from the shadowy bottom of neoliberalism's global hierarchy. Suggests Habell-Pallán, "El Vez's performances thus enable the possibility of building alliances in communities [...] on the basis of 'horizontal affiliations,'"[36] whereby marginalized groups, recognizing how they are similarly positioned, might join together in opposition.

Writing in the wake of California's anti-immigration Proposition 187, a voter referendum denying education, health care, and other services to undocumented immigrants that was passed in 1994 but later deemed unconstitutional, both Saldívar and Habell-Pallán interrogate how El Vez performances provide a meaningful counternarrative to the anti-immigrant discourses circulating during that time. Saldívar stresses that colonialist narratives villainizing Latinx subjects within the United States—citizens, documented immigrants, and those without documentation alike—positioned the United States as "the golden nation-state [...] being invaded by so-called illegal aliens, corrupting and polluting pure cultural spaces." In contrast, El Vez's performances "make space for an alternative narrative of what can now be called the ethno-racialized cultures of displacement."[37] They work against ethno-nationalist discourse by giving voice to the displaced and the downtrodden. Yet, through his melding of pop culture with his Latinx specificity, Saldívar notes that Lopez "does not celebrate protonationalist Chicano movement wholeness but makes room for a heterogeneous fragmentariness."[38] His art resists *any* gesture toward ethno-nationalism—be it white or Latinx. Additionally, Habell-Pallán provides an assessment of the post-9/11 rhetoric of the Bush Administration, noting the "shrinking public outlets for the circulation and discussion of alternative and oppositional perspectives"[39] and discussing how El Vez's performances create a space for counternarratives to emerge.

My analysis adds to these the perspective of time and its peculiar repetitions. Though immigration policies and race relations could hardly be seen as progressive or productive during either the Bush or Obama Administration, under Trump they took a decidedly dark turn back toward the Proposition 187 years, in both rhetoric and policy, and remain stuck under the Biden Administration.[40] As Lopez jokes, "Everything new is old again!"[41] Really old—never in my life did I expect to see (Tiki) torch-wielding white supremacists march with impunity through Southern towns, nor did I expect a sitting president to make concessions toward them. I would not have thought possible the devastating policy of family separation would be instituted to such a degree that small children, taken from their parents, would stand trial in immigration courts before being haphazardly relocated throughout the nation. Or that Make America Great Again (MAGA) governors would adopt the language of the Confederacy in their anti-immigration stances against the Biden Administration. Indeed, Trump not only harnessed the anti-immigrant rhetoric out of which El Vez emerged, but he also fully weaponized it. A key component of his 2024 platform called for the mass deportation of millions of undocumented immigrants, a position embraced by nearly every MAGA candidate.

Additionally, there has been an outpouring of academic writing theorizing how neoliberalism has come to impact our society, and this underlies my thinking through El Vez. Neoliberalism refers to economic and political ideology enacted through specific policy. It values competition and entrepreneurship among individuals, just as it favors corporatism, the privatization of public entities, deregulation, and the reduction of state power and state social support. Moreover, neoliberalism encourages us to imagine all aspects of human life through market logic. Wendy Brown astutely notes that "neoliberalism assaults the principles, practices, cultures, subjects, and institutions of democracy understood as rule by the people."[42] Because neoliberalism deploys market values to new configurations, things once deemed outside the logic of capitalism (such as religion, education, health care, individual identity, and the very notion of a public) have become economized. She warns that "when the domain of the political itself is rendered in economic terms, the foundation vanishes for citizenship concerned with public things and the common good."[43] Brown suggests that the current state of political rancor and partisanship directly stems from the dominance of neoliberalism.

In *Neoliberal Culture: Living with American Neoliberalism*, Patricia Ventura offers a deep analysis of the way neoliberalism in the United States operates not simply as an economic and political ideology enacted through policy but also as what cultural theorist Raymond Williams has identified as a "structure of feeling," that informs our lived realities as "sensibilities and unthought assumptions that suffuse daily life."[44] States Ventura:

> Neoliberal culture as a structure of feeling impels us to extend the market, its technologies, approaches and mindsets into all spheres of human life, to move the ideology of consumer choice to the center of individual existence, and to look to ourselves rather than larger social-welfare structures or society as the source of our success or the blame for our failure—indeed, to define "success" and "failure" in market terms.[45]

She traces how U.S. neoliberalism inflects such terms as freedom and family so that both represent a move away from the collectivity of the democratic state toward an atomized individuality. Ventura also usefully notes that the ideal neoliberal subject is "an individual that views himself or herself as primarily a consumer rather than a producer."[46] This has resulted in the increased vulnerability of working USAmericans, especially as state support for workers' rights and collective bargaining have eroded with neoliberalism's emphasis on the individual and with the offshoring of manufacturing under globalization. Ventura suggests that neoliberalism has also increased anti-immigrant sentiment, noting "the intensity of globalization with its cross-border flows explains the intensity of the effort to highlight the border and border control."[47]

Patricia Ybarra adds to the field of neoliberalism by charting its specific impacts on Latinx artists and analyzing their innovative artistic answers to it. She notes that neoliberalism normalizes its violence by forwarding discourses that "rhyme with longer-standing racist U.S. discourses used to explain away inequality as a result of laziness, lack of ambition, or failure to assimilate to mainstream U.S. (capitalist) culture."[48] Though many connect the rise of neoliberalism to the Reagan Administration, Ybarra clarifies that the U.S.'s first experiments with neoliberalist policy date back to the mid-1960s,[49] and they directly impacted Latinx subjects on both sides of the Southern border. Therefore, she continues, "Latinx theater has always been responding within, if not to, neoliberal conditions understood as such."[50]

This is surely true of Lopez's life and career: from his very first forays into performance as a teenaged punk rocker in the 1970s, his career has been intentionally shaped by neoliberalism. Indeed, his most prolific years—the 1990s—coincide with and in fact mirror neoliberalism's global heyday (El Vez was a global phenomenon then, too), even as his songs critiqued with precision the way marginalized subjects were debased and displaced by neoliberal economic systems. Lopez's art directly engages with democratic principles; thus, the very messages he conveys (of equality, of liberty, of community) are under assault. Yet, at the same time, because he is a working musician who self-funds all of his projects (Lopez has never applied for grant money), he very much practices entrepreneurship in forging his career. Ybarra further posits that "Latinx theater artists are theorists, undoing hierarchies of knowledge production that position people of color, particularly artists of color, as authenticity and content providers in an outdated ethnographic frame."[51] As I will discuss throughout, Lopez resists essentialist narratives and tropes of authenticity in productive ways.

Though El Vez reached his peak in the late 1990s, Lopez continues to work as a performer and musician today. Thus my inquiry offers a unique perspective, documenting the continued labor of an artist who is much less in the limelight than he had once been. At the same time, I submit that his punk rock sensibility allows him to speak with clarity about the current political moment, as does his age. Though he now records less frequently and tours less robustly, Lopez continues to both adapt existing work and generate new projects that offer needed perspective for deploying critique in partisan times. He also offers a model of engagement that might bypass the extreme partisanship rampant in our national discourse.

The key innovation of *Make the Dream Real*, however, is methodological. I analyze the performances of El Vez through what I call a dramaturgical methodology, informed by my theatrical praxis as a dramaturg as well as from my training in performance studies and theatre scholarship. Whereas Saldívar studied El Vez through a borderlands approach to cultural studies, and Habell-Pallán added a music-focused methodology to her analysis, I marry theoretical inquiry to theatrical practice, putting both to work in the interrogation of the various texts, performances, sociohistorical context(s), and institutional settings that create meaning in the performances of El Vez. Moreover, because dramaturgy hones an awareness of both artistic intent and audience reception, I analyze both throughout the book.

A dramaturgical methodology begins with dramaturgical thinking. In his foundational text, *Toward a Dramaturgical Sensibility: Landscape and Journey*, Geoff Proehl describes what he dubs the dramaturgical sensibility, a devotion to inquiry that "exposes us to landscapes and journeys that confirm both how much we have to gain and how much we have to lose in the acquisition of the most trivial piece of information."[52] Proehl posits that a dramaturgical sensibility is fueled by "the sometime sublime potential of *knowing*,"[53] referencing those thrilling, almost transcendent moments in which art opens up and speaks to the most profound aspects of the human condition. Proehl charts four components that are key to a dramaturgical sensibility: the desire for—and questioning of—deep knowledge marked by both abundance and loss; an awareness of one's subjectivity and one's situated knowledges, which allow for distances and intimacies between scholar and scholarship; the importance of time and the impact of temporality in any engagement; and finally, a relentless commitment to inquiry, through which new discoveries continually unfold.[54] Each of these core components is evident in my research practice. For instance, the deep knowledge I have of Lopez and his art results from the extensive time I have spent on this project. I have seen countless versions of El Vez shows over the years, often attending multiple nights of the same tour. I am keenly aware of the innovations he makes to keep his music and his critiques vitally relevant. I have seen him perform everywhere from street fairs to art centers; small bars to big clubs; at festivals and in grand concert halls, and I consider how each of those settings impacts the meanings made. We have even collaborated on projects that combine his artistry with my scholarship. I embrace the multiple positions I maintain—fan, researcher, fellow artist, and friend—by clearly articulating and situating myself in them and asking questions of them.

Stressing the importance of engaging in sustained intellectual and emotional inquiry, Proehl also suggests that dramaturgy necessitates a "deep, often personal, even idiosyncratic understanding of the forms and rhythms crucial to a play as written or conceived and performed."[55] Thus, beginning with my own fandom, I consider how El Vez performances create meaning through the many performative components, and how they mean differently in different moments, in different venues, and with different audiences. Because I regularly attend El Vez performances throughout the United States, I often use an autoethnographic methodology to assess my experience as an audience member and my interactions with other audience members. This, of course, is complicated, as gauging audience response is necessarily imprecise. While it is possible to get a general read of the room, and to conduct a loose demographic assessment of the audience members, it is more challenging to see moments of dissatisfaction. Normally, people who are not having a good time leave. Occasionally, however, audience members have visibly performed their own dissent directly to Lopez as he performs. I rely on his accounts—and, in some instances, my own witnessing—to analyze these moments.

A dramaturgical methodology values intellectual and methodological flexibility; dramaturgs select from and sometimes combine various research methodologies in order to best serve the project. Theatre historiography, cultural studies, and performance studies theory factor into my analysis. I engage in qualitative analysis through my ongoing dialogue with Lopez, and autoethnography as a participant-observer at El Vez shows. Caroline Heim's participant-observer methodology, which includes adhering to an ethos, watching and listening, prizing, and above all, maintaining adaptability, resonates with my own.[56] Like Heim, I always introduce myself as a researcher, which is not only ethical but also puts people at ease and often prompts them to volunteer their opinions to me. I also rely heavily on reflexive autoethnography, which Deborah Reed-Danahy defines as "a form of self-narrative that places the self within a social context."[57] Tony E. Adams, Carolyn Ellis, and Stacy Holman Jones recognize autoethnography's power to capture how "personal experience is infused with political/cultural norms and expectations."[58] They posit that autoethnography can speak against dominant cultural scripts, thereby filling in gaps in knowledge and articulating insider understandings about "aspects of cultural life that other researchers may not be able to know."[59] Specific to the theatre, Signy Lynch suggests that autoethnography can be used to make visible "the subjectivity and individuality of audience response, and the political stakes of interpretation" while it also "untangle[s] the complexities and affective nuances of audience experience."[60] In my practice, I offer thick descriptions of El Vez shows that include my intellectual, emotional, and somatic responses. I seek to capture the full experience, using lively, detailed prose "to create evocative and specific representations of the culture/cultural experience and to give audiences a sense of how being there in the experience feels."[61]

A dramaturgical methodology also involves breaking down a performance into its constitutive elements. Indeed, Lee Devin's query, "What are the parts of this thing? How do they go together?"[62] is so frequently cited by dramaturgs that it has become almost a mantra. As Devin elaborates, "These questions address materials and arrangements of materials. They focus our attention on form [...] They are at the heart of that part of play-making we call dramaturgy."[63] I adopt Devin's approach, addressing the different pieces of El Vez's performances to consider how the materials are brought together. As detailed later in this introduction, each chapter tackles a different performative element. Breaking an El Vez show down to focus on each of these pieces of meaning-making is necessary, as each aspect offers a complex mode of engagement that contributes to the dramaturgy of the performance overall and its capacity for world-building. Interrogating them individually offers a focused study of what happens simultaneously in concert.

A final aspect of my dramaturgical methodology includes setting aside calls for objectivity and instead embracing critical proximity. Dramaturg Shelley Orr stresses that we have much to gain by practicing critical proximity, suggesting that while "several benefits accrue, the most notable is an increased level of trust among the collaborators."[64] Orr traces critical proximity to its roots in feminist research and cultural studies when scholars sought to make their personal investments clear. Rather than striving for objective distance, critical proximity instead encourages the scholar to bring her whole creative self to a project. The field of fan studies similarly grapples with subjectivity through its concept of the aca-fan, where the researcher occupies both positions. Notes Henry Jenkins in the twentieth-anniversary edition of *Textual Poachers*:

> There are at least three things at stake in the use of the aca-fan concept: the acknowledgement of our own personal stakes in the forms of popular culture we study, the accountability of the ethnographer to the communities we study, and the sense of membership or affiliation with the populations at the heart of our research.[65]

Jenkins suggests that the aca-fan is invested in their fandom, but treats it with appropriate critical rigor. One difference between Jenkins's project and my own is disciplinary focus: put simply, fan studies seek to produce knowledge about fans and their fandom, whereas a dramaturgical methodology seeks to elucidate the meaning-making and world-building that occurs in and through performance and the creative labor of the artist in its production.

Undeniably—and unapologetically—I'm still a fan, taking pleasure in the performances. My familiarity with the El Vez oeuvre allows me to see what is new—some funny bit of stage banter, a particularly apt pop culture reference, a unique interaction with an audience member, a performance goof that Lopez covers with improvisational skill, and the inventive reworking of the music and the inclusion of new songs. Like Jenkins, my research is marked by "a constant movement between these two levels of understanding [academic and fan] which are not necessarily in conflict but are also not necessarily in perfect alignment."[66] Being an aca-fan surely presents challenges. Because I believe in Lopez's project and stand in allegiance with the worldview he presents as El Vez, I am perhaps prone to overlook issues within his work, or might fail to formulate criticisms of it. I might also find his performances to be more or differently impactful than other audience members do. Yet, I believe the benefits of critical proximity outweigh the risks, by allowing me to move into a deeper understanding of El Vez and Lopez. Ideally, following Ruth Behar, it allows me to grapple with "the dialectic between connection and otherness that is at the center of all forms of historical and cultural representation."[67]

Moreover, critical proximity cultivates openness and generosity between the researcher and the artist, which enlivens deep conversations about the art, the process, and its aims. It has also made possible a wealth of research opportunities. Lopez has been exceedingly welcoming, allowing me to peek behind the curtain, as it were: I have jumped in the El Vez tour van and stayed in his hotel rooms and at his house. I have rooted through his costume closet and manned his merch table. And I have seen countless shows. Applying critical proximity to my El Vez scholarship means considering the full scope of the labor of a touring musician, what Lopez describes as:

> [A]n odd 24 hours to experience one hour [of performance] and that one hour can be a great one, which can make it all worthwhile, or that one hour can be horrible and why am I doing this and spending 24 hours a day? And when you're in a group, it's not just yours, it's my entourage of nine. One person's bad mood can affect everyone else, so it's a unit thing.[68]

My relationship with Lopez allows me to glimpse the totality of the work: the hours spent on the road; the unique relationships of an ensemble; the hauling, sorting, packing, unpacking, and upkeep of costumes, props, and merch; and the experience of walking into a new venue, doing the same show each night to a brand-new audience.

The unique relationship that I have with El Vez and with Lopez speaks to the difficulty "of knowing, and not knowing yet"[69] that lies at the heart of the dramaturgical sensibility. When I first saw El Vez, I arrived at First Avenue with no foreknowledge of the event. Not recognizing the irony in the ad for the show, I had expected El Vez's performance to be totally earnest and, most likely, terrible. I had not anticipated social commentary, productive spectacle, or musical virtuosity. Having talked to audience members across the nation, I have found that this not knowing what to expect, or anticipating something totally different, is common among first-time attendees. They initially come for a variety of personal reasons, but they always seem surprised by what El Vez offers. So it was with me: I was elated by the performance, physically energized and intellectually enthused, buzzing with enjoyment, and I became an instant fan.[70] Of course, a first encounter is, by definition, not repeatable. Whatever I felt then, I cannot feel quite the same now. That night is locked in my memory, and yet I know that my initial encounter with El Vez was brief and unremarkable.

After decades of study, I now know Lopez incredibly well, and consider him not just a research subject but also a dear friend. We text, email, and talk regularly. We have drinks together. He even officiated my wedding, which means his signature is on my marriage certificate. From the very first email I sent him, he has been willing to share his thoughts about the art he creates. In practical terms, this means that the evidence to my analyses of Lopez's art is comprised equally of more formal sources including articles, interviews, recordings, and notes on performances, as well as much more familiar (and therefore messy) sites such as late-night conversations in cars or in bars, text messages, joking responses on social media, and rambling emails. Our relationship is much more collaborative than it is objective.

There is much that connects Lopez and me, just as there are many aspects in which we differ. He once joked about this at a performance at an academic conference in Manhattan, Kansas, calling out the knowing and not knowing that Proehl describes. Sitting on my lap with his arms draped around me, Lopez-as-El-Vez introduced me as "the woman who has a PhD in El Vez." Calling out my whiteness, he then proclaimed, "I thought her name was Martínez, that's why I gave her access to my life."[71] Even that was a performance of sorts—we did not know each other extremely well at that time. The truth is that he is simply an open performer who was willing to answer my emails and grant my requests for interviews. Since then, however, he *has* given me incredible access to all aspects of his life, and even if it muddies my role as a scholar, it surely enhances it.

A dramaturgical methodology takes both time and familiarity, as it results from what Proehl characterizes as the "thoughtful and persistent engagement with the ways that theatrical performances emerge from their first dreamed indeterminacies to their most recent staged incarnations."[72] I have learned much from Lopez, especially regarding the business end of El Vez. In fact, this has taught me to recognize my own blind spots: I tend to view El Vez solely as artistic expression, and am sometimes surprised by the pragmatism with which Lopez approaches his business decisions, as he always must consider how different aesthetic choices will impact his income. I have been able to speak with Lopez about the ideas and references he layers into performance, gaining access to his originary ideas while also analyzing how they operate in the moment of performance. I have developed a professional relationship with Lopez and with his collaborators, and I rely on their insights and perspectives, especially in researching past tours that predate my exposure to El Vez.[73] Critical proximity has benefitted my research tremendously, granting me access to insider knowledge and the ultimate primary source: Robert Lopez. *Make the Dream Real* reflects our deep dialogues. I strive toward inquiry that is critically engaged and intellectually rich, even though this act of knowing is complicated by subjectivity, with its intimacies and its distances.

Do Not Shelter This Dream, Make It Real: World-Building at the Cat's Cradle

In constructing his El Vez performances, Lopez is unafraid to voice subversive statements, to harness controversial imagery, to irreverently lampoon culturally sacred icons, and to invite his audience to take pleasure in the revelry. Though Lopez has a clear point of view, he prefers for El Vez shows to remain open for audience interpretation, even if it can lead to unexpected misreadings. In discussing the overabundance of references and images he deploys in his shows, he notes:

> Because of that you get misinterpretations, because of that you get wriggle room [...] And it's also done in a theatrical way: "What did I mean? Did you really want me to kill the President?" Which was a whole jester part of the show.[74]

Lopez says a lot in these few sentences. He signals that he does not expect his audience to walk out of his shows spouting his ideas. Although he hopes they will be thinking, he is fine with radical misreads of his show, as when the young men at the Cat's Cradle thought he was literally calling for George W. Bush's assassination (he assured them it was a metaphor and informed them that his song was an adaptation of an earlier hit). This quote also demonstrates his awareness of his own theatricality, and how he uses multiple elements in performance to create meaning. Here I want to delve into the Cat's Cradle performance, taking time to unpack its rich intertextuality and depth of meaning by offering an analysis of it.

Though song lyrics are a key mode of engagement in El Vez performances, they are not the only way Lopez expresses subversive content. Indeed, the lyrics to "George Bush on the Guillotine" are very straightforward, calling for the end of the Bush Presidency. The recording hints at the way other performative elements contribute to meaning-making in rock performance, augmenting or altering what is expressed in the lyrics. For instance, toward the end of the phrase, "And people like you / Make me feel so old inside," the audience again bursts into hoots and applause. Clearly *something* happened onstage to prompt the response. Was it something scripted, such as a costume change or an interaction with the Elvettes? Or was it something impromptu, like an evocative gesture or an exchange with a member of the audience? Without further context, the listener is left to guess what might have occurred.[75] Thus, the recording marks both presence and absence, tracing the outline of something that must be seen and not heard.

What we can hear, however, provides greater insight into the multiple ways that Lopez makes meaning in his El Vez performances. Take, for example, the proliferation of references found in the monologue he speaks near the end of the song:

> Give us your hands! Whatever happens tonight, I love you! I might not make it to the Mountain[top], but you can. I have a dream and you were in it. It's up to us to keep America free. America is the home of the brave and the land of the free. You have the vote, you have the power. Do not be afraid to use it. You have the right. Fight like your life depended on it. America is great and you need to keep it that way. Is it up to us? We the people, by the people, for the people. We *are* the people. This is a great country, and you need to keep it free because America belongs to you; America belongs to [...] (*gunshots*).

The speech, replete with juxtaposed verbal allusions to stirring rhetoric, nationalistic myths, and pop culture catch phrases, accumulates to offer a complex view of what it is to be an USAmerican citizen.

In citing Dr. Martin Luther King, Jr., Lopez-as-El-Vez calls up the importance of principled resistance to sustained injustice. Joining his famous "I Have a Dream" refrain with Dorothy's exclamations from *The Wizard of Oz* grafts more meaning onto this moment: like Dorothy, we, too, might arise from the dark and confusing nightmare of the Bush Administration[76] enlightened and appreciative of the home around us. At the same time, placing quotes from MLK's famous speeches alongside lines from *The Wizard of Oz* calls attention to the way both phrases, extremely well known and often overused, risk being spoken purely for affect and thereby have their message diluted or completely emptied of meaning.[77]

El Vez arguably puts them to rousing use in his monologue, an example of world-building in which he urges the audience to join with him to fulfill his dream of fighting to keep the nation free. Though it is always difficult to determine just who the "we" of an audience is, Lopez-as-El-Vez defines this by addressing the crowd first as a collective "you," which implies that the listener—those in the 2004 Cat's Cradle audience as well as those listening to the recording—joins together to become a collective "we" who hear his address. He quickly broadens the collective to include himself, the Lovely Elvettes, and the Memphis Mariachis, noting that "it is up to us." This is further underscored later in the speech, when he stresses that "We *are* the people." Indeed, he underlines the importance of collective action: we are in his dream because he needs the "you" of the audience to join with him and his entourage to make an "us." He stresses the power of political action while also foreshadowing the potential costs of such action—King's "Mountaintop" speech was famously delivered the night before his assassination.

In his call for collective political action, Lopez-as-El-Vez offers another critique through signifyin(g), using "repetition with a signal difference."[78] He inverts the language of the national anthem, calling America "the home of the brave and the land of the free,"[79] perhaps suggesting that social hierarchy, which was enforced along racial and gender lines when Francis Scott Key penned the now-famous lyrics, should be revised. Moreover, after forging the collective we of the audience, he similarly proclaims them full heirs to the nation's history, the "We the people" of the Constitution. He also assures them that they are vital actors in the government of and by the people President Lincoln lauded in the Gettysburg Address. Recalling this bloody battle waged over slavery connects to the MLK reference that started the monologue while also charting the slow progression of civil rights for African Americans and other people of color in the United States. Yet, these contentious moments of history, in which people fought for equal citizenship and inclusion, perhaps stand as evidence to El Vez's assertion that "This is a great country." Indeed, hearing El Vez, The Mexican Elvis—who clearly aligns himself with immigrants and minoritized subjects[80]—assert his rights to USAmerican citizenship is a powerfully subversive moment, and, within the narrative of the show, a dangerous one. Before he can say the "me" that will finalize his claim to the nation—"America belongs to you, and America belongs to"—he is "shot."

A mock assassination is not the usual fare for rock performance, which tends to focus on music over more overt forms of storytelling. However, El Vez's performances are carefully structured by Lopez, and often framed by a narrative conceit. These are perhaps most evident in the El Vez for Prez tours, which have a built-in fiction that helps define the show: El Vez is running for president. The format and storytelling surrounding El Vez's election bid change from tour to tour to be in conversation with the most prominent issues of the actual campaigns, but in all EV4P tours, a narrative plays out. Lopez's liner notes describe this particular moment as, "one of the tunes where I died on stage. It's happened many times with many songs in many ways. This show version was the secret service guy from the top of the show turning rogue and killing El Vez."[81] Perceiving El Vez to be a danger to the nation—whether because he calls for the guillotine (a symbol of popular revolt against an out-of-touch and frivolous elite) or because he claims America for himself and for his fans—the agent executes him in order to preserve the status quo.

In considering the musical references embedded in the song, the complex layering of meaning further multiplies. The base melody is an adaptation of a Morrissey song, released on his first solo album, *Viva Hate*.[82] Lopez's use of Morrissey is significant: the morose white rocker raised in a working-class Irish family in Manchester has a huge Latinx fan base, and is especially popular among the Chicanx culture of Southern California in which Lopez was born and raised.[83] By covering "Moz," as Morrissey is affectionately known among his Latinx fans, Lopez subtly calls attention to the sorts of transracial and transcultural border crossings that music makes possible—those of Morrissey, and his own. It also evidences their mutual respect for each other. After El Vez opened for the Santa Barbara and Las Vegas shows of Morrissey's 1999 ¡Oye Esteban! tour, Morrissey stated in an interview, "I saw El Vez recently and I'd like to have a go at stealing his ideas,"[84] which was powerful praise from an international star. When Morrissey appeared on Saturday Night Live in 1992, he wore an El Vez T-Shirt for the curtain call. Of course, it must be noted that Morrissey's endorsement, though meaningful when the interview was conducted, is tarnished now due to Morrissey's recent privilege-laden and bigoted comments.[85] Still, his influence and import within the Latinx community made him excellent source material for Lopez in 2004.

Thematically, the two songs align to rebuke the policies of the sitting governmental leaders. The Morrissey original sets its target on then-Prime Minister Margaret Thatcher.[86]

Thatcher's tenure as PM—and her positive relationship with President Ronald Reagan—helped secure the predominance of neoliberalism. The "Iron Lady" ushered in deregulation, privatization, and the cutting of social services, and was known for her antipathy for union labor and her proclivity for armed conflict. Lopez stated that he simply "[c]hanged who the hate is pointed at" and "added a front and end."[87] In this way, Lopez calls attention to the way Thatcherite policies resonate with those of the Bush Administration that he criticizes in performance sixteen years after the release of the Morrissey song, and the way they continue to resonate today.

Lopez melds two other songs into his version, each adding nuance to the critique levied through the performance. His version opens with electric guitar playing the Pink Floyd song "Brain Damage." This augmentation offers a subtle, yet scathing, criticism of President Bush. First released in 1973 on *The Dark Side of the Moon*, the lyrics begin with the repetition of the line "The lunatic is on the grass." Though El Vez does not sing these words in performance, they were certainly on Lopez's mind in his selection of the Pink Floyd song. He notes, "I was thinking of a Bush Rose Garden Speech,"[88] suggesting that (at least to its critics) the Bush Presidency was guided by a kind of mental incapacity wrapped in protocol. The song also builds on political connections already made by Pink Floyd in their performances. The band's 1994 The Division Bell tour featured a giant arched structure and a massive screen onto which video was projected. In their performance of "Brain Damage"—easily viewed on YouTube—images of Thatcher, President George H. W. Bush, Bill Clinton, Ronald Reagan, Mikhail Gorbachev, Saddam Hussein, and other world leaders engaged in ceremonial photo ops are intercut with black and white archival footage of armed conflict. These accumulate to suggest that history is simply the folly of world leaders played out violently onto the bodies of the citizenry.

Similarly, Lopez adds to the meaning of his performance by layering in The Beatles' song "Sun King" to underscore his monologue at the end. The guitar seamlessly segues into the Beatles melody, with an Elvette singing the gibberish Romance language lyrics under his monologue (which, wrapped in the performance of The Mexican Elvis, sound like Spanish), "Quando paramucho mi amore de felice carazón."[89] Other lyrics from The Beatles original, these unsung, include the lines "Here comes the sun king [...] Everybody's laughing / Everybody's happy." This bit of musical allusion works in several ways.[90] It again heightens the fact that Lopez-as-El-Vez momentarily embodies four different Kings in performance: the Sun King, Martin Luther King, Jr., Elvis, and The Mexican Elvis. Indeed, he begins the monologue with the use of the royal we, heightening this read. It also suggests that, were El Vez to accomplish his dream of ending the Bush Presidency, laughter and happiness would ensue. But Lopez more specifically uses this to again criticize Bush. As the offspring of a former president, Bush's rule is made to parallel the decline and demise of the French aristocracy, which moved from the heights of the Sun King to the bloody beheadings by the guillotine of Citizen Louis Capet. Lopez adds that his use of the song "was also referring to Louis the 15th, who was seen as foolish for his opulence. I was using the foolish for Bush."[91] Thus, he again stressed how the Bush Administration—deemed both crazy and foolish—should be overturned.

In parsing out the meaning of this piece as part of the overall performance event, it is crucial to note that the show continues after El Vez's assassination ends the song. Through the magic of show business, El Vez comes back to life, with a quick costume change into "the white reincarnation jumpsuit like Evel Knievel." Toys Lopez, "He jumps over death?"[92] El Vez returns to the stage to launch into a revision of Robbie Williams's pop hit "Let Me Entertain You," mashed up with his "JC Sí Lowrider Superstar," an anthemic medley that closes the show.[93] In his reworked lyrics, El Vez heralds his triumph over death while further emphasizing the need to vote Bush out of office:

> Hell is gone and heaven here
> He won't last another year
> I'm still alive so don't you fear
> My dear
>
> [...]
>
> We all know the right is wrong
> Come and sing a different song
> It's time to vote so come along
> My dear.[94]

The lyrics again call the audience members into collective action, aligning them against the policies of the right and urging them to head to the polls. This message is reinforced by both the dramaturgy of the assassination narrative and the conventions of rock performance. El Vez is clearly situated as the hero of his own shows; thus his return elicits screams and applause from the audience, which is energized by El Vez's ability to cheat death. The searing guitar licks and up-tempo music also build the momentum, signaling that the end of the concert is near and encouraging fans to abandon themselves to the revelry, and to side with El Vez.

Though it has taken me pages of thick description to hint at the many allusions Lopez includes in his performance and the potential meanings these create, in performance, this all happens quickly, so quickly that it is virtually impossible that any one audience member might catch everything that occurs. Indeed, the entire event—song, monologue, assassination, and rebirth—spans only a few minutes. "George Bush on the Guillotine" is a short 2:30 minutes, the monologue takes approximately 45 seconds to deliver, and "Let Me Entertain You" lasts just 1:46 minutes. This rapid-fire and extremely broad approach by Lopez is tactical. The speed with which his allusions accumulate aid his project: they function not as a unified vision, but rather as "seeds for ideas." He notes, "mixing of ideas is the whole idea of El Vez [...] mixing everything is what I do. They are all reference points [...] it's the collage process, especially in today's mass info society."[95] Moreover, the rapidity of his delivery also works to effectively short-circuit knee-jerk objections to his stances. Because things happen so quickly, the audience can get swept up in the energy of the performance. Lopez creates an environment where audience members might still dance along, even if they disagree with his politics.

Lopez's decision to follow the more provocative "George Bush on the Guillotine" with "Let Me Entertain You" emphasizes a final tactic he deploys in his art. Lopez avers that entertainment is paramount to his performances. Indeed, he places as his sole responsibility to the audience "to be entertained, I suppose. That's about it. No moral or ethical or leadership responsibilities lay on my shoulders. That's for them to decide."[96] Though this perhaps sounds like a move of absolution through which Lopez distances himself from any artistic culpability, I in fact take it as a key mode of audience engagement as well as a respect for the genre in which he operates. After all, he normally plays rock clubs, and audiences at a rock club expect a strong musical performance. Notes Lopez:

> [Y]ou shouldn't have to read a book before you go in [...] So, the main thing [the performer has] to do to grab them on is entertainment, be it the sexy, be it the flashy, be it the rocking, be it the energy you exude.[97]

Indeed, Lopez stresses that it is the responsibility of the performer to make the audience want to listen. Audience members should be able to come into the show with no expectations, other than to have a good time. Still, he adds that by knowing the history and the ideas that he engages with "you'll get so much more when you laugh harder or get angrier or know the crux better, but you can't be expected to [walk in with that knowledge]."[98] Lopez strives to ensure that all audience members can take pleasure in the show by giving them multiple entry points into the performance.

Lopez is meticulous about crafting a show that overflows with rock star bravado and humor, is replete with spectacle, and is musically innovative and energizing. In fact, I argue that by focusing on entertainment, he is able to more effectively express his own perspectives in performance. Lopez himself downplays this, especially because he realistically views his reach, noting, "It's not a crusade.

I'm not thinking I can change the world with rock and roll." Yet in the same breath, he speaks to his ability to influence his audience, adding, "but I *can* put something into a different light or make them see something in a way they didn't think of before."[99] Indeed, it is because of his deep knowledge of rock performance that he is effectively able to use the form to inform:

> I do know that the medium is the message, and that medium [rock performance] I know how to do and I know that medium can get your attention and while I get your attention I give you the message [...] a beat can move you, get your attention. The harder the beat, the harder the attention, the harder the message I can get in.[100]

That is, he relies on music—its hooks, its rhythm, its melodies, its kinesthetic effects on the body—to help captivate the audience's attention and open them up to different ideas. Lopez refers to this as "the medicine in the ice cream. Like, 'oh I was so entertained, oh maybe I'm going to think about that differently.'"[101]

Lopez has an exceptional understanding of how to gauge an audience. He states:

> [Y]ou have to have, I think, a bit of care about the audience, but there is certain mind think that is easy to direct the crowd at times, if you know how to read it [...] in El Vez speak, [give them] something they care about, something that will get them fired up.[102]

This does not necessarily mean feeding an audience what it wants to hear. Interestingly, other than including pointed local references in his banter, "naively or bravely,"[103] Lopez does not adapt his shows to different areas when touring. He instead perceives his audience primarily "as [potential] fans and they are up to the challenge of where I decide to take them."[104] Lopez trusts that, by focusing on entertainment and by offering multiple levels through which to take pleasure in his performances, he can win any crowd over. They may not agree with him, but they can still rock with him.

Lopez acknowledges that he hopes to impact the audience, to make them think through the issues and ideas he presents. He states, "people need to talk about it [social issues] rather than blindly accept it and walk through it in a daze."[105] But he also recognizes that making people think does not always equate to political victories or social change. Indeed, in 2004, El Vez did not see his dream come true. Despite the enthusiasm of the Cat's Cradle crowd, North Carolina went for Bush, who in his re-election bid indisputably won both the Electoral College and the popular vote. In fact, thirteen of the states El Vez toured during the 2004 El Vez for Prez went red. Thus, the reach of art—especially a very niche art such as that of Lopez—is necessarily limited.[106] Yet, that does not negate its power: its power to offer new ways of engaging with processes of identification, its power to reorient our thinking about some of the most contentious social issues we face, its power to build worlds that engender inclusive social spaces, its power to plant seeds of ideas.

My Traveling Companions La Virgen, Miss Liberty, a Map, and my MEChA Books: An Overview of Chapters

Lopez's performative approach and aesthetic sensibility rely on his innovative use of Elvis as an icon steeped in pop culture. In Chapter 1, I unpack the theoretical foundations upon which El Vez is built, taking a deep dive into Henry Louis Gates, Jr.'s discussion of signifyin(g) alongside José Esteban Muñoz's disidentification, and consider how both contribute to the world-building of El Vez shows. From there, I turn to the very beginnings of El Vez. After reflecting on Lopez's experience in the early L.A. punk scene, which continues to inform the art he creates, I discuss El Vez's legendary origin story: The Elvis Show that Lopez curated at the L.A. art gallery La Luz de Jesus, which led to his first performances in Memphis as part of Weep Week. I loosely chart the growth of the idea from a one-off into a highly polished tour. I also comment briefly on the working life of touring performers in the late twentieth and early twenty-first centuries, a topic I return to in the conclusion. Indeed, musicians occupy a unique, and uniquely precarious, social position in contemporary USAmerica, as they often lead lives deemed non-traditional by neoliberalist standards, yet must at the same time perfect the entrepreneurship required by neoliberalism.

Chapter 2 interrogates the expansive range of issues that Lopez can explore through El Vez, especially tracking how irony and inauthenticity function in his performances, in contrast to a reliance on empathy and authenticity. El Vez disallows the easy equivalencies of empathy in favor of connections that bridge difference rather than elide it. Because it does not prescribe a "feeling with" each other as either a starting point or an end goal, El Vez's use of irony expands his message to reach his diverse audience base. By emphasizing ironic engagement over empathetic entrapment, and performativity over the real, El Vez's performances reimagine relationships between commonly held conceptions of cultural identity, prompting the audience to become active in the meaning-making and world-building of the show. In this chapter, I also consider Auslander's substantial work on music as performance, focusing on his theorization of Glam Rock and musical personae. Auslander usefully takes up both authenticity and performed identity in rock performance, and offers ways to further consider the relationship of Lopez to El Vez. Finally, I dissect instances where the use of irony in El Vez shows prompted negative responses, making visible moments of tension that arise through the capacity for multiple interpretations of his performances. Irony in an El Vez concert allows for the revelation of both alliances and differences across multiple subject positions, which makes possible the world-building of an ethical community enacted through thought, reflection, and rock and roll.

More than many rock performances, El Vez shows make extensive use of costumes. These objects maintain a high degree of agency as they perform both on stage and off. Chapter 3 considers all the work that costumes and merch do in an El Vez show. I lean heavily on Aoife Monks's scholarly engagement with costumes and the actor's body to analyze the various ways that costumes collaborate with Lopez and the other performers to create meaning and assist in the world-building of his shows. The theatricality of the costumes makes possible Lopez's ironic and inauthentic performance as El Vez, both masking and bringing forth different bodies in process through performance. Costumes also provide dramaturgical structure, reinforcing a narrative arc, as I track through the analysis of *The Gospel Show in Madrid*. This chapter also uses a thing-centric analysis to consider El Vez merchandise, which allows the show to live on in the minds of the audience while granting audience members access to the man himself—after every show, El Vez greets his public, talking briefly with his fans while signing their merchandise. These items perform as mementos of the live performance event, and continue the world-building that happens at the shows. At the same time, they provide a much-needed revenue stream to support Lopez's work as a touring musician.

Chapter 4 delves into the musical mash-ups and sonic imaginings of El Vez shows. Lopez's genius is evident in his ability to rewrite and refashion popular songs to evoke a subversive political stance. Lopez audibly performs subversion in a variety of ways: through the accent he adopts, the humorous stage banter and audience interaction he employs, the lyrics he rewrites, and most importantly, the vast wealth of musical forms that he merges within his shows. Knowing that music is racially coded, he purposefully blends genres to disrupt the essentialized understanding of sound and racialized listening. Lopez unleashes a powerful sonic critique by destroying music's containing mechanisms. His shows manifest what Josh Kun has described as an "audiotopia," an alternate space made through music. I consider how Lopez at once sustains the politically marginalized while also inviting everyone to join in the fun he creates.

In the Conclusion, I consider the impact of COVID-19 on artists and on a sustained, self-produced art project like El Vez, turning again to the precarity that exists within neoliberalist capitalism. Due to the restrictions of the pandemic, theatre and live music performances all but stopped in early 2020. Artists from all sectors had their incomes cut off; they needed work. At 61, Lopez found himself doing what he had done at 16: he got a job delivering pizza, suddenly becoming an essential worker. He reflected on this in one of his first post-pandemic shows, *Stand & Deliver, Pizza!*, which he performed at Seattle's Triple Door in August 2021. The show brought together pieces from some of Lopez's different projects – Mr. Bob, Covid Cola, and El Vez – using art to reflect on the collection trauma of COVID-19.

Each chapter will begin with a close read of a different El Vez site—a music video, a poster for sale, a costume piece, a performative moment, a text—as a point of entry into the specific area of focus and element of production that will be interrogated. Like my analysis of "George Bush on the Guillotine," these engagements not only frame the theoretical argument of the chapter, but they also grant readers a taste of the expansive and complex art that Lopez creates. Similarly, every chapter title and subtitle in the book comes from Lopez and/or El Vez; they include song lyrics, bits of banter, lines from emails, and other interpersonal exchanges. Throughout, I attempt to capture his wit, his thoughtfulness, and his performative skill as I unpack the richness of El Vez's performances. I also hope that these descriptions and snippets will inspire readers to continue the conversations that might begin here, by going out to experience the pleasure of an El Vez performance for themselves.

Some Call Me Culture, Some Say El Rey: A Brief Note about Terminology

Though in his performances Lopez prefers to blur boundaries and layer meaning on top of meaning, it is prudent to pause to clarify some terms. First, the name: says Lopez, it is "a funny Mexicanization of Elvis." He adds, El Vez "started as a one-off, so I didn't put the most thought to the name at first."[107] Now decades into his character, Lopez plays with its literal translation "the time/this time" to provide a bit more nuance and backstory to the character. For example, the liner notes to *Endless Revolution*, the 2004 "Service Re-Issue" of *G.I. Ay, Ay! Blues*, repeatedly mentions how El Vez taps into the urge for revolution found in "these times."

As I will discuss in Chapter 2, Lopez's relationship with the character of El Vez is exceedingly unique, as the two are quite different from each other. As Lopez describes it, "Robert Lopez is a director. So I'm directing the El Vez dialogue, and action, and points I want to get across."[108] I refer to the shows as El Vez performances or El Vez shows, as this is how they are billed. In analyzing the meaning of his art and the tactical decisions made in the presentation, I cite Lopez as the active agent, whereas, in discussing the persona, I refer to El Vez. However, often these two very distinct personalities seem to co-exist, especially in the stage banter surrounding the songs in performance. To discuss such moments of juxtaposition and complexity, I use Lopez-as-El-Vez.

Identity markers are particularly free-flowing within El Vez performances. Lopez usually self-identifies as Chicano, but as El Vez—in performance, interviews, liner notes, and websites, he generally uses the term Latino or Latinx over Chicano. Lopez notes, "the modern kids don't use the term [Chicano] much [...] Latino is more inclusive."[109] With that said, within the lyrics of his songs, he uses a variety of identity markers: Chicano/a/x, Latino/a/x, Mexican, Mexican American, Zapatista, Mijo, Mija, La Raza, etc. He refuses to claim one term as preferential and thereby allows his audience members to self-identify as they choose. This is both powerful and pragmatic, especially as the language continues to evolve, with many now electing to use Latine or Latiné over others. Carla Della Gotta discusses the continually shifting terminology, noting:

> Language is in constant change: Latinx use terms including "Latin," "Latino," "Latino/a," "Latina/o," "Latin@," "Latinx," and now at times "Latine" or "Latiné" to describe themselves and their cultures. I use "Latinx" because it acknowledges that gender is not a binary, it is intended to be inclusive to all, and because it contrasts with the gendered language of Spanish; it is not a word in any language, and for me, it encompasses the spirit of language play.[110]

Similar to Della Gotta, I primarily use the broad term Latinx when discussing the character of El Vez, the music, and its impact. Moreover, the language play that she identifies in the term resonates nicely with Lopez's project and his embrace of expansive possibility over didacticism. However, when describing Lopez's own identity, I use the term Chicano and explore how it, and his openness to all identity markers, operates within his art.

Finally, our nation. I consciously use the term USAmerican in my critical engagement with the social, cultural, and political structures of the United States, recognizing that the Americas span a hemisphere. Similarly, in naming the nation, I will use the United States, U.S., or perhaps USA. At times, however, I quite specifically use the term America or American to address the mythologized and often melodramatic vision of our nation as the bastion of freedom, equality, and democracy at home and abroad—often in reference to "The American Dream." This usage is meant to suggest the way such visions of the nation have been coded; full access to this America has been reserved for straight, white, monied, Christian males; it is to this past configuration that many Christian nationalists would like to return. Sources I quote often do not make this distinction, and I leave their words as they are printed.

NOTES

1. All citations of the performance are transcribed from the live performance track, recorded October 29, 2004, on El Vez, *God Save the King: 25 Years of El Vez*, Munster Records, 2013.
2. Todd S. Purdum, "The Nation: Focus Groups? To Bush, the Crowd Was a Blur," *New York Times*, February 23, 2003, accessed April 17, 2018, https://www.nytimes.com/2003/02/23/weekinreview/the-nation-focus-groups-to-bush-the-crowd-was-a-blur.html.
3. Ron Suskind, "Faith, Certainty, and the Presidency of George W. Bush," *The New York Times Magazine*, October 17, 2004, accessed April 17, 2018, https://www.nytimes.com/2004/10/17/magazine/faith-certainty-and-the-presidency-of-george-w-bush.html.
4. These include, but are not limited to, deregulation, the mortgage crisis, the Great Recession, Karl Rove's exacerbation of political partisanship, the messianic rhetoric surrounding our enemies along the Axis of Evil, the normalization of torture, the passage of disastrous educational policies, the exploitation of the culture wars, and the lauding of faith-based rhetoric over scientific analysis.
5. Unsurprisingly, left-leaning writers stress this sentiment. Noting the return to the headlines of key figures from the Bush White House, including John Bolton and Gina Haspel, Sarah Jones writes that "Trump is no deviation, no mutation, no surprise. He is a continuation." Jones, "Donald Trump is the New George W. Bush," *The New Republic*, March 15, 2018, accessed May 9, 2018, https://newrepublic.com/article/147477/donald-trump-new-george-w-bush. Ryan Grim and Alexander Zaitchik concur, stating, "Without Bush's two most fateful decisions—letting Wall Street run amok and invading Iraq—it's hard to imagine Trump's metamorphosis from a second-rate reality star to president of the United States." Grim and Zaitchik, "George W. Bush Gave Us Donald Trump. Now He Wants To Be Forgiven," *The Huffington Post*, March 18, 2018, accessed May 9, 2018, https://www.huffpost.com/entry/george-w-bush-trump-forget-history_n_58c6e69ee4b0598c66989c6e. I would add that Trump's blatant appeal to racist tropes, particularly through his promotion of birtherism levied against President Barack Obama, also played a significant role in his appeal to white voters.
6. "About," accessed April 18, 2018, https://www.catscradle.com.
7. Robert Lopez, text message to author, April 8, 2018.
8. Trump made this particular statement in a May 2018 White House meeting in which he inveighed against California's sanctuary laws, but he has consistently dehumanized immigrants and people of color since he first announced his candidacy. Julie Hirschfield Davis, "Trump Calls Some Unauthorized Immigrants 'Animals,'" *New York Times*, May 16, 2018, accessed May 17, 2018, https://www.nytimes.com/2018/05/16/us/politics/trump-undocumented-immigrants-animals.html.
9. Transcript of President Trump's January 6 speech on the Ellipse, printed as part of an article by Brian Naylor, "Read Trump's Jan. 6 Speech, a Key Part of Impeachment Trial," *NPR*, February 10, 2021, accessed September 3, 2023, https://www.npr.org/2021/02/10/966396848/read-trumps-jan-6-speech-a-key-part-of-impeachment-trial.

10. Trump said this during the debate with Joe Biden on September 29, 2020, in response to prompting from moderator Chris Wallace. Kathleen Ronayne and Michael Kunzelman, "Trump to far-right extremists: 'Stand back and stand by,'" *APNews*, September 30, 2020, accessed March 23, 2024, https://apnews.com/article/election-2020-joe-biden-race-and-ethnicity-donald-trump-chris-wallace-0b32339da25fbc9e8b7c7c7066a1db0f.
11. The Southern Poverty Legal Center tracks hate crimes, preparing its own reports and also analyzing reports issued by the FBI. The SPLC documents that hate crimes and the number of hate groups rose from the election of 2016 throughout 2017. After Charlottesville, when public outrage led to the "deplatforming" of alt-right websites and social media accounts and a disruption to their funding sources, there was a slight decline in violent activity. However, hate crimes have continued to rise in the United States with the persistence of white nationalist rhetoric in the media and on social media.
12. A line in "Immigration Time" that I will discuss in more detail in Chapter 2. El Vez, *Graciasland*, Sympathy for the Record Industry, 1994.
13. Lines in "Mexican Can" El Vez, *Boxing with God*, Sympathy for the Record Industry, 2001.
14. Diana Taylor, *The Archive and the Repertoire: Performing Cultural Memory in the Americas* (Durham, NC: Duke University Press, 2007), 19. Taylor notes that because of its seeming permanence, the archive is often used to sustain power, while the repertoire enacts embodied memory, though "the actions that are the repertoire do not remain the same" (20). Yet, Taylor warns against considering the archive and the repertoire as binaries; rather, they exist in relation to each other and interact with each other; thus it is valuable to consider them together. Taylor, 16–32.
15. Taylor, *Archive and Repertoire,* 2–3.
16. Dorinne Kondo, *Worldmaking: Race, Performance, and the Work of Creativity* (Durham, NC: Duke University Press, 2018), 27. Kondo's book considers how performance offers both the possibility for imagining new ethical communities and for causing harm through affective racial violence.
17. Taylor, *Archive and Repertoire*, 20.
18. Kondo, *Worldmaking*, 26.
19. Kondo, *Worldmaking*, 26.
20. Philip Auslander, *Liveness: Performance in a Mediatized Culture* (London: Routledge, 1999), 40. Auslander's substantial work on musical performance informs much of my thinking about El Vez, and is especially vital in Chapter 2.
21. Though I limit my discussion of neoliberalism to its effects in the United States, this is not to suggest that it does not violently play out throughout the world. Indeed, the entire hemisphere of the Americas has suffered greatly with the rise—and exportation—of U.S. neoliberalist policy throughout the latter half of the twentieth century. Throughout the world, neoliberalism threatens individuals, particularly people of color, women, and the impoverished.
22. As I will discuss later in this chapter, Michelle Habell-Pallán's work tracks how El Vez performances in Germany resonated with Turkish immigrants during this time period.

23. Long-term members who have overlapped with my study of El Vez include Elvettes Crissy Guerrero, Lysa Flores, Pinky Turzo, and Tana the Tattooed Lady and Mariachis Pierre Smith, Slim Evans, Kim Serene, Pat Beers, Lety Beers, Ashley Paul Ryu, Stephen Rey, and Declan Halloran. All of these artists are active in their own projects as well.
24. Rachel Rubin, "Interview with El Vez," *Journal of Popular Music Studies* 16, no. 2 (August 2004), 217.
25. Rubin, "Interview," 217–18, original emphasis.
26. Lopez shared that Eva Gardner, a bass player who has toured with artists including Pink, Cher, Gwen Stefani, Veruca Salt, Tegan and Sara, and her own group The Mars Volta, performed as a Memphis Mariachi in 2003, doing a short tour that included an outdoor performance at the opening of the Philadelphia El Vez Restaurant. Lopez recounted that Gardner said she specifically wanted to tour with El Vez because she "had heard it was a good boot camp, a hard show and a good workout." Lopez, interview with author, March 4, 2024. I confirmed this with Gardner when I met her in Las Vegas in 2024.
27. Lopez, text message to author, April 20, 2018.
28. Most El Vez songs include the melodies of several songs; the main melodic strand will be interrupted with brief "samples" of a few measures of other songs, performed live by the Memphis Mariachis. He also embeds lyrical allusions to different songs within his pieces; many of these moments are described throughout the book. As his band members have anecdotally noted, and as the Eva Gardner endnote above points to, it's an incredibly challenging gig.
29. During this time, Lopez notes that he was also creating and performing in other bands, including The Zeros and Trailer Park Casanovas. Lopez recalls touring Europe in the mid-late 1990s, jetting from one city to the next to perform different shows with these different projects. Lopez, interview with author, March 4, 2024.
30. José David Saldívar, *Border Matters: Remapping American Cultural Studies* (Berkeley, CA: University of California Press, 1997), xii.
31. Saldívar, *Border* Matters, xiv.
32. José David Saldívar, "In Search of the 'Mexican Elvis': Border Matters, 'Americanicity,' and Post-State-Centric Thinking," *MFS Modern Fiction Studies* 49, no. 1 (Spring 2003), 88.
33. Saldívar, "In Search of," 96.
34. Michelle Habell-Pallán, *Loca Motion: The Travels of Chicana and Latina Popular Culture* (New York: New York University Press, 2005), 6.
35. Habell-Pallán, *Loca Motion*, 184.
36. Habell-Pallán, *Loca Motion*, 202.
37. Saldívar, *Border Matters*, 7.
38. Saldívar, *Border Matters*, 195.
39. Habell-Pallán, *Loca Motion*, 6.

40. Indeed, as I make the final revisions to this manuscript, the immigration debate has grown ever more vitriolic in the run-up to the 2024 election, with several states seeking to enact immigration policies in violation of the supremacy clause of the Constitution and Trump pledging to begin mass deportations on day one of his presidency.
41. Lopez, interview with author, May 22, 2018. He uses this inversion of the *All That Jazz* song title "Everything Old Is New Again" in different iterations, as noted here and as recorded in the Foreword and Conclusion.
42. Wendy Brown, *Undoing the Demos: Neoliberalism's Stealth Revolution* (New York: Zone Books, 2015), 9.
43. Brown, *Undoing*, 39.
44. Patricia Ventura, *Neoliberal Culture: Living with American Neoliberalism* (Surrey: Ashgate/Taylor & Francis, 2012), 2.
45. Ventura, *Neoliberal Culture*, 2.
46. Ventura, *Neoliberal Culture*, 23.
47. Ventura, *Neoliberal Culture*, 28. Ventura offers detailed analysis of how government policy, specifically NAFTA, impacted workers in the United States and in Mexico. NAFTA enabled corporations to relocate their production facilities to Mexico, impacting workers and undercutting their collective bargaining power in the United States. These corporations also displaced Mexican farmers off of once publicly held lands, while speculation by U.S. interests negatively impacted the Mexican working and middle classes, all of which contributed to increased immigration, 25–28.
48. Patricia Ybarra, *Latinx Theater in the Times of Neoliberalism* (Evanston, IL: Northwestern University Press, 2018), xi.
49. Ybarra points to the U.S. government's 1964 termination of the Bracero Program, which had allowed Mexican migrant farm laborers to work legally in the United States, and Mexico's Border Industrialization Act of 1965, which allowed for the opening of maquiladoras on the border, as the "first incursions of neoliberal capital in the Americas." Ybarra, *Latinx Theater*, 3.
50. Ybarra, *Latinx Theater*, 3.
51. Ybarra, *Latinx Theater*, 10.
52. Geoff Proehl, *Toward a Dramaturgical Sensibility: Landscape and Journey* (Madison, NJ: Fairleigh Dickinson University Press, 2008), 17.
53. Proehl, *Dramaturgical Sensibility*, 6, original emphasis.
54. Proehl, *Dramaturgical Sensibility*, 16–17.
55. Proehl, *Dramaturgical Sensibility*, 20.
56. Caroline Heim, "Participant Observation in Practice and Techniques for Overcoming Research Insecurity: A Case Study at the Deutsches Theater," in *Impacting Theatre Audiences: Method for Studying Change*, edited by Dani Snyder-Young and Matt Omasta (London: Routledge, 2022), 29.
57. Deborah Reed-Danahay, *Auto/Ethnography: Rewriting the Self and the Social* (Oxford: Berg, 1997), 9.

58. Tony E. Adams, Carolyn Ellis, and Stacy Holman Jones, "Autoethnography," in *The International Encyclopedia of Communication Research Methods*, edited by Jorg Matthes, Christine S. Davis, and Robert F. Potter (Wiley Online Library, 2017), 1.
59. Adams, Ellis, and Holman Jones, "Autoethnography," 3.
60. Signy Lynch, "The Gaze Turned Inward: A Reflexive Autoethnographic Approach to Theatre Research," in *Impacting Theatre Audiences*, edited by Dani Snyder-Young and Matt Omasta, 88, 97.
61. Adams, Ellis, and Holman Jones, "Autoethnography," 2–3.
62. Lee Devin, "Conceiving the Forms: Play Analysis for Production Dramaturgy," in *Dramaturgy in American Theater: A Source Book*, edited by Susan Joans, Geoff Proehl, and Michael Lupu (Fort Worth, TX: Harcourt Brace College Publishers, 1997), 209.
63. Devin, "Conceiving the Forms," 209.
64. Shelley Orr, "Critical Proximity: A Case for Using the First Person as a Production Dramaturg," *Theatre Topics* 24, no. 3 (2014): 242, https://doi.org/10.1353/tt.2014.0036. While Orr's article primarily focuses on the production dramaturg in the rehearsal space, it can be broadened to discuss research practice.
65. Henry Jenkins, *Textual Poachers: Television Fans and Participatory Culture* (New York: Routledge, 2012), xiii.
66. Jenkins, *Textual Poachers*, 5.
67. Ruth Behar, *The Vulnerable Observer: Anthropology That Breaks Your Heart* (Boston, MA: Beacon Press, 1996), 20.
68. Lopez, interview with author, July 16, 2023.
69. Proehl, *Dramaturgical Sensibility*, 16.
70. Having assisted at the merch table for Lopez at different events, I have seen my own reaction played back to me by other new attendees.
71. *Entertainment! Cultural Studies Conference*, Kansas State University, Manhattan, KS, 2007.
72. Proehl, *Dramaturgical Sensibility*, 20.
73. I have heard so many stories from both Lopez and his bandmates that help to paint a picture of life on the road and the sorts of relationships that the artists maintain during (and outside of) touring. Though many of these stories do not directly make it into the book, they add depth to my understanding. They also make me chuckle. For instance, following the 2023 Merry MeX-Mas concert in L.A., Lopez—notorious for misplacing things—was on a frantic search for the keys to the truck he had borrowed from a friend. As is often the case, the whole group was called into the search. Pat Beers said to me, "I hope your book has a chapter listing all of the things that Robert has lost on tour." When Lopez found the keys (which he had had the entire time), we joked that this chapter should catalog the items lost, the length of the time missing, and the story of how he eventually found the items and had never lost them to begin with. Pat Beers, conversation with author, L.A., December 22, 2023.

74. Lopez, interview with author, May 22, 2018.
75. In this instance, I am that listener. I was unable to see the 2004 EV4P tour. Days before El Vez was slated to perform at the legendary Minneapolis rock club, First Avenue, in my then-hometown, the venue unexpectedly closed when the owner declared bankruptcy. It is also lost to Lopez (who remembers a surprising amount of detail from his decades-long career) and to the band members to whom he reached out. This suggests that perhaps this moment was not a pre-planned bit, but rather an improvisational response to something that unexpectedly happened during the performance. Yet, this is still conjecture: whatever it was eludes the record.
76. Both the 2004 and 2008 EV4P tours negatively situate the Bush Administration, calling for an end to his policies.
77. A particularly egregious example includes a 2018 Superbowl commercial for Dodge Ram Trucks that put excerpts of an MLK speech in service to selling trucks. Audio from "I Had a Dream" had previously been better used to underscore an advertisement for the NBA that put forth a narrative touting the league's history of racial inclusion.
78. Henry Louis Gates, Jr., *The Signifying Monkey: A Theory of African-American Literary Criticism* (Oxford: Oxford University Press, 1988), xxiv. I will discuss Gates's theory in more depth in Chapter 1.
79. He also makes this inversion in his song "Immigration Time," when he sings, "Wanting to live with the brave in the home of the free."
80. Many El Vez standards unambiguously call for the acceptance and protection of immigrants and assert equality of all minoritized subjects. A set list from the tour reveals that "George Bush on the Guillotine" was preceded by "Mexican American Trilogy," which, like Elvis's American Trilogy, combines the melodies of "Dixie," "The Battle Hymn of the Republic," and "All My Trials" with rewritten lyrics that celebrate Latinx culture.
81. El Vez, *God Save the King*, liner notes.
82. *Viva Hate* is interpreted to reflect on Morrissey's emotional state with the break-up of his band The Smiths, which ended acrimoniously with several lawsuits. His use of Spanish perhaps foreshadows his future proclamations of love for Latinx people during his ¡Oye, Esteban! tour in 1999.
83. The Latinx love of Moz is well documented in the popular press. Many point to Morrissey's melancholic vocal style, which is similar to that of ranchera music. Others point to his outsider status; having grown up minoritized culturally and economically as an Irish Catholic in Protestant England, he sings of an oppression and alienation with which many Latinx subjects can connect. In fact, scholar Iván Alejandro Ramos devotes an entire chapter of his dissertation (now book, cited later) to Morrissey, and the way the negative feelings evoked by his excessive melancholia "are essential to expanding our understanding of the physical and psychic landscapes in which Latino/a subjects dwell." Ramos, "Sonic Negations: Sound, Affect, and Unbelonging Between Mexico and the United States" (PhD diss, University of California, Berkeley, CA, 2015), 77–78. His recently published monograph is entitled *Unbelonging: Inauthentic Sounds in Mexican*

and Latinx Aesthetics (New York: New York University Press, 2023). Morrissey has embraced his Latinx fan base, declaring during his ¡Oye, Esteban! tour that he wished he had been born Mexican. Reflecting its Latinx population, the City of L.A. declared November 10, 2017 "Morrissey Day." Mayor Eric Garcetti called up the artist's ability to connect with oppressed populations, noting "Morrissey Day celebrates an artist whose music has captivated and inspired generations of people who may not always fit in—because they were born to stand out." "Los Angeles Declares Morrissey Day," *Music Connection*, November 8, 2017, accessed July 23, 2018, https://www.musicconnection.com/los-angeles-morrissey-day/. See also Javier Cabral, "Why Do Mexican Americans Love Morrissey So Much?" *The Washington Post*, October 8, 2014, accessed July 23, 2018, https://www.washingtonpost.com/posteverything/wp/2014/10/08/why-do-mexican-americans-love-morrissey-so-much/; Raf Noboa y Rivera, "Morrissey and Mexico Fit Together like Hand in Glove. Is That Really So Strange?" *The Guardian*, March 7, 2016, accessed July 23, 2018, https://www.theguardian.com/commentisfree/2016/mar/07/morrissey-popularity-mexicans-smiths-chicanos-california; Alex Zaragoza, "In Honor of LA Declaring Nov. 10 Morrissey Day, Here's Why Mexicans Love Moz So Damn Much," *Mitú*, November 10, 2017, accessed July 23, 2018, https://wearemitu.com/street-culture/why-mexicans-love-morrissey/.

84. Alex Needham, "Q & A: Morrissey," *The Face*, November 1999, accessed July 23, 2018, https://www.morrissey-solo.com/news/1999/620.shtml. Lopez casually informed me that he and Morrissey went on a couple of dates during this period. Lopez, interview with author, March 3, 2024.
85. In 2018, Morrissey not only claimed that "Hitler was left wing," but also he seemed to defend sexual predators Harvey Weinstein and Kevin Spacey while disparaging their victims, mocked London mayor Sadiq Khan, implied that halal butchers are terrorists affirmed by (and thus supporters of) ISIS, and suggested that "the modern Loony Left" accuses anyone and everyone of racism as a way of "changing the subject." Articles accessed on the *Consequence of Sound* website and elsewhere, June 14, 2018.
86. Upon Thatcher's death, Morrisey submitted a piece to *The Daily Beast* website, some of which was previously published in a 2012 interview in *Loaded* magazine. He describes Thatcher as a "Barbaric" leader who "hated the miners, hated the arts [...] hated the English poor and did nothing to help them." He concludes that she "was a terror without an atom of humanity." *The Daily Beast*, April 8, 2013, accessed April 23, 2018, https://www.thedailybeast.com/morrissey-thatcher-was-a-terror-without-an-atom-of-humanity. In his memoir, Morrissey reports that he was interrogated by Scotland Yard after the release of *Viva Hate,* "to determine whether he posed a threat to the then-Prime Minister." Sophie Jane Evans, "Smiths Singer Was Quizzed by Scotland Yard over Controversial Thatcher Song Margaret on the Guillotine," *The Daily Mail*, October 18, 2013, accessed April 23, 2018, https://www.dailymail.co.uk/news/article-2465742/Smiths-singer-Morrissey-quizzed-Scotland-Yard-controversial-Thatcher-song-Margaret-Guillotine.html.

87. Lopez, text message to author, April 8, 2018.
88. Lopez, text message to author, April 18, 2018.
89. As published by EMI, recording. Accessed via Google, April 26, 2018. As noted, The Beatles stressed that these were gibberish, but they include phrases such as "when" "my love" and "happy heart."
90. In discussing this musical selection, Lopez suggested that he initially based his decision to include it as much on the musical similarities between the songs as any political point. Lopez, interview with author, March 4, 2024.
91. Lopez, text message to author, April 18, 2018.
92. Lopez, text message to author, April 17, 2018.
93. The 2004 EV4P slightly modified this El Vez standard, recordings of which appear on the *G.I. Ay, Ay! Blues* (1996) release and on the *Endless Revolution G.I. Ay, Ay! Blues Service Re-Issue* (2004). The song combines the Broadway musical showstopper "Jesus Christ Superstar" with Elvis's version of "C. C. Rider." Lopez added the Robbie Williams song to the beginning of the medley specifically to sing of his rebirth.
94. El Vez, "Let Me Entertain You (Live)," unreleased track, email to author, April 19, 2018.
95. Lopez, email to author, September 20, 2005.
96. Lopez, email to author, September 20, 2005.
97. Lopez, interview with author, May 19, 2018.
98. Lopez, interview with author, May 19, 2018.
99. Lopez, email to author, September 29, 2005, emphasis added.
100. Lopez, interview with author, May 19, 2018.
101. Lopez, interview with author, May 19, 2018.
102. Lopez, interview with author, May 22, 2018.
103. Lopez, interview with author, May 19, 2018.
104. Lopez, interview with author, May 19, 2018.
105. Lopez, interview with author, August 27, 2008.
106. In 2016, EV4P condemned the xenophobic, ethno-nationalist rhetoric of Donald J. Trump. Once again, Lopez's art was unsuccessful in swaying the election.
107. Lopez, email to author, October 28, 2014.
108. Lopez, interview with author, August 27, 2008.
109. Lopez, email to author, October 28, 2014.
110. Carla Della Gotta, *Latinx Shakespeares: Staging U.S. Intracultural Theater* (Ann Arbor, MI: University of Michigan Press, 2023), 5.

1

If There Is Any Hope for a Revolution: Activating Elvis

The video for "Say It Loud! I'm Brown and I'm Proud!" begins with grainy black and white footage. A young Latino boy walks through a bustling urban setting, replete with signs in both English and Spanish (it is in fact the Giant Penny store, an old five-and-dime opened in 1945, which was located on Broadway and 3rd St in Downtown L.A. before it closed in 1998). The boy approaches a photo booth, where he finds a pair of gold metallic Elvis sunglasses sitting on the stool. After giving them a thorough examination, he puts them on and slides a coin in the slot. Immediately, the music kicks in, the world turns to color, and an alternate reality opens up: El Vez, The Mexican Elvis looks back out at him, wearing the same gold glasses. After a series of shots that cut back and forth from El Vez to the boy, now also in color, we see that the photo booth has been transformed. Lined with an ever-changing backdrop of El Vez posters, Mexican flags, Che Guevara banners, United Farm Workers flags, Virgen de Guadalupe prints, and other Mexican and Chicanx iconography, the tightly framed shots cut from El Vez to the Lovely Elvettes to the Memphis Mariachis to various others—mostly, but not exclusively, Latinx—who sing and dance along to the music, raising their fists, kissing, and otherwise posing for the camera. Occasional exterior shots in black and white show the young boy grooving along as he sits on the stool of this enchanted place. The video suggests that he is a young El Vez who, by donning the Elvis glasses, glimpses his future greatness. That is to say, he sees that by performing *as* and *through* Elvis, he is able to engage in world-building while expressing Latinx pride and Latinx power.[1]

This chapter delves into Lopez's punk rock revisioning of Elvis, establishing the theoretical foundations of his art and tracing the early history of his career. Lopez activates Elvis, critiquing the status quo The King is seen to represent and harnessing the many discourses attached to Elvis as a pop culture icon.

Primary among these is a critique of race and ethnicity, as Lopez performs a sophisticated disidentification through his embodiment of The King through which he signifies on and through his iconicity. However, as much as Lopez plays with race and ethnicity in performance, he also goes beyond it, critiquing any number of issues that have been made to sing in tune with the oppression of neoliberalism. Indeed, with over three decades of performance experience under his Flying Eagle replica belt, Lopez has created an extremely expansive artistic frame that grants him the capacity for world-building, through which he creates social spaces that reimagine USAmerican culture and society. Finally, this chapter will offer a brief retrospective of Lopez's origin and history as El Vez.

The Peanut Butter and Chocolate Have Made a Format: Theoretical Underpinnings

In describing his El Vez performances, Lopez notes, "Good art at times needs to be framed. The frame is ELVIS/MEXICAN."[2] That is, his performances exist at the intersection of two distinct loci of identification: Elvis and his position as a pop culture icon, and that of Lopez's own Chicano background—with a dash of rock star thrown in for good measure. This perhaps sounds cavalier, but Lopez is indeed quite specific about hitting these layers of meaning in performance while also staying in conversation with current events. He asserts, "Whatever thing I [do] can work at least three levels—of a Chicano stance, an Elvis stance, a rock and roll stance."[3] In analyzing Lopez's ELVIS/MEXICAN frame, it becomes clear that Lopez performs two sophisticated actions through his art. Drawing upon Elvis's status as a pop icon and making use of the wealth of visual and linguistic iconography that surrounds The King, Lopez signifies on Elvis and Elvisness. Drawing from his own personal identity as a gay Chicano punk, he also creates a disidentificatory performance that not only transforms the cultural logic of white supremacist heteronormative capitalism embedded in Elvis's status but also allows for world-building to occur through his shows. If signifyin(g) critiques the society that made Elvis, disidentification allows Lopez to make Elvis from his own gay punk Chicano culture.

The liner notes to the 1996 El Vez release *G.I. Ay, Ay! Blues: Soundtrack for the Coming Revolution* make clear how Lopez harnesses Elvis to voice a progressive social message. A Phil Ochs quote is displayed prominently in the CD materials and is printed on the back of the "Che It Loud" T-shirts sold as merch during the accompanying Rock & Revolution tour, which feature El Vez's face superimposed onto the iconic image of the beret-wearing Che (Figure 1.1):

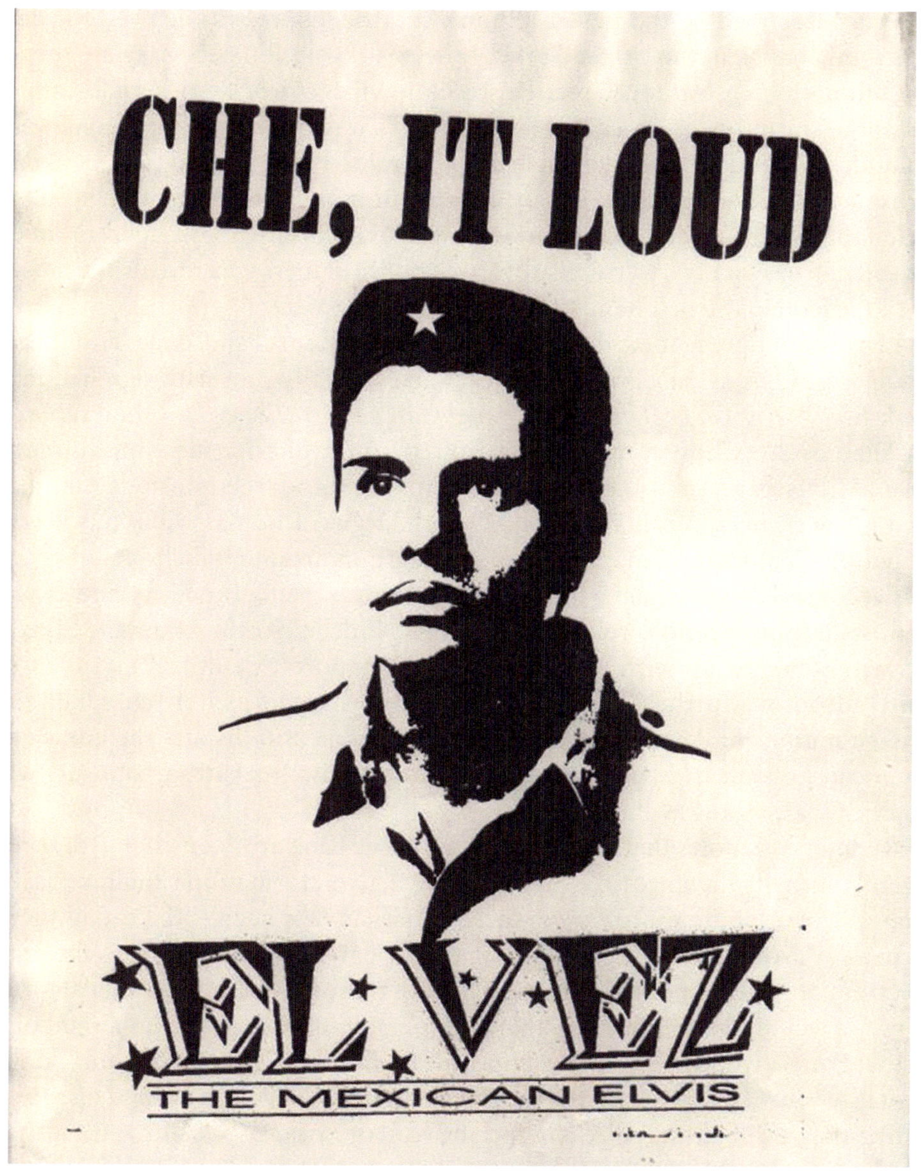

FIGURE 1.1: The El Vez Che It Loud T-shirt design: El Vez becomes Che Guevara, *c.*1995. Courtesy of Robert Lopez's collection.

If there is any hope for America it lies in a Revolution
If there is any hope for a Revolution
It lies in Elvis Presley becoming Che Guevara[4]

The quote, echoed by the El Vez album's subtitle, expresses the need for deep, structural change in the United States. It deems revolution necessary and beneficial, our nation's great hope. Yet, it also acknowledges USAmerica's adoration of consumerism and celebrity culture, suggesting that revolution will not come solely from ideas and ideals—it must instead be heralded by a pop culture icon. That Ochs identifies Elvis as the celebrity capable of motivating revolution speaks to the unique position The King occupies in popular culture; that Lopez, taking up the call, harnesses Elvis to voice subversive political messages reveals the flexibility of the icon in the deft hands of an imaginative artist.

Elvis is omnipresent on the USAmerican pop culture landscape, and it is the ubiquity of Elvis as an icon that makes it an especially powerful signifier. In his book *Elvis After Elvis: The Posthumous Career of a Living Legend*, Gilbert D. Rodman dissects how a multitude of often contradictory meanings circulate around Elvis as a symbol, each of them tapping into larger tensions that mark the USAmerican cultural landscape. As such, argues Rodman, Elvis has become a mythological formation, a point of articulation around which sets of related myths coalesce—particularly those involving race, gender identity and expression, sexual orientation, religion, and class. Indeed, states Rodman, Elvis "is intimately bound up with many of the most important cultural myths of our time."[5] Rodman further asserts that these myths are intimately entwined with understandings of America, and are used to define and dispute the concept of American-ness itself. Elvis as an icon exists as a site for battling out just what America was, is, and will be.

Rodman also notes that understandings of The King are "consistently linked to several mutually incompatible myths within a given formation simultaneously," each of them tapping into larger social tensions.[6] As such, "the mythological formation around Elvis seems flexible enough to be invoked across the entire spectrum of political positions associated with these broader mythological formations," which situates Elvis as "a figure who simultaneously stands as a symbol for all that is most wonderful and most horrible about [the American] dream."[7] Lopez capitalizes on the way that Elvis is linked to competing mythologies and discourses. Rather than trying to stabilize any specific read of Elvis, Lopez allows these many meanings to circulate throughout his performance. Contentious cultural discourses are layered on top of each other, allowing for new and surprising resonances to open up between them in the process. Prominent among these, and specifically called out by the ELVIS/MEXICAN framework, is race and ethnicity.

In *American Skin: Pop Culture, Big Business, and the End of White America*, Leon E. Wynter heralds as the heart of USAmerican culture the transracial exchange that has occurred in our nation since its founding. Historically, what set white U.S. residents apart from their European forebears was the interaction and exchange with the racial Other at home. Wynter notes, "Whatever is distinctly American yet somehow universally appealing in our most immortal works of popular culture flows from the alchemy of racial amalgamation peculiar to the United States."[8] Wynter draws an important distinction between this transracial flow as it played out politically and culturally. Because white supremacist policies and practices bestow power and privilege on white citizens, it was they who historically were granted the ability to play with and profit from transracial performance. With the *de jure* and *de facto* social, economic, and legal benefits that whiteness bestows (what Wynter dubs political whiteness) safely kept intact, white performers could put aside their cultural whiteness through transracial performance, instances in which they would either present themselves *as* or borrow (some would say steal) *from* the racial Other. Racial privilege granted them the opportunity to appropriate what they wanted from minoritized cultures through performance, and then safely return to their privileged racial position after the performance was finished. The most popular USAmerican cultural exports, including minstrelsy, jazz, rock and roll—and Elvis—were marked by this transracial exchange.

For many, Elvis's prominence epitomizes racial inequality and oppression: Elvis was a white man who became rich and famous playing Black music, while Black musicians were barred access to that path. He stole from Black culture and was crowned The King for his thievery. In Wynter's terms, his political whiteness allowed him to adopt cultural Blackness and profit from it. In contrast, others hold that Elvis's massive popularity made visible—and unavoidable—the fact that cultural mixing forms the vibrant core of USAmerican culture. His music was not the watered-down stylings of a Pat Boone, but rather was authentic to the lived experience of his upbringing, marked as it was by transracial exchange that occurred within impoverished, rural Mississippi. Without ignoring the pervasive racism that enabled Elvis's ascendency, a more hopeful read of the cultural mixing at the core of Elvis's sound and aesthetic sees it as a precursor to much greater racial integration to come.

By inserting his racially marked body into Elvis's familiar bell-bottomed jumpsuits, Lopez evokes these discourses as he perturbs the privileged place of whiteness within USAmerican culture. Lopez can then use the intersections established through the iconicity of Elvis to discuss the racial discourses to which The King is already bound while deconstructing these same tropes. Indeed, he strategically amplifies his racial difference by linking it to nationality, calling himself The *Mexican* Elvis. Because Lopez is in fact a U.S. citizen, born and raised in Southern California, his name also seems to mimic the racist habit, recently practiced by Donald J. Trump, of linguistically rendering all Latinx individuals "Mexicans," a tactical move that speaks to the way race, nation, and Otherness has been used to suggest inferiority and impose the precarity of second-class citizenship. Lopez uses the materiality of his body along with the difference inscribed in the El Vez name to effectively underscore the way we are trained to see race.

What is exciting is that with El Vez, it can be all ways. If one believes that Elvis was a white thief of Black culture, then El Vez is the Latinx trickster who is stealing it back. Through performance, he calls attention to the racial politics that enabled this theft and granted Elvis superstardom while blocking access to other artists of color. Conversely, if one believes that Elvis was a charismatic and powerful performer deserving of his superstardom, then El Vez celebrates that legend through impersonation. And, if one is conflicted about Elvis's legacy, one can simply take pleasure in the music and spectacle that Lopez creates. Through performance, Lopez can make visible how racial inequality *made* Elvis, while also claiming The King's legacy as his own. He asserts an equality of access to this icon by showing that The King is not solely a white hero: Elvis can *belong to* everyone. In fact, by revealing how Elvis borrowed from other cultures—how he in fact *came from* everyone—and by performing a similar borrowing back, El Vez reminds his audience that the Elvis icon represents more than Elvis the man. That is to say, Elvis Presley the artist appropriated multiple cultural traditions, which all were folded into his racially (un)marked white body to create Elvis the icon, whose superstardom exceeded even his own embodied experience. El Vez unpacks the icon, revealing the multiplicity of cultural traditions at play and marking each as distinct, and yet somehow compatible. His use of Elvis pushes back against essentializing discourses. Through El Vez, Elvis becomes a conduit for world-building, for the creation of a progressive social space that affords the inclusion of all identities.

I should note that not all critics embrace Lopez's use of Elvis as a sign. In her chapter "My Love/Hate Relationship with El Vez," Bernadette Marie Calafell, a communications studies scholar, critiques Lopez's use of Elvis. As the chapter title suggests, Calafell is "an ambivalent fan,"[9] who raises important questions about the relationship between Lopez, El Vez, and Elvis. While she acknowledges the subversive political messaging at play in El Vez's performances, noting both the potency of his song lyrics and his use of pop culture references and imagery, Calafell expresses considerable discomfort with Lopez's embodiment of Elvis. She notes that she is not alone in articulating this concern, offering a summary of her students' reactions to El Vez, whom she teaches in class. Says Calafell, "All too often students of color chastise Lopez for presenting his message through a 'white sign' (Elvis), arguing that his reappropriation is not enough, that whiteness is still privileged."[10] Indeed, this is a valid critique, especially given the fact that white supremacist culture absolutely enabled Elvis's superstardom. Yet, such a reading of Elvis is just one of the many discourses attached to the Elvis sign, and, I would suggest, it is a reading that is rooted in the kinds of essentialized understandings of race and culture that El Vez performances seek to undo. Moreover, such a reading overemphasizes how Lopez situates Elvis in El Vez's performances. Though The King is certainly present, he is hardly centered. Rather, the highly inauthentic figure of El Vez reigns supreme. Elvis is called up, but, as Lopez readily notes "self-reference is kind of the name of the game with El Vez."[11]

Henry Louis Gates, Jr.'s discussion of signifyin(g)[12] offers a means of analyzing how El Vez performances use the playful (re)doubling of language, images, and sound to defer, repress, hide, or altogether set aside "official" meaning so that new meanings can be brought forward.[13] Gates defines signifyin(g) as "a theory of criticism that is inscribed within the black vernacular tradition and that in turn informs the shape of the Afro-American literary tradition."[14] That is, it is specifically located within Black culture. Gates traces its roots back to the Yoruban trickster figure Esu-Elegbara through "all of the rhetorical play in the black vernacular"[15] and into a sophisticated literary tradition that creates narrative space to present a double-voiced utterance that exists beyond literal, sanctioned meanings. As discussed above, Lopez's use of Elvis as an icon as well as his engagement with popular culture supports using this theory as a means of analyzing El Vez's performances, even as the theory travels across racial lines to a Latinx specificity. Clearly, Elvis is inextricably tied to Black culture, even as his physical body absents it. In essence, Lopez's signifyin(g) calls up the Blackness that Elvis erased. Moreover, popular culture—and especially popular music—functions as a vibrant site of transracial exchange, one in which Black culture carries great influence. Finally, like African Americans, Latinx individuals have faced a long history of oppression in the United States, thus the need to speak through double-voiced utterances that vacate and subvert the rhetoric of dominant whiteness is shared among these groups.

The intertextuality of an El Vez performance allows for his signifyin(g), through which he ultimately offers revisions—with a signal difference—to USAmerican culture itself. El Vez's performances are replete with linguistic, visual, sonic, and musical references to other texts. For instance, his album covers (Figure 1.2) and many of his publicity photos visually signify on work by other artists, including Elvis, David Bowie, and Paul Simon, just as his album titles, lyrical revisions, and stage banter bring in even broader allusions. These references come from all over: from Lopez's Chicano background and personal history, popular culture and advertising, music, politics, art, propaganda, literature, and film. States Lopez, "it's really trying to connect the millions and millions of dots that is life, politics, [society]."[16] Lopez crafts an experience that connects the dots and then "throw[s] them into the air, like Chinese sticks, to see where they land."[17] As I will discuss in further detail in Chapter 2, not only does Lopez give his audience members different entry points, but he also allows them multiple interpretations, which can co-exist together.

Take, for example, the song and video with which I opened this chapter, "Say it Loud! I'm Brown and I'm Proud," a song he describes in the *Endless Revolution* liner notes as his "call to arms for Latinos of today."[18] In it, El Vez speaks out against the misrepresentation of Latinx subjects in order to interrogate how racist policy is predicated on the deployment of a distorted image. He begins by singing James Brown's original lyrics, repositioned through El Vez to focus on Latinx individuals:

> Some say we got a lot of malice
> Some say we got a lot of nerve
> I say we won't quit until we get what we deserve.

In both songs, these opening lyrics describe how Black and Latinx subjects, in seeking equal rights, are characterized by those in power ("some say") as dangerous, angry, and uppity in their desire to overturn social hierarchies. The lyrics then recast this ("I say") as a political action that seeks to expand freedom and equality. In the video, which features a mix of Latinx and non-Latinx people, men and women, and straight and queer couples, Lopez visually reinforces both the Latinx pride the song exudes and the inclusivity he seeks.[19] Similarly, the iconography is Mexican, Chicanx, and USAmerican.

Lopez goes on to critique the codification of racism into law through the specificity of the Latinx experience in California. Though these lyrics, which reference Proposition 187 and Governor Pete Wilson, are temporally grounded in the mid-1990s, they continue to resonate with anti-immigration discourse circulating today:

> I've worked all day with my hands and my feet
> And all the time we're running from some Governor name Pete
> 187 tried to keep us down
> That won't happen just because I'm brown
>
> [...]
>
> Now we demand a chance for better, higher education
> We're tired of being in our homeland with this feeling of alienation
> Now we are people too, we like the birds and the bees
> But we'd rather die on our feet
> Than keep on livin' on our knees.

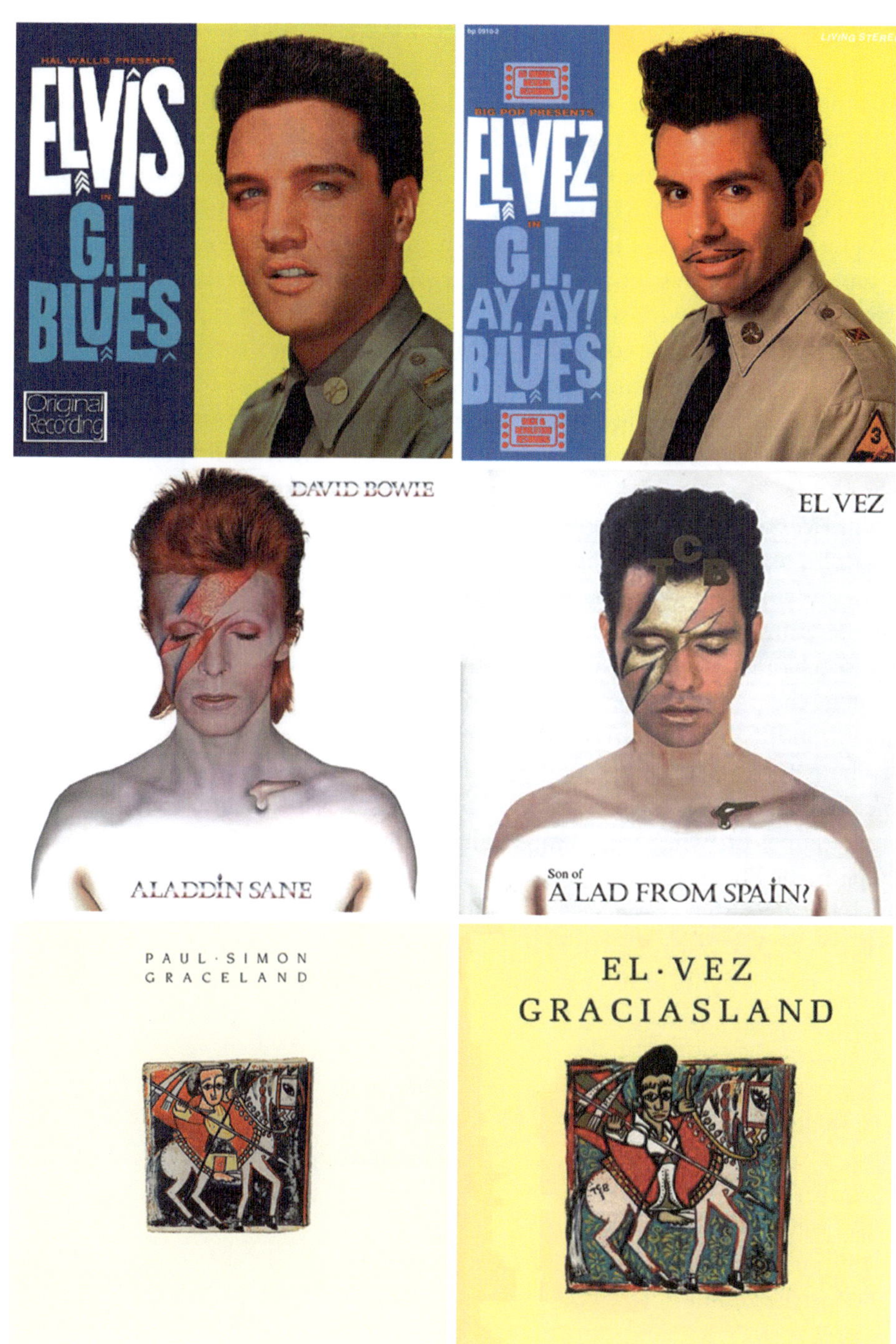

FIGURE 1.2: El Vez album covers next to the original covers they signify on: Elvis's *G.I. Blues* (1960) becomes El Vez's *G. I. Ay, Ay! Blues* (1996); David Bowie's *Aladdin Sane* (1973) becomes El Vez's *Son of a Lad from Spain?* (1999); Paul Simon's *Graceland* (1986) becomes El Vez's *Graciasland* (1994).

The song clearly refers to the way political discourse vilifies Latinx individuals based on their perceived racial markers—the very material aspects that Lopez highlights in his performance of El Vez. Latinx citizens and non-citizens alike are dubbed outlaws; they are brown, and they are therefore dangerous pollutants.

As Lopez reworks the James Brown original into the El Vez cover, he engages in "repetition and revision, or repetition with a signal difference."[20] Through his key revisions of Brown's hit, Lopez is in effect signifyin(g) on an original that is perhaps itself signifyin(g) on white culture. Thus, Lopez's rewrite simultaneously grounds the piece in Latinx specificity, forges connections between brown and Black culture by revealing the similar oppressions both groups have faced, and celebrates the way that popular music acts as a vehicle for subversive expression.

Sonically, "Say It Loud!" marks an interesting departure from many of Lopez's earlier El Vez songs in that it does not directly reference Elvis. Rather, the song follows a playful referential chain that leads back to Elvis, which evidences Lopez's skill at aural signifyin(g). El Vez cleverly uses indirection, metaphor and image, humor and irony, rhythm and sound, rhyme, puns and wordplay, and semantic and logical surprise to craft a mode of teaching that resists lapsing into didactic preaching, which heightens the pleasure we as audience members can take from it.[21] The version of "Say It Loud!"[22] featured in the video samples several Public Enemy tracks, and the full album borrows heavily from them, often creating a cacophonous aural landscape replete with sirens, scratches, and loud bass lines. Public Enemy, in turn, frequently samples James Brown, perhaps most famously in "Fight the Power." Via this circuitous path, the Elvis connection becomes clear: in the third verse of "Fight the Power," Chuck D says, "Elvis was a hero to most, but he never meant shit to me / Straight up racist, the sucker was / Simple and plain" followed by Flavor-Flav's "Mother fuck him and John Wayne." El Vez responds to this line in his version, singing:

Elvis was a hero to me
You've got to remember he was the first public enemy
PE backwards spells Elvis Presley
If you can't stand the man, then don't stand next to me
So say it proud and say it loud
¡Viva Elvis! Viva paper towels
I'm a quicker picker upper, I wipe up impersonators
TCB to the faithful
To hell with Elvis haters.[23]

Chuck D's line speaks to the racism embedded in the music industry. El Vez responds that Elvis's music marks the fact that cultural exchange across racial lines has always occurred, starting first and foremost with his own Elvis fandom.[24] Though his delivery of these lines sounds strident, he undercuts what he says by coupling it with humor through the seemingly silly pop culture reference to Viva paper towels.[25] Yet, this joking moment in fact layers more meaning onto his words. It of course references Elvis's *Viva Las Vegas*, both the movie and the song, which further recalls the linkage of Elvis (both the young Elvis of the movie and the fatter, tackier, drug-addled Elvis who held a Vegas residency at the end of his career) to the city. The Viva paper towel reference also notes how the dominant culture will appropriate and commodify the Other, in this case transforming the Spanish expression ¡Viva! (usually translated as "Long Live!") into a brand name. Lopez takes this back by appropriating the slogan "The quicker picker upper" and uses it, with pure MC bravado, to mark his own prowess as an Elvis impersonator. He adds in the additional reference of "TCB," an Elvis mantra and emblem, to signal his alliance with The King and against Elvis haters.[26] Moreover, in this moment he acknowledges that the persona musical artists adopt is always performative, as is the relationship between the persona and the characters of the songs (more on that in Chapter 2).[27] Through music, artists often seek to make a strong statement, and controversy sells, as do commercial slogans. Indeed, Chuck D has repeatedly asserted that his Elvis line was not about the man, but about the white supremacy embedded in USAmerican culture that lauded him as it erased the Black musicians he cited. In September 2014, Chuck D told *Guardian* reporter Adrian Deevoy:

> I never personally had something against Elvis. But the American way of putting him up as the King and the great icon is disturbing. You can't ignore black history [...] So, Elvis was just the fall guy in my lyrics for all of that. It was nothing personal—believe me.[28]

The exchange between these two songs exemplifies Rodman's assertion that Elvis is a mythological formation around which discourses of race and racism coalesce.

Lopez acknowledges that there is an inherent irony in his adoption of Elvis, whose iconicity he uses to speak subversive political commentary and create progressive social spaces; remarks Lopez, Elvis:

> never was political, and he hated that. But even being non-political is a kind of political statement. And so when you are dealing with people and audiences, it turns into a forum, and a forum to me is always a political element.[29]

Moreover, Lopez stresses that Elvis was considered more of a joke during the early years of El Vez:

> there was also the stereotype on the Elvis. It was like, okay, Elvis is already, especially in the mid-80s, a court jester. It was the lucky period to latch onto that, Elvis

> was already a silly character, a caricature [...] It's like, okay, let's gild that lily even more, put a moustache on it, put a sombrero on it, and then while you've got their attention, then you slip in the other thing. That was the whole, for me, the one good that I could do.[30]

When Lopez began performing as El Vez, Elvis and Elvis impersonators were objects of ridicule. Lopez layered his own jokes on top of this—stereotypes on top of stereotypes, in his words—which became the conduit for him to slip subversive content into his performance by creating what he describes as "a symposium of ideas under the Elvis frame. To make [the audience] think is the most important thing."[31] Through El Vez, a joke becomes something more, and Elvis becomes a revolutionary.

Signifyin(g), as I am applying it to El Vez performances, is a potent means of using the knowledge of the marginalized to call out the absurdities of structural oppression in USAmerican society. Excluded from and therefore external to the dominant culture, signifyin(g) subverts "official" discourse, calling attention to the distance between the lofty rhetoric of equality and the lived realities of minoritized subjects. The trickster can speak truth to power precisely because that truth is double-voiced—a seeming homage to The King is reworked to lambaste white supremacy, heteronormativity, misogyny, and more. Moreover, the double voice is lasting. Notes Lopez, his audiences, having heard his reworkings, "will never think about [the Elvis originals] the same way, even though his have been around for longer than mine. But I put a mustache on it."[32]

If signfyin(g) speaks from the external position of the marginalized, the second half of the ELVIS/MEXICAN frame operates differently, using disidentification to place the self within exclusionary discourses and thereby create new social spaces. As José Esteban Muñoz posits in *Disidentifications: Queers of Color and the Performance of Politics*, political power is encoded into cultural fields, making a "phobic majoritarian public sphere" that is hostile to minoritized subjects.[33] Signifyin(g) uses playful indirection to critique these structures of oppression from without; disidentification enacts a more personal language of "identities in difference" to "transform [their] cultural logic[s] from within."[34] That is, disidentification allows a disempowered subject to read the self—a self that is marginalized due to race, gender, sexuality, or other identificatory categories—into an antagonistic representational hierarchy. Notes Muñoz:

> The process of disidentification scrambles and reconstructs the encoded message of a cultural text in a fashion that both exposes the encoded message's universalizing and exclusionary machinations and recruits its workings to account for, include, and empower minority identities and identifications. Thus, disidentification is a

> step further than cracking the code of the majority; it proceeds to use this code as a raw material for representing a disempowered politics or positionality that has been rendered unthinkable by the dominant culture.[35]

Through disidentificatory performance, the minoritized subject not only lays claim to the dominant culture, revealing how it aids oppression but also simultaneously remakes and decolonizes it. In so doing, disidentification engenders a new social space that "would be the blueprint for minoritarian counterpublic spheres."[36]

As noted earlier, Lopez capitalizes on the way Elvis functions as a site of mythological formation. That flexibility of meaning is heightened through the disidentificatory performances of El Vez. As Muñoz notes, "disidentification does not dispel those ideological contradictory elements."[37] Rather, suggests Muñoz, "Disidentification is about recycling and rethinking encoded meaning."[38] Through performance, Lopez infuses his own sensibility (and oftentimes, his own biography) into the Elvis icon, scrambling Elvis into El Vez and creating a forum from which to speak a different truth.

Muñoz notes that "to disidentify is to read oneself and one's own narrative in a moment, object, or subject that is not culturally coded to connect with the disidentifying subject."[39] And what can be further from Elvis Presley than a self-described formerly chubby, gay, Chicano punk rock outsider?[40] I will speak more directly about the *how* of Lopez's disidentification—the specific techniques of using irony and inauthenticity to create a gap between Lopez as artist and El Vez as persona, which creates a critical distance that contributes to his world-building—in the next chapter; here I want to focus on the *why* of it, considering aspects of his biography that might compel Lopez to embrace this style of performance as well as the experience he curates for the audience, which amounts to the sort of world-building that disidentificatory performances make possible.

Born in 1960, Lopez grew up in the San Diego suburb of Chula Vista, where he was one of a handful of Latinx students in the school. Chula Vista is far more racially diverse today than it was in Lopez's youth. He states that in his elementary school:

> from kindergarten to sixth [grade] I was [one of] one, two, there might have been ten Latinos in the whole school [...] So that's not, it wasn't something you thought about but when you think about it now, you go wow, that's not much at all.[41]

By high school, there were more Latinx students, but they were still a small percentage of the student body. Lopez notes that he did not feel particularly ostracized, stating, "that was just the way it was. We were the only Latinos on our block [...] No, there were Puerto Ricans right next to [us], but they were fancy Puerto

Ricans—they had more money than us."[42] He notes in "Punk-Rock Teenage Heaven" that "My family floated somewhere between middle and lower-middle class. Our diet included government cheese and something we called 'poor people's chop suey' a few times a week."[43] He would go on to pen songs contemplating race and class in his work as El Vez.

He recalls that he was a "library lunch time by myself" kind of kid, a "Misfit, I would say."[44] His isolation was dictated by his interests as much as by any particular hostility on the part of his peers, though he does acknowledge that he "was overweight and picked on a lot"[45]; if his school had a "surfer, stoner, sosch" vibe, he was drawn more to avant-garde art along with trash, glitter, and glam bands that he read about in underground music magazines like *Creem* or *Rock Scene*.[46] He adds, "I think by 14 [...] the idea of music and theatre and music was my in, it was my invitation to the theatre of Iggy [Pop] and [David] Bowie, of [theatricalized rock] performance."[47] His social position also allowed him to experiment with and through music, he suggests that "you already knew you were a misfit so you already knew you could be free to make mistakes [...] so the idea of experimentation at age 16 was a good chance."[48] He joined with Javier Escovedo, Baba Chenelle, and Hector Penalosa to become the punk band The Zeros.

Punk rock is foundational to Lopez's artistic sensibility, and his time spent experimenting in the L.A. punk scene of the late 1970s informs the strategies he would adopt in building El Vez into an international phenomenon. In *Loca Motion: The Travels of Chicana and Latina Popular Culture*, Habell-Pallán situates Lopez as part of a group of artists generationally distanced from first-wave Chicanx[49] activism and animated instead by a punk sensibility of resistance. Picking up on the revisioning of the popular at the heart of Muñoz's discussion of disidentification, she notes:

> In addition to constructing individual and collective identities, popular performance culture, as a hybrid form, often articulates social and historical conflicts and allows those who have little access to ways of intervening in the dominant modes of representation (film, television, print) to represent themselves in their own terms.[50]

Marginalized from power, the impulse behind punk rock was to engage with popular culture in order to disrupt it.

This sentiment is echoed by legendary punk rocker Alice Bag, a past Elvette and dear friend of and collaborator with Lopez. Bag reflects on the inclusivity of the early punk movement while also highlighting the outsider status that animated many punk artists, noting:

> Early punks were rich, poor, gay, straight, male, and female, with a good sampling of L.A.'s ethnic diversity [...] united only in the sense of having been identified as

> "outcasts," either by society or by themselves [...] Early punk was as much a rejection of the status quo as it was the product of the rejects of the status quo.[51]

Lopez echoes this, noting how punk forged vital connections that stood in opposition to concerns he might have faced in school: "at 16, when you're an outcast and you aren't going to the prom, this is your prom."[52] Punk was an exercise in carving out their own social spaces and creating community around alternate values and new ways of being—that is, the sort of world-building that Lopez continues to do through El Vez performances. Furthermore, Bag situates punk as a vital node in a long history of social activism, noting, "Punk attitude continues to inform counterculture, protest movements, and popular actions aimed at societal change."[53] Punk, and its relationship to the popular, offers a necessary critique of societal norms, and it activates different social configurations.

Lopez specifically notes the sort of "message-in-a-bottle romantic idea" embedded in the early punk scene, that they were reaching out to an unknown audience through flyers advertising underground events:

> the idea of putting up a flyer up on Santa Monica Boulevard and you know Santa Monica Boulevard goes on for miles and still the idea is like, "Oh, who walks in L.A.?" everyone's driving, but then again people who don't have cars, which was us, that was our only access to advertising and to think of it now which is a great thing [...] But it's that idea that you were reaching out to people that you did not know, to whom you did not have a link, and [with] what images? The images were usually antisocial, be it a car crash or something violent, or some odd word or some odd face that's not going to say, "Oh, we're friendly, come and see us!"
>
> It was obviously confronting you in a sense, and artistically, hopefully, and something askew and akimbo and not of the norm. And so you have to think, oh, that has got to reach out to somebody [who will then] say, "Look at that, that looks interesting, I have no idea who those people are [... but this] dismembered arm or amputated leg with a little chain around the toe or something like that is cute and funny." And they say, "Oh, that represents us!"[54]

Lopez describes a model that at once targets a specific audience while also leaving room for their own imaginings of the event. That is, the flyers spoke to certain conditions: people who were walking, who didn't have cars; people who knew to look for flyers in the first place; people to whom the antisocial images and a skewed vision of the norm would appeal. But they also were ambiguous, asking potential audience members to determine how they might situate themselves in the event.

Lopez's musings speak to the importance of the DIY (do-it-yourself) ethic embedded in punk. If punk deliberately places itself outside of mainstream culture, by and for Bag's outsiders and rejects, it follows that the culture would need to be created by its participants, especially during its early years. The DIY ethic refers to the way punks literally built their own culture on the fly, creating bands, booking and advertising shows, covering the scene in zines, developing styles and aesthetics, and recording albums. Stephen Duncombe emphasizes how the DIY ethic not only offers a cultural critique but also prompts agency:

> Doing it yourself is at once a critique of the dominant mode of passive consumer culture and something far more important: the active creation of an alternative culture. DIY is not just complaining about what is, but actually doing something about it.[55]

Joe Mageary adds that DIY as an "ethical and practical stance now pervades punk shows [...] It is such an integral element of punk that many participants [...] cannot separate the two."[56] And Ryan Moore and Michael Roberts suggest that the DIY ethic "plays a constitutive role in resource mobilization and other organizational aspects of a social movement,"[57] considering it a mobilizing structure through which culture is built and organized.

The DIY ethic stands in opposition to the slick professionalism and corporate interests of the mainstream. Instead, it celebrates amateurism. Notes Duncombe,

> Beginning in the mid-1970s as a reaction against the professionalization of rock music, punk took music back to its R&B, hillbilly, thoroughly unrespectable, roots. Songs were loud and fast and short: pure blasts of adrenaline with little pretense to studied musicianship.[58]

Lopez avers this description, noting, "A lot of people, this was their first time to pick up a thing and do it, which is a different aesthetic—learning your trade as you perform on stage."[59] Still, Lopez points to the varying levels of performance knowledge within the early years. Artists such as Tomata du Plenty would:

> confront us with theatre [...] his knowing of performance was opposed to us [The Zeros] where we were shoegazing and standing there. He knew how to command the stage, and one of the things, of course, was dancing around, but he also [embraced] the idea of just standing still, which is a great theatre knowledge, to know you can command presence just by doing nothing, if you have the gumption to do it.[60]

The theatricalism of (some of) the performances was combined with sonic experimentation, which again was rooted in the DIY ethic. States Lopez, "people were experimenting and learning and that's how you could get weird sounds and noise, and that opened the floodgates."[61] Thus, the DIY ethic, with its rejection of professionalism in favor of a more earnest musical expression, allowed for different performance aesthetics to emerge.

A second aspect of the DIY ethic, at least for Lopez, was educational; he learned lessons about his profession not only by being in the scene, keenly observing what other punk artists were doing but also by being somewhat outside of it. As Lopez describes it, he and his Zeros bandmates were insulated by their geography and their youth. They traveled to L.A. from Chula Vista to play gigs, but then were back home attending high school during the week:

> We were young sponges so we were absorbing every musical style [...] so it was pretty exciting and more energetic. Then you would get home. And I think since we were there for the weekends or a show and then back home, it gave us time to ponder, to contemplate.[62]

They not only were recognized as peers by other punk rockers but also were able to step away, to "go home, regroup, get your ideas about how we can do better."[63] This space allowed Lopez to both be an artist and a student of the art, learning key lessons that would eventually allow him to step into the role of lead singer and creative director as he created the rich, exciting art of El Vez, The Mexican Elvis.

When I Was Just a Little Vez: The El Vez Origin Story

The El Vez origin story is well-documented, relayed in many newspaper articles and interviews, but the lead-up to this artistic creation is worth mentioning if only to make visible the hustle of a punk rock kid against the backdrop of L.A. of the 1970s and 1980s. Over the next decade, Lopez would officially relocate to L.A., with a quick trip to New York described in his chapter in *Under the Big Black Sun*. He would work a series of different jobs: as a waiter at Straw Hat Pizza in Hollywood (his first official L.A. job); at the Supply Sergeant on Hollywood Boulevard (near the Pussycat Theater, which screened X-rated movies; the theatre sat above Brendan Mullen's legendary punk performance space The Masque, housed in the building's 10,000 square-foot basement/nuclear fallout shelter[64]); as a cashier at El Coyote on Beverly Boulevard; as a barista at Coffee Land in Century City; working the overnight shift at Drake's adult book store on Melrose; and at the Continental Hyatt House on Sunset Boulevard—nicknamed the Riot House—where Little Richard dubbed him "Little Robert" (a story that he often shares in performance, especially in the context of his band The Little Richards).[65] Eventually, Lopez became the curator for the groundbreaking underground art gallery La Luz de Jesus, an artistic offshoot of L.A.'s storied Soap Plant and Wacko, stores owned by Billy Shire. As part of his gallery curation, he would produce monthly openings to celebrate the different shows and artists. These openings became star-studded events, and have been described as having "gathered something of a cult following"[66] and as "wildly popular [...] raucous and subversive."[67] In May 1988, he curated *The Elvis Show*, a folk-art celebration of Elvis featuring the work of 36 different artists. For this, Lopez hired an Elvis Impersonator to perform, while he took on the role of manager Colonel Tom Darker (a play on Elvis's manager Colonel Tom Parker). The impersonator was mediocre at best; Lopez realized he could be a better Elvis, and a legend was born.[68] Lopez recounts:

> Some friends of mine said the place to go was Memphis, for the anniversary of Elvis' death, August 16th, and I dared myself to go there. I said, "I can make a fool of myself, I don't know anyone there, so it's OK." Someone gave me a number, I pretended I was an agent booking El Vez, and they said, "Oh, yeah, we've heard of him." They hadn't, of course, because I'd never done it before. I rewrote some of the words on the plane, practiced once in my hotel room, they gave me a band, I wore gold lamé pants and a gold sombrero, a jacket covered with Elvis buttons, so I made a splash.[69] (Figure 1.3)

Lopez in fact had contacted Bad Bob's Vapors Club, the Memphis venue that hosted a contest for Elvis impersonators—unsanctioned by the Elvis estate, yet very popular—during Elvis International Tribute Week (also affectionately known as Weep Week or Death Week).[70]

One of the first people to have seen El Vez perform in Memphis was Belinda Gordon, a Memphis native who served as Lopez's local connection when he first arrived in the city in 1988.[71] Gordon describes late-1980s Memphis as a fascinating place: like many Southern cities, it was rather conservative, but also featured a "weird little arty scene."[72] It was also a city synonymous with music: it had long been a hub for groundbreaking blues, jazz, gospel, rockabilly, and rock and roll music, and Memphis sites including Beale Street, Sun Records, Stax Records, and Ardent Records are storied within USAmerican popular music history. And, of prime importance to this story, Memphis is where Elvis got his start, at Sun Records, and where he met his end, at Graceland. Notes music journalist Robert Gordon:

> Memphis—my Memphis—*likes* the unquantifiable. Nashville, New York, and Los Angeles—they promise stardom. Had Elvis gone there, he might have enjoyed minor success as the lame-ass Perry Como imitator he thought he was supposed to be. Elvis needed Sam [Phillips, legendary music producer] to identify and affirm his renegade spirit, to allow him to express what he felt rather than what he imagined others expected. Memphis wants something different.[73]

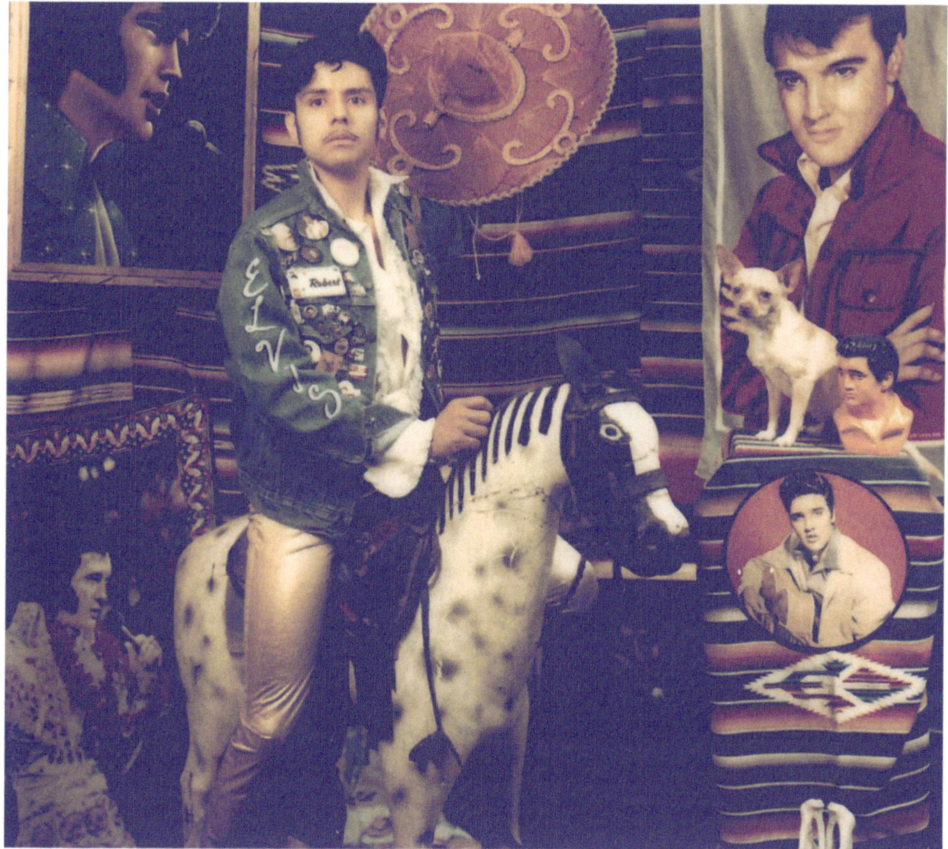

FIGURE 1.3: El Vez's first publicity photo, in which he wears a custom-made jean jacket and gold lamé pants as a costume, *c.*1988. Courtesy of Robert Lopez's collection.

Though Elvis is interwoven into Memphis culture, his position in 1988 was contradictory. Just over ten years after his death, his status as an icon was clearly in formation, but it was met with a fair share of skepticism—especially from locals, a feeling highlighted in much of the national journalism of the time. A *New York Times* article cites Shelby County mayor Bill Morris, Jr. reflecting, "The Elvis Presley syndrome after death continues to startle and amaze even the people closest to Elvis [...] I'm not certain scholars will ever come up with a consensus of who or what was Elvis Presley."[74] A 1987 *Washington Post* article emphasizes the new music being made in Memphis, relegating Elvis (and his diehard fans) to a pitiable nostalgic past. Moreover, it slights Elvis fans in gendered and classist ways, for instance when it notes in a parenthetical aside, "(The average fan, according to a survey commissioned by RCA, Elvis's longtime label, is a woman between 35 and 50, a resident of the South and the wife of a blue-collar worker, who listens to 'contemporary' radio.)"[75] The article goes on to quote Harry Chapman, bartender at Beale Street's Rum Boogie Cafe as saying, "We don't like Elvis too much around here."[76] Gordon recalls a similar attitude in her own Memphis experience. Discussing Elvis's death and the events that built up around it, she notes, "People were shocked. I mean, he was only 42, but then it was also kind of a little bit of sneering going on, you know, not when he died, but later."[77]

Perhaps what Weep Week in 1988 makes clear is how many different authors, across so many different political and social positions, would descend upon Memphis to simultaneously write their own Elvis myths. For one, there were the aims of Elvis Presley Enterprises (EPE), a corporate entity created in 1981 by the Elvis Presley Trust, under Priscilla Presley's leadership. At EPE's founding, the estate was struggling, due in part to the exploitative contract Colonel Tom Parker had maneuvered with Elvis, which continued after Elvis's death when his father Vernon became executor, and was set to continue after Vernon's death until it came under the review of Probate Judge Joseph Evans. Parker's contract stipulated that he would receive 50 percent of the estate's income, an arrangement Evans rightly deemed exploitative. After a thorough investigation by court-appointed attorney Blanchard Tual, who was also ordered by Evans to serve as Lisa Marie's financial guardian, the judge severed the relationship between the estate and Parker, and further ordered the estate to bring suit against him.[78] To correct their financial fortunes, EPE moved to codify Elvis's public image by strictly stewarding his music, image, and intellectual property. As a business enterprise, EPE sought to control the narrative and meaning of Elvis's life and work while also profiting from it, sanctioning events as part of the official Elvis Week schedule. Elvis Impersonators were decidedly NOT a part of this, and would not be officially welcomed into the festivities until 2007—after Lisa Marie Presley's sale of 85% of EPE to the branding firm CKX[79]—when EPE first sponsored the Ultimate Elvis Tribute Artist Contest.[80] Lopez reports that he was once told by an EPE employee, "About half of us love what you do as El Vez and half of us hate it."[81] He further recounts that Priscilla reportedly said, "We like El Vez, he does what he does and & leaves us alone …"[82] However much EPE's relationship to tribute artists may have evolved, it is clear that in 1988, the entity was still invested in asserting strict control over Elvis's image.

Yet, Elvis fans who celebrated The King—and their relationship with him—did so both inside and outside of the official structure of EPE. Gordon stresses that many events in fact originated as spontaneous actions by Elvis's admirers; "Death week wasn't something that Elvis Presley Enterprises came up with. That's just something that happened, and they started calling it Death Week. But I mean people have been going [to Graceland] every August since he died."[83] As many scholars have noted, devoted Elvis fans often feel a deeply emotional connection to Elvis. In her study of Elvis impersonators, Lynn Spigel notes that they and their fans engage in an act of popular memory, which is:

> bound up with its use value in the present [...] The memories of Elvis that impersonators revive serve to open up a space for common experiences among a group of devoted fans who also want to remain in contact with The King and what he represents to them.[84]

Benson P. Fraser and William J. Brown similarly recognize how "Elvis fans and impersonators identified with Elvis in very personal and intimate ways as a father, a relative or culturally similar brother, a lover, and as a lover of music."[85] Spigel notes a tendency among devoted fans to speak of Elvis with a sort of spiritual reverence, which is activated through performance. She suggests that the impersonator, "works as a medium who channels the spirit of a savior, all the while opening up a public space where people can express their mutual faith in an abstract principle that no one can name."[86] Fraser and Brown similarly note that "The Elvis fans and impersonators interviewed here have integrated their internal values and beliefs with those derived from a mediated image of Elvis Presley, such that the fabric of their self-identity is intricately interwoven with their image of Elvis"[87] (Interestingly, the authors, who interviewed Lopez for this article, seem to set him outside of this framework, noting, "Robert's identification with Elvis is a means to an end and not an end in itself."[88]) Thus to his truest fans, participation with Elvis impersonators is often imbued with spiritual and identity-affirming resonance.

Though she herself attended the impersonator contest at Bad Bob's more ironically, Gordon's description of the event clearly captures the sort of grass-roots meaning-making described by scholars. Gordon recalls:

> Once there was this woman, I think she had said [that she had] just gotten over cancer. She was real skinny, she had short hair and she was just thin, so thin and pale, and she had this plain brown jumpsuit.[89]

Though she was by no means good, Gordon muses that "in a weird way, she's trying, and somehow it's reaching her." Yet she stresses that "even though we had our own respect for Elvis," the impersonators at Bad Bob's were largely fodder for jokes.[90] She recalls:

> When you went to the impersonator contest during Death Week, it was always like the saddest thing that you just drank beer to and laughed at. I remember being there and going [...] this is the Slim Pickens Elvis, this is the Morey Amsterdam Elvis—that's how bad it was [...] And it was always very ramshackle [...] Now others might come

> along and say, "She's crazy! It was the greatest thing ever!" but it was kitschy and mirth-provoking.[91]

Gordon notes a general preference among impersonators for the costume and spectacle of Elvis's later years, a fact that Spigel also comments upon. Indeed, Spigel draws a connection between Elvis impersonation and a religious revival, highlighting how the performers and audience collectively build a memory. She suggests, "Popular memory is history from below that comments back—although in indirect ways—upon the larger confusion and alienation of our time."[92] That is, the impersonators and their audience perform Elvis nostalgia in order to fix the past and thereby cope with the present. And this, above all, is Gordon's recollection of Bad Bob's:

> They'd always do the American Trilogy. It was never young, good-looking Elvis with his gold lamé suit [...] Elvis would be fat and sweaty [...] people love to get a bunch of beer and watch them and say, "That's the way it was."[93]

The ramshackle nostalgia of the Bad Bob's impersonators provides the necessary context to Gordon's description of her first phone conversation with Lopez. Thinking they would share a laugh at the impersonators, she invited him to the show:

> And Robert says, "I'm going to be in that contest." So I immediately think, "Oh boy. Oh no!" I remember calling my friend and saying, "Oh my God, this guy is coming, and I don't know him, and he's going to be in the impersonator contest!"[94]

Of course, even in its first iteration, Lopez's performance was subversive, operating with a different modality from the other impersonators. Avers Gordon, "Robert—he had a plan from the get-go [...] I know for a fact he knocked those impersonators for a loop."[95] Indeed, during that first trip to Memphis, El Vez caused quite a stir. A *Los Angeles Times* article cites Jon Bok (Lopez's then-boyfriend, or, as the article calls him, "Lopez's roommate and a furniture artist whose work is exhibited at galleries throughout the world") recalling, "At Graceland, someone started a rumor that El Vez was the little boy in 'Fun in Acapulco.' Everyone wanted to have their picture taken with him."[96]

Lopez affirms the thinking that went into these early performances, even as he acknowledges its DIY nature. He credits his ability to balance intentionality with improvisation to his years coming up in punk rock. Punk, he suggests, trained artists to embrace both "proficiency and letting loose of your proficiency as another way of working. And at some point they would meet."[97] This willingness to boldly commit to making it up as he went along served Lopez well. When he returned to L.A., he immediately received media coverage. In fact, he was booked as a guest on the short-lived national television show *2 Hip 4 TV*, hosted by Ahmet Zappa and Colin Quinn. By his own admission, "I got to go national before I had done anything, really, and it just kind of snowballed from there."[98] Punk had taught him to step into these situations, to embrace the performance of already having "made it," even if it was—at least for the moment—more fantasy than reality.

Lopez very quickly began gigging around L.A., refining the critical foundation for the performance—the combination of subversive political content with a punk sensibility that deftly balanced social critique, caricature, and lively entertainment—while building up his act:

> El Vez was, in my mind, more calculated. I wanted to be more Mexican than you, and at the same time more American than you, to exemplify what Mexican-American is [...] and so it was more of an art concept piece. But it still used the punk rock ideas, because the very first year, all my shows I did with Karaoke tapes that I bought at Graceland. And it was like me singing louder than the vocals on the tapes, so they're going "Suspicious Minds," and I'm going "Immigration Time!" The shows were at clubs, so it was like guerilla theater in a punk rock venue.[99]

From the start, he garnered acclaim. Coverage of "'Sabor!' a party to celebrate 'the best Latinos in Los Angeles'" in November 1988 declares him a "Triumph," noting that "Though the air was thick with glamour and sophistication, even the ritziest guests seemed to anticipate the final act, a Mexican Elvis impersonator—*El Vez.*"[100] A January 1989 article about an *L.A. Style* magazine party describes how El Vez "wowed the likes of Nicolas Cage, Scott Baio, Ray Manzerak, Michael Des Barres, and Fred Dryer," name-dropping hot celebrities of the time.[101] His performance at a *LACE* (*Los Angeles Contemporary Exhibition*) benefit in February 1989 garnered him critical praise along with the recognition of Bobcat Goldthwait, who so enjoyed his performance that he invited him to open his April 1989 comedy show at L.A.'s Wiltern Theatre. The 30-minute performance contained all of the elements that would become even more developed in future shows: multiple costume changes (including one backlit by strobe lighting behind a sheet), props (including a giant sombrero, a Cadillac, and four-foot-tall gold letters spelling out "El Vez," all constructed with "a cardboard-and-glitter budget"), and excellent singing paired with thoughtful lyrical rewrites.[102] By May 1989, he landed a feature story in the *Los Angeles Times.*

Throughout the first year of El Vez, Lopez continued to work at La Luz de Jesus. Owner Billy Shire fostered a flexible, creative environment in which his employees—most of whom were artists and musicians—were able to pursue their own projects through the hub of the store. Lopez describes it as "a bed of creativity," noting that "Billy, being the mother hen, allowed us to take time off, or promote or come to the shows," while Shire called it "punk rock college," since so many of his employees had been active in the punk rock scene and continued to develop art projects once the music had become more mainstream and appropriated.[103] It proved an excellent training ground for crafting and promoting El Vez; notes Lopez, "the whole gallery experience is where I developed the 'they came for this but give them that' [...] so the story has two different angles or points: A kicker for a media story. A surprise for a live performance."[104] Moreover, he was able to cross-promote both El Vez and La Luz de Jesus, attracting film crews as he promoted gallery shows in the character of El Vez. Lopez notes:

> Being the curator and also being in charge of PR, it was where I turned all this knowledge onto myself. And it just kind of snowballed, the idea of being living art myself, as the performance of El Vez, The Mexican Elvis.[105]

This helps unpack the rumor of the *Fun in Acapulco* boy that circulated at Graceland. It was, of course, Lopez who started it. He states, "I never did the full math, but I knew enough facts when quizzed in Memphis. I was impersonating him. But then it's the set up for the second lie I ran,"[106] one that he carried into much of his early press and his onstage banter, that El Vez is the love child of Charo and Elvis. He describes the publicity posters he made for those first Memphis performances as reading "Elvis Was Mexican!"[107] Lopez playfully brands this "Aztec Futurism, using the re-imagined past" to create the imagined story of a Mexican Elvis. Lopez believes he stepped away from his curator position in 1990, reporting, "I remember my dad saying, 'Are you sure?' 'cause I got such a big Xmas bonus that year of 89."[108] He then made El Vez his career, progressing from tapes purchased at Graceland to playing with live musicians in different cities to assembling a dedicated live band who understood the way he intercut different musical phrases, songs, and lyrics together and embraced the theatricality of the shows.

The 1990s were a prolific time for Lopez. He composed the bulk of his oeuvre, which includes multiple singles, EPs, and the albums *How Great Thou Art: The Greatest Hits of El Vez* (true to his "self boasting funny"[109] approach to El Vez, his Greatest Hits is among the first albums Lopez released), *Graciasland, G.I. Ay, Ay! Blues*, and *Merry MeX-mas* (*Boxing with God* and *Sno-Way José* would be released in the early 2000s), and he developed the tours that supported these releases—themed tours including Graciasland, Rock & Revolution, El Vez for Prez, and The Gospel Show interrogated issues of Americana, revolution and social change, politics, and religion through performance, while his Merry MeX-Mas tours considered the holiday through a Latinx lens. A glance at the "Historia" page on his website documents the extensive national and international touring he, the Lovely Elvettes, and the Memphis Mariachis undertook, spending weeks to months on the road.[110]

He also staged pop-up events, interweaving El Vez into the pop culture of the times. For example, he performed at the Hollywood Post Office on January 8, 1993, Elvis's birthday and the first day the Elvis stamp became available. Lopez notes:

> By that time I was pretty savvy of doing interviews with CNN, local news, and MTV, and [...] the stamp was a big to-do, there was a whole old or young Elvis [debate], and me knowing how to stir a pot.[111]

At the celebration, he was the first person in California to purchase a sheet of Elvis stamps, and used one to mail a letter to President-Elect Bill Clinton, suggesting that he invite El Vez to perform at his inaugural ball later that month. He said:

> Clinton is a big Elvis fan [...] this is the new era he's taking [us] into—cultural diversity, multiculturalism [...] What better way to usher in this era [than] with El Vez, a multicultural Elvis impersonator, you know? I'm going to take us to the new, new frontiers of Elvisness.

He further reflected on Elvis's importance noting:

> Elvis Presley has always been a part of American culture, but now he is sanctified by the U.S. government by having his own official stamp. This means he's officially part of American culture, a stronghold, a pillar of society, because, you know, you lick the back of his head and put him on letters.[112]

He distributed his own El Vez stamps (Figure 1.4a and b) along with cake (with peanut butter and banana filling), pitched his 1-800-KING-MEX phone number (playing with another fad of the time—free and pay-per-minute call-in lines), and performed "Está Bien Mamacita" and "Maria's the Name (of his Latest Flame)."[113] The event demonstrates the PR and production knowledge Lopez honed at La Luz de Jesus.

In reflecting on the visibility he garnered during the 1990s and early 2000s, Lopez notes that his ability to create televised events was crucial to his success. He jokingly states, "TV is an amazing unifier [...] I mean, I'm a unifier, but I'm also there to say, 'Step away from the mass, count yourself as one—all together now!'"[114] In addition to having national coverage on NBC, Regis and Kathie Lee, and Oprah, Lopez continues:

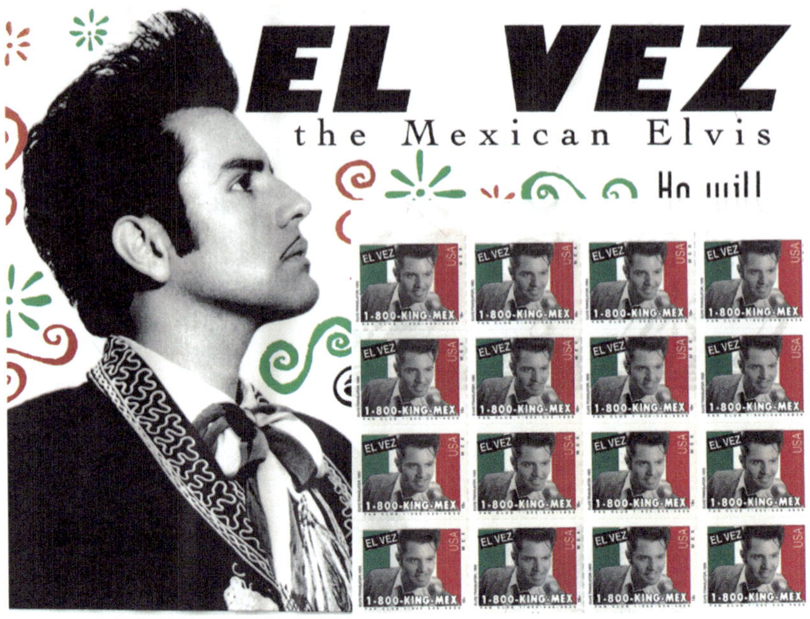

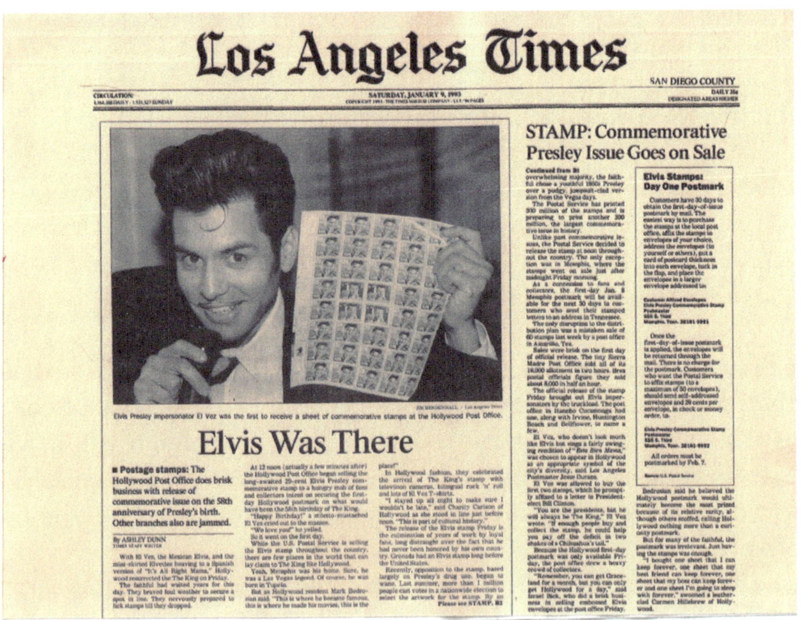

Los Angeles Times

SAN DIEGO COUNTY

SATURDAY, JANUARY 9, 1993

Elvis Presley impersonator El Vez was the first to receive a sheet of commemorative stamps at the Hollywood Post Office.

Elvis Was There

■ Postage stamps: The Hollywood Post Office does brisk business with release of commemorative issue on the 58th anniversary of Presley's birth. Other branches also are jammed.

By ASHLEY DUNN
TIMES STAFF WRITER

With El Vez, the Mexican Elvis, and the mini-skirted Elvettes heaving to a Spanish version of "It's All Right Mama," Hollywood resurrected The King on Friday.

The faithful had waited years for this day. They braved foul weather to secure a spot in line. They nervously prepared to lick stamps till they dropped.

At 12 noon (actually a few minutes after) the Hollywood Post Office began selling the long-awaited 29-cent Elvis Presley commemorative stamp to a hungry mob of fans and collectors intent on securing the first-day Hollywood postmark on what would have been the 58th birthday of The King.

"Happy Birthday!" a stiletto-mustached El Vez cried out to the masses.

"We love you!" he yelled.

So it went on the first day.

While the U.S. Postal Service is selling the Elvis stamp throughout the country, there are few places in the world that can lay claim to The King like Hollywood.

Yeah, Memphis was his home. Sure, he was a Las Vegas legend. Of course, he was born in Tupelo.

But as Hollywood resident Mark Bedrosian said, "This is where he became famous, this is where he made his movies, this is the place!"

In Hollywood fashion, they celebrated the arrival of The King's stamp with television cameras, bilingual rock 'n' roll and lots of El Vez T-shirts.

"I stayed up all night to make sure I wouldn't be late," said Charity Carlson of Hollywood as she stood in line just before noon. "This is part of cultural history."

The release of the Elvis stamp Friday is the culmination of years of work by loyal fans, long distraught over the fact that he had never been honored by his own country. Grenada had an Elvis stamp long before the United States.

Recently, opposition to the stamp, based largely on Presley's drug use, began to wane. Last summer, more than 1 million people cast votes in a nationwide election to select the artwork for the stamp. By an

Please see STAMP, B2

STAMP: Commemorative Presley Issue Goes on Sale

Continued from B1

overwhelming majority, the faithful chose a youthful 1950s Presley over a pudgy, jumpsuit-clad version from the Vegas days.

The Postal Service has printed 300 million of the stamps and is preparing to print another 200 million, the largest commemorative issue in history.

Unlike past commemorative issues, the Postal Service decided to release the stamp at noon throughout the country. The only exception was in Memphis, where the stamps went on sale just after midnight Friday morning.

As a concession to fans and collectors, the first-day Jan. 8 Memphis postmark will be available for the next 30 days to customers who send their stamped letters to an address in Tennessee.

The only disruption to the distribution plan was a mistaken sale of 60 stamps last week by a post office in Amarillo, Tex.

Sales were brisk on the first day of official release. The tiny Sierra Madre Post Office sold all of its 16,000 allotment in two hours. Brea postal officials figure they sold about 8,000 in half an hour.

The official release of the stamp Friday brought out Elvis impersonators by the truckload. The post office in Rancho Cucamonga had one, along with Irvine, Huntington Beach and Bellflower, to name a few.

El Vez, who doesn't look much like Elvis but sings a fairly swinging rendition of "*Esta Bien Mama*," was chosen to appear in Hollywood as an appropriate symbol of the city's diversity, said Los Angeles Postmaster Jesse Durazo.

El Vez was allowed to buy the first two stamps, which he promptly affixed to a letter to President-elect Bill Clinton.

"You are the presidente, but he will always be The King," El Vez wrote. "If enough people buy and collect the stamp, he could help you pay off the deficit in two shakes of a Chihuahua's tail."

Because the Hollywood first-day postmark was only available Friday, the post office drew a heavy crowd of collectors.

"Remember, you can get Graceland for a month, but you can only get Hollywood for a day," said Israel Bick, who did a brisk business in selling embossed Elvis envelopes at the post office Friday.

Bedrosian said he believed the Hollywood postmark would ultimately become the most prized because of its relative rarity, although others scoffed, calling Hollywood nothing more than a curiosity postmark.

But for many of the faithful, the postmark was irrelevant. Just having the stamps was enough.

"I bought one sheet that I can keep forever, one sheet that my best friend can keep forever, one sheet that my boss can keep forever and one sheet I'm going to sleep with forever," swooned a leather-clad Carmen Hillebrew of Hollywood.

Elvis Stamps: Day One Postmark

Customers have 30 days to obtain the first-day-of-issue postmark by mail. The easiest way is to purchase the stamps at the local post office, affix the stamps to envelopes of your choice, address the envelopes (to yourself or others), put a card of postcard thickness into each envelope, tuck in the flap, and place the envelopes in a larger envelope addressed to:

Once the first-day-of-issue postmark is applied, the envelopes will be returned through the mail. There is no charge for the postmark. Customers who want the Postal Service to affix stamps (to a maximum of 50 envelopes), should send self-addressed envelopes and 29 cents per envelope, in check or money order, to:

All orders must be postmarked by Feb. 7.

FIGURE 1.4a–b: El Vez stamps, sold as merch starting in 1993. The stamps are affixed to a reused El Vez *Graciasland* publicity poster, with a copy of a news article featuring El Vez from the *Los Angeles Times*. The stamp photo signifies on the Elvis stamp, and the entire object features a DIY aesthetic. Courtesy of the author's collection.

> I was on MTV all the time, hosting things, and I did local things all the time. I mean, that's what most of my people across the nation said, they could say, "Oh we saw you on TV!" which gets played again and again for other things. [...] I was on [MTV] a lot. And then the UK equivalent. At one point, I was even going to be a regular host on the Munich channel and they were, "would you consider moving here?" which is really silly because I don't speak any German, but they—that was part of that whole stupid 80s—late 80s—TV personality like, you would go grab the camera like David Lee Roth as of that period, for lack of a better word, of here, let me grab the camera, let me tell you about this, which was Cyndi Lauper, David Lee Roth, characters on TV. It's like, that—the birth of that. And I was self-aware, and I was adding extra depth but tons of funny and goofy. But no, I was doing lots of TV and added to that.[115]

In short, Lopez knew how to both play the part that networks wanted, while also subverting those standard tropes by leaning into controversial topics. For instance, he recalls a German television appearance during the Rock & Revolution tour. As implied by the name (and the Phil Ochs quote cited above), the tour called for social change; the music was loud and strident, peppered with samples of sirens and gunfire, and heavy guitar riffs, and it visually employed revolutionary iconography—Che Guevara, the UFW flag, camouflage costumes, and even toy machine guns. As he remembers, the stakes were even more heightened because Mark Spitz was also a guest on the program (Spitz, a Jewish American swim star, had won seven gold medals at the 1972 Munich Olympics, just before Palestinian terrorists took Israeli athletes and coaches hostage. In all, eleven Israelis were killed, along with five of the eight terrorists and a West German policeman). Notes Lopez, "I had German El Vez fans be terrorists and storm the Tonight Show equivalent in Berlin." He ponders, "How could you even do that now?"[116] And yet the effect of the performance was festive and hopeful.[117] As in the Cat's Cradle example cited in the previous chapter, Lopez's performance tactics and commitment to entertainment allow him to live on that razor's edge. Looking back, he expresses some amazement, "I think—wow, look at those things I've done, would those have landed now?"[118] And yet, as quickly as that question sets in, he declares, "That was a lucky period for me, to be that much in the limelight, and say those things. And I would still say those things now, if I was in the limelight."[119]

The Wall-to-Wall Is Calling, It Lingers, Then You Forget: After the Limelight

The music industry has always been fickle—tastes change as new sounds emerge, bands (and bandmates) come and go, and yet the music plays on. Artists, especially those like Lopez who operate independently of a major label, are familiar with precarity. They bear the financial risks of touring and production, fronting the costs for travel, hotel, artist payments, and per diems; they also reap the rewards when they clear those costs. As discussed above, El Vez did well. He was extremely visible throughout the 1990s and early into the 2000s, attracting industry, media, and scholarly attention. He opened for such luminaries as David Bowie (who thanked El Vez onstage)[120] and Carlos Santana, played festivals with attendees in the tens of thousands, and was even courted by several television producers. He was the subject of a documentary, *El Rey de Rock 'n' Roll*, and was featured in *Americanos: Latino Life in the United States*,[121] and was on television frequently. In early 2004, Lopez relocated from L.A. to Seattle, where he performed for many years with Teatro ZinZanni, bringing the El Vez persona, costumes, and music to the Spiegeltent.

Perhaps unsurprisingly, the heights of celebrity Lopez achieved in those early years did not last; the El Vez limelight faded. Moreover, the music industry itself has changed dramatically. We now consume music digitally, often through individualized playlists. We interact with artists and learn about shows primarily through social media. As an artist whose performances make use of popular music while also existing somewhat outside of it, these changes make El Vez a bit more difficult for potential audiences to discover. Similarly, the economics of touring changed as well, with fewer and fewer venues offering guarantees—that is, a set payment guaranteed to the artist, regardless of ticket sales. Without guarantees, tour budgeting becomes more difficult, and the possibility of losing money increases. As a result, Lopez's U.S. tours are now much shorter and geographically concentrated in order to minimize costs and maximize profits (consider, as an example, gas costs on a passenger van big enough to transport El Vez, the Lovely Elvettes, and the Memphis Mariachis, plus their costumes, instruments, and personal luggage).[122] And as rock performance resumes again after the global pandemic, it is probable that touring will become even more challenging for musicians and venues alike.

And yet, despite the fluctuations and disruptions, some 40+ years after stepping onto a punk stage with The Zeros, and 30+ years since inventing El Vez, Lopez continues to make art. And perhaps this is what most fascinates me. If it is ever easy to be a working performer, it is when you have plenty of coverage, lucrative bookings, ecstatic audiences, and a hefty income. It seems unlikely that El Vez will again achieve the heights he once held. Still, he has had incredible, sometimes surprising reach through his art. Once, while in Memphis for a series of performances, Lopez spotted Chuck D. The MC was perusing the gift shop at Sun Records, of all places, where Elvis recorded his first sessions. Recounts Lopez:

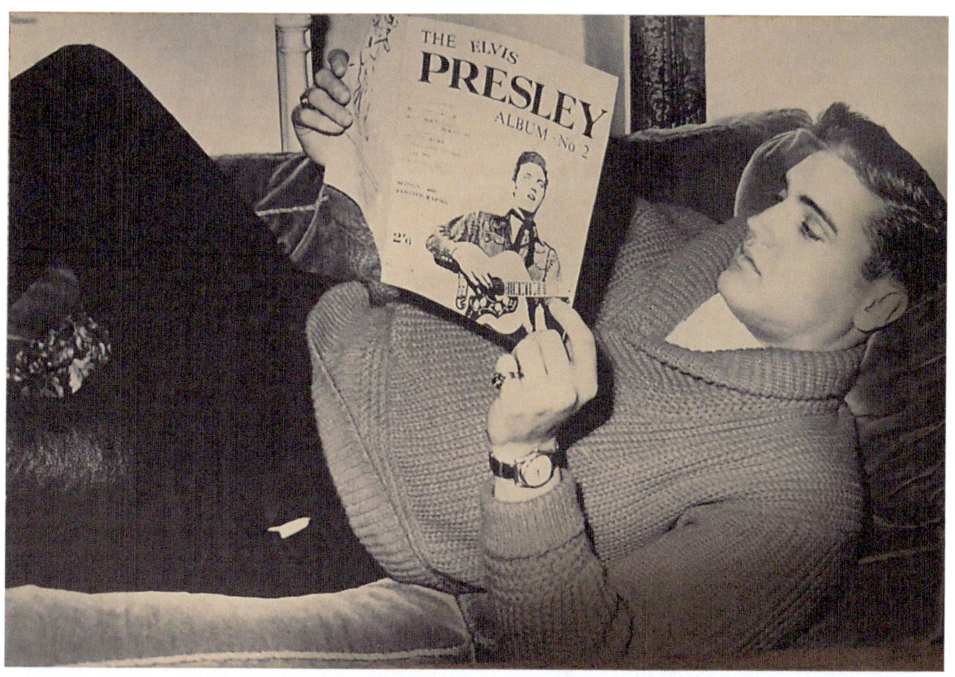

FIGURE 1.5a–b: An Elvis postcard, signed by Chuck D at Sun Records, *c.*1990–91. Courtesy of Robert Lopez's collection.

> I saw him in the gift shop and I knew it was him. I walked up to him and introduced myself—he was excited to see me! He said, "Man! I was just talking about you this morning!" I was so glad he knew who I was and my work.[123]

Chuck D autographed an Elvis postcard with the message, "Keep Rockin" (Figure 1.5a and b), which is what Lopez continues to do. I am fascinated by Lopez's ability to continually reinvent El Vez to meet the times, without it becoming what is the norm for Elvis Impersonators: "a tired old cliché oldie show"[124] or a "kitschy abyss of novelty."[125] Like the boy in the video with which I opened the chapter, through his performances as El Vez, Lopez has built worlds: the imagined world of a Mexican Elvis through which audiences can explore and embrace the tensions, ugliness, and beauty of the United States; and also the real world in which Robert Lopez has built a life through his art. And he builds worlds for his audiences as well, social spaces that engender community, one big enough for The King, Chuck D, and so many more.

NOTES

1. The video can be viewed on YouTube, accessed September 19, 2014, https://www.youtube.com/watch?v=XczYSiwYZmY. Directed by Pablo Prietto, it won a Golden Spire award in the music video category of the 1998 San Francisco International Film Festival.
2. Lopez, email to author, September 29, 2005.
3. Lopez, interview with author, May 22, 2018.
4. Ochs was a committed leftist, aligned with the Yippies and the peace movement. The Elvis quote came out of a March 27, 1970 performance at Carnegie Hall where, wearing a gold lamé Nudie suit like that of Elvis, Ochs proclaimed himself to be a symbol of America, and spoke about being remade into "the Elvis Presley all-time commercial plastic gold lamé everything you want in America." Part performance art, part indictment of capitalism, racism, genocide, and injustice, Ochs played two very strange shows, featuring many covers of other artists, including an Elvis medley that was booed. Based on reviews and the audible audience response from the recording, the audience would have preferred a more straightforward set of his greatest hits. A recording of the second show can be found on the Internet Archive at https://archive.org/details/phil_ochs_1970-03-27_New_York_NY/18+I'm+Gonna+Say+It+Now.flac, accessed June 13, 2020. A&M Records released an edited album of the concert, entitled *Gunfight at Carnegie Hall*, five years later. As I note in endnote 57 of Chapter 2, this iconic performance has been understood in different ways. Auslander reads it as Ochs anticipating changes in rock performance, and having his clearly costumed, theatrical performance rejected by his countercultural fans.
5. Gilbert D. Rodman, *Elvis After Elvis: The Posthumous Career of a Living Legend* (London: Routledge, 1996), 40.

6. Rodman, *Elvis After Elvis*, 42. As I discuss in Chapter 2, Lopez-as-El-Vez also has the capacity to draw fire from opposing sides of an issue.
7. Rodman, *Elvis After Elvis*, 41.
8. Leon E. Wynter, *American Skin: Pop Culture, Big Business, and the End of White Culture* (New York: Crown Publishers, 2002), 27.
9. Bernadette Marie Calafell, "My Love/Hate Relationship with El Vez," *Latina/o Communication Studies: Theorizing Performance* (New York: Peter Lang, 2003), 86.
10. Calafell, "Love/Hate," 73.
11. Lopez, interview with author, August 27, 2008.
12. Special thanks to Faedra Chatard Carpenter, who suggested that El Vez performances engaged in signifyin(g) (and effectively co-signed my application of the theory to El Vez) when I participated in the 2014 ASTR Working Group "Facing the Other," convened by Carpenter and Marvin McAllister.
13. Henry Louis Gates, Jr., *The Signifying Monkey: A Theory of African-American Literary Criticism* (Oxford: Oxford University Press, 1988), 45–51.
14. Gates, *The Signifying Monkey*, ixx.
15. Gates, *The Signifying Monkey*, 53.
16. Lopez, interview with author, August 27, 2008.
17. Lopez, interview with author, August 27, 2008.
18. El Vez, *Endless Revolution: G.I. Ay, Ay! Blues Service Re-Issue*, Graciasland Records, 2004. The lyrics are from the liner notes to the original release, *G.I. Ay, Ay! Blues: Soundtrack for the Coming Revolution*, Big Pop, 1996.
19. In a chapter that engages with the way we visibly read race through the materiality of the body, it is important to note that there are no Black performers in the video. This absence of Black bodies is perhaps offset by the heavy sampling of Public Enemy and James Brown. Aurally, this not only calls up the artists but also the way that their songs explore race and racism as it plays out in and on the Black community. Blackness is present sonically.
20. Gates, *The Signifying Monkey*, xxiv.
21. Gates, *The Signifying Monkey*, 94.
22. Lopez often records, mixes, and releases multiple versions of his songs.
23. These lyrics are transcribed from the music video. El Vez changes the lyrics slightly in the "Say it Loud! PE-Remix" released on his *Son of a Lad from Spain?* Album. He says, "PE backwards means Elvis Presley," and after the Viva paper towels line he substitutes "I got the big bells, I got the most cake / Impersonate so real" at which point he samples Courtney Love of Hole singing "So real / I am beyond fake."
24. Lopez recounts seeing Elvis in *Viva Las Vegas* when he was a young boy. He was convinced that The King was Latino. Interview with author, September 13, 2013.
25. Lopez juxtaposes seriousness and playfulness throughout the piece, which also includes lines such as "We've been 'buked, we've been scorned / We call it maize, while you're still calling it corn."

26. TCB stands for Taking Care of Business. Lopez notes, "TCB is an old Black saying [...] Elvis took it as his symbol adding the lightning bolt to the TCB letters. He made endless jewelry with the symbol for his friends and people." Lopez, text message to author, May 9, 2024.
27. These lyrics not only condense the distance between the persona of El Vez and the character of the song but also point back to the real person of Lopez, terms I discuss in greater depth in the next chapter.
28. Adrian Deevoy, "Chuck D: I Smack Myself Twice in the Face and I'm Good to Go," *The Guardian*, March 26, 2014, accessed September 18, 2014, www.theguardian.com/music/2014/mar/26/chuck-dinterview-public-enemy-fight-the-power.
29. Lopez, interview with author, August 27, 2008.
30. Lopez, interview with author, May 22, 2018.
31. Lopez, interview with author, August 27, 2008.
32. Lopez, interview with author, May 19, 2018. As a personal anecdote, it's true. I only knew the biggest Elvis hits when I first saw El Vez, and I tend to sing El Vez lyrics over the originals now.
33. José Esteban Muñoz, *Disidentifications: Queers of Color and the Performance of Politics* (Minneapolis, MN: University of Minnesota Press, 1999), 4.
34. Muñoz, *Disidentifications*, 6, 11–12.
35. Muñoz, *Disidentifications*, 31.
36. Muñoz, *Disidentifications*, 5.
37. Muñoz, *Disidentifications*, 12.
38. Muñoz, *Disidentifications*, 31.
39. Muñoz, *Disidentifications*, 12.
40. Robert Lopez, "Punk-Rock Teenage Heaven," in *Under the Big Black Sun*, edited by John Doe with Tom DeSavia and Friends (Boston, MA: Da Capo Press, 2016), 95–109.
41. Lopez, interview with author, May 22, 2018.
42. Lopez, interview with author, May 22, 2018.
43. Lopez, "Punk-Rock Teenage Heaven," 95. In an interview with Weirdo Music Forever, he shares the recipe: "It was like Hamburger Helper without the package: ground hamburger, bok choy, soy sprouts, and a lot of soy sauce. It was cheap to make, so we had it many times," December 26, 2016, accessed April 18, 2024, http://www.weirdomusicforever.com/weird-news-and-interviews/2016/12/26/robert-lopez-on-the-unhappy-hour-el-vez-the-early-days-of-la-punk-and-more.
44. Lopez, interview with author, June 6, 2018.
45. Lopez, interview with Weirdo Music Forever, December 26, 2016.
46. Lopez, "Punk-Rock Teenage Heaven," 95–96.
47. Lopez, interview with author, June 6, 2018.
48. Lopez, interview with author, June 6, 2018.
49. As noted in the previous chapter, Lopez usually uses the term Chicano. He notes "I like CHICANO cause it's a kinda dying term. It was very 60–70s from my aunts' and uncles'

era of activism." Personal email to author, October 28, 2014. In keeping with current terminology, I use the word Chicanx here.

50. Habell-Pallan, *Loca Motion*, 6.
51. Alice Bag, "Work That Hoe: Tilling the Soil of Punk Feminism," *Women & Performance: a Journal of Feminist History* 22, no. 2–3 (December 2012): 236.
52. Lopez, interview with author, June 6, 2018.
53. Bag, "Work That Hoe," 233.
54. Lopez, interview with author, June 8, 2018.
55. Stephen Duncombe, *Notes from Underground: Zines and the Politics of Alternative Culture* (London: Verso, 1997), 117.
56. Joe Mageary, "'Rise Above/We're Gonna Rise Above': A Qualitative Inquiry into the Use of Hardcore Punk Culture as Context for the Development of Preferred Identities" (PhD diss., California Institute of Integral Studies, ProQuest Dissertations Publishing, 2012), 63.
57. Ryan Moore and Michael Roberts, "Do-It-Yourself Mobilization: Punk and Social Movements," *Mobilization: An International Journal* 14, no. 3 (September 2009): 276.
58. Duncombe, *Notes from Underground*, 118.
59. Lopez, interview with author, June 6, 2018.
60. Lopez, interview with author, June 6, 2018.
61. Lopez, interview with author, June 6, 2018.
62. Lopez, interview with author, June 6, 2018.
63. Lopez, interview with author, June 6, 2018.
64. Lopez notes that RuPaul (who was a punk contemporary; both grew up in the San Diego area, but RuPaul went to New York and joined that punk scene, while Lopez went to L.A.) now owns the building that housed The Masque, and has preserved all of the graffiti on the walls dating back to the 1970s. Lopez and RuPaul traveled in similar circles, though their paths did not actually cross. For example, RuPaul's break came at the Pyramid Club in New York. El Vez also played there early on and got a big break: an invitation to perform at the Roskilde Festival. El Vez performed between Patti Smith and Elvis Costello. Lopez recounts that he was sent plane tickets and a "pot of money" to play the festival, which allowed him to put together a full band. This "led to all that followed." Lopez, interview with author, March 4, 2024.
65. Lopez, personal text to author, May 13, 2021. Lopez recalls that he was back and forth between various jobs and multiple music projects during this time. He regularly played in the Johnnys, Catholic Discipline (featured in Penelope Spheeris's documentary *The Decline of Western Civilization*), and The Boneheads. Notes Lopez, both Catholic Discipline and The Boneheads featured "boys and girls" in the band: Phranc (The All American Jewish Lesbian Folk Singer) played guitar in Catholic Discipline, and Alice Bag, Chase Holiday, Elissa Bello, Trudie Arguelles-Barrett all played with The Boneheads. Lopez continues this gender mixing with El Vez, intentionally resisting the gender stereotypes that continue to mark music performance. Lopez also notes that musician/music critic Craig Lee, who

played in both Catholic Discipline and The Boneheads, was his first friend to die of AIDS. Lopez, interview with author, March 4, 2024.

66. Beth Ann Krier, "El Vez: Colorful Impersonator Gets a Big *Ole*," *The Los Angeles Times*, May 12, 1989, D1+. Consulted via ProQuest Historical Newspapers, ASU library, on April 15, 2021.
67. Jean Trinh, "Soap Plant & WACKO Turns 50: A Look Back at Its Underground Art Scene and Legendary Parties," *KCET Online*, June 8, 2021, accessed July 16, 2021, https://www.pbssocal.org/shows/artbound/soap-plant-wacko-turns-50-a-look-back-at-its-underground-art-scene-and-legendary-parties.
68. Trinh, "Soap Plant and WACKO."
69. Susan Larson, "Rock and Revolution: An Interview with El Vez, The Mexican Elvis," *Arizona Journal of Hispanic Cultural Studies* 1 (1997): 144.
70. Elvis died at his Graceland estate in Memphis on August 16, 1977.
71. Gordon was born and raised in Memphis. When I interviewed her in 2018, she lived in Skokie, IL and was teaching at Lake County Community College. She became acquainted with Lopez through Brad Dunning, a friend whom she had grown up with who knew Lopez in L.A.
72. Gordon, interview with author, June 18, 2018.
73. Robert Gordon, *Memphis Rent Party: The Blues, Rock & Soul in Music's Hometown* (New York: Bloomsbury, 2018), 9.
74. Patricia Leigh Brown, "A Decade After Elvis: Faithful at the Shrine," *New York Times*, August 14, 1987, accessed May 25, 2021, https://www.nytimes.com/1987/08/14/us/a-decade-after-elvis-faithful-at-the-shrine.html.
75. Eve Zibart, "Echoes of Elvis in Memphis," *Washington Post*, August 14, 1987, B1+. Consulted via ProQuest Historical Newspapers, ASU library, on May 25, 2021. Rodman delves into the classist and gendered critiques of Elvis in his book.
76. Zibert, "Echoes of Elvis."
77. Gordon, interview with author, June 18, 2018.
78. This history is documented in Sam O'Neal, *Elvis Inc.: The Fall and Rise of the Presley Empire* (Rocklin, CA: Prima Publishing, 1996), 47–76, as well as other sources. A years-long financial battle between Presley's family members and Parker as well as RCA Record followed Judge Evans's decision; a settlement was reached in 1983. O'Neal, *Elvis, Inc.*, 74. The Presley Estate is today worth approximately $400–500 million, and it continues to make around $40 million annually, second only to Michael Jackson in earnings by deceased performers.
79. In 1993, when Lisa Marie Presley turned 25, the trust automatically dissolved (as Lisa Marie's legal guardian, Priscilla previously had been the trust executor). Lisa Marie formed a new trust, with Priscilla and the National Bank of Commerce continuing to serve as coexecutors. In 2005 Lisa Marie sold 85 percent of EPE to CKX; it was later sold to Authentic Brands Group (ABG). She retained sole ownership of Graceland and 15 percent ownership of EPE until her death on January 12, 2023; these assets now belong to her remaining children, Riley, Harper, and Finley Keough.

80. An Associated Press article cites EPE marketing chief Paul Jankowski discussing the inclusion of tribute artists, stressing, "It's all about paying tribute to the life and legacy of Elvis." Woody Baird, "Graceland Finally Embraces Elvis Impersonators," *Reading Eagle*, August 17, 2007, accessed June 2, 2021. Bobbie Hoover, who once ran the Elvis Presley Museum in Virginia and later the Images of the King contest, claims to have coined the term "Elvis Tribute Artist" to replace impersonator; it is meant to denote a more talented, respectful performer, and is used by several entities, including EPE. Susan Ellis, "Everybody Elvis," *Memphis Flyer*, August 11, 2011, accessed June 2, 2021.
81. Lopez, interview with author, August 28, 2021.
82. Robert Lopez [@mr.robertlopez], post, *Instagram*, January 13, 2023. In this post, he reflects further on his relationship with Lisa Marie Presley, noting that thought they did not interact directly, they crossed paths in Los Angeles and were at times in similar circles. He remembers them both being at Roman and Sophia Coppola's parties. Says Lopez, "I literally rubbed her elbow w/my elbow as we squeezed into the kitchen, so I could say 'we rubbed elbows.'" There were other connections; Michael Lockwood, Lopez's first El Vez guitarist (who dated one of the Lisa María Elvettes), went on to marry Lisa Marie Presley. Lopez's brother, Guy, also gave Lisa Marie an El Vez Che T-shirt at one of her concerts. Lopez [@mr.robertlopez], post, *Instagram*, 13 January 2023.
83. Gordon, interview with author, June 18, 2018.
84. Lynn Spigel, "Communicating with the Dead: Elvis as Medium," *Camera Obscura* 8, no. 2 (1990): 180.
85. Benson P. Fraser and William J. Brown, "Media, Celebrities, and Social Influence: Identification with Elvis Presley," *Mass Communication & Society* 5, no. 2 (2002): 198.
86. Spigel, "Communicating with the Dead,"193.
87. Fraser and Brown, "Media, Celebrities, and Social Influence," 202.
88. Fraser and Brown, "Media, Celebrities, and Social Influence," 197.
89. Gordon, interview with author, June 18, 2018.
90. Gordon, interview with author, June 18, 2018.
91. Gordon, interview with author, June 18, 2018.
92. Spigel, "Communicating with the Dead," 199.
93. Gordon, interview with author, June 18, 2018.
94. Gordon, interview with author, June 18, 2018.
95. Gordon, interview with author, June 18, 2018.
96. Krier, "El Vez," D1+.
97. Lopez, interview with author, June 6, 2018.
98. Larson, "Rock and Revolution," 144.
99. Peter Heyneman, "BYT Interview: El Vez!," December 3, 2009, accessed June 4, 2021, http://www.brightestYoungThings.com/el-vez [password protected].
100. *Los Angeles Times*, November 23, 1988, G3, via ProQuest Historical Newspapers, accessed June 8, 2021.

101. Patrick Goldstein, "POP EYE," *Los Angeles Times*, January 29, 1989, 86K. Consulted via ProQuest Historical Newspapers, ASU library, on June 8, 2021.
102. Krier, "El Vez," D1+.
103. Trinh, "Soap Plant and WACKO."
104. Lopez, personal text to author, July 16, 2021.
105. Trinh, "Soap Plant and WACKO."
106. Lopez, personal text to author, July 27, 2021. In fact, the boy in the film was played by Larry Domasin, a child actor from L.A.
107. Lopez, interview with author, July 9, 2022.
108. Lopez, personal text to author, July 16, 2021.
109. Lopez, personal text to author, July 16, 2021.
110. For example, 1996 and 1997 were particularly heavy touring years, with El Vez on the road most months, including several extended tours through Europe.
111. Lopez, interview with author, March 4, 2024.
112. All quotes are transcribed from a publicity video posted to YouTube. Electric Earl, "EL VEZ at Hollywood Post Office 1/8/93 (Part 1)," YouTube, uploaded by ElectricEarldotcom, January 5, 2012, accessed June 8, 2024, https://www.youtube.com/watch?v=J9NdalnXvCM.
113. The way the stamp piece of the puzzle came together is its own story. Sandra Bernhard (who, coincidentally, was trying to date Gladysita [Lopez's cousin Michelle Chenelle], but was rebuffed) was originally going to create the stamp/phone number to promote her comedy, but she backed out of the arrangement. Someone at the company then suggested El Vez as a replacement. Recalls Lopez, "And I said, 'yes, let's do this, but let's coincide with the [Elvis] stamp coming out and do this whole thing.'" He then got the stamp company to pay for the two cakes (one decorated with the Elvis stamp image and one with the El Vez stamp image). He was also in communication with the L.A. Post Office, who tried to steer him away from the Hollywood Post Office, "because Hollywood Boulevard then was pretty gritty." But he insisted due to Elvis's connection to Hollywood. Another funny note is that no one had told the Postmaster General that Lopez would also be promoting his own El Vez stamps; he was shocked when El Vez presented him with a sheet of stamps right after receiving the Elvis stamps. Lopez, interview with author, March 4, 2024.
114. Lopez, interview with author, May 22, 2018.
115. Lopez, interview with author, May 22, 2018.
116. Lopez, interview with author, May 22, 2018.
117. Lopez notes that they all went out for drinks with Spitz after the show, and Lopez got Spitz's autograph for his aunt. Lopez, interview with author, March 4, 2024.
118. Lopez, interview with author, May 22, 2018.
119. Lopez, interview with author, May 22, 2018.

120. Because this was during the Rock & Revolution tour, El Vez would have played a version of Bowie's "Rebel Rebel," making this onstage appreciation even more meaningful. Lopez, interview with author, March 4, 2024.
121. *El Rey de Rock 'n' Roll*, directed by Marjorie Chodorov was released in 2001. *Americanos: Latino Life in the United States*, directed by Susan Todd and Andrew Young was released in 2000.
122. Lopez, interview with author, September 13, 2013.
123. Personal email to author, September 17, 2014.
124. Gordon, interview with author, June 18, 2018.
125. This quote comes from one of my anonymous peer reviewers, who praises Lopez's work as a citizen artist who stays relevant and avoids kitsch and nostalgia, a quote that I shared with Lopez. Ever the contrarian, he replied, "Hmmm I think I jump into that abyss of kitsch and novelty. It is within K&N that we find truth Where (or at least a section) society is at now. You can quote me professor." Lopez [@mr.robertlopez], message to author, *Instagram*, February 28, 2024. I have so much gratitude for my reviewers, whose comments made this book much better. I hope whoever this person is finds joy in seeing their words El Vez-ified.

2

You May Call Me El, You May Call Me Vez: Lopez and El Vez in Performance

El Vez's piercing brown eyes stare out from his El Vez for Prez publicity poster with all the seriousness of the iconic Uncle Sam visage he adopts (Figure 2.1). Though the overall effect of seeing The Mexican Elvis, complete with his pencil-thin moustache, dressed up in the red, white, and blue of our national personification is humorous, the somber visual tone is not misplaced: it hints not only toward the contentiousness of electoral politics but also the dangers of the discourse he enters into through his performance. El Vez wraps himself in the emotionally charged images of patriotism and speaks frankly about USAmerican politics—a risky business.[1] However, by establishing an ironic distance from the images and rhetoric he deploys, El Vez both protects himself from and warns us against the double edge of empathy, where "feeling with" can become distorted in colonizing and propagandizing ways. His performances, though they often prompt emotional responses, disallow the easy equivalencies of empathy in order to engender a deeper form of connection and engagement among his audience base through irony and inauthenticity. Because it prevents his audience members from fully putting themselves in the *huaraches azules* of *El Rey*, irony in an El Vez concert contributes to its world-building, empowering the audience to actively decode the performance and allowing for the revelation of alliances across multiple subject positions to create an ethical community enacted through thought, reflection, and rock and roll.

The clever inversion that flips Uncle Sam's famous "I want you" into El Vez's "You want me"—an ostensibly silly joke completely in keeping with the rock star tradition in which El Vez situates himself—in fact voices a motivating impulse that marks encounters across lines of difference: desire. "You want me," asserts El Vez in the poster. Yet his accusatory finger seems to challenge the viewer, demanding, "What exactly is it of me that you want?" Of course, the desire for difference is not necessarily harmful in its intent. Indeed, as Doris Sommer suggests, it provides the lifeblood of democratic negotiation within diverse societies; she notes, "Precisely because citizens cannot presume to feel, or to think, or to perform alike, their ear for otherness makes justice possible."[2] At its best, wanting to hear and learn from

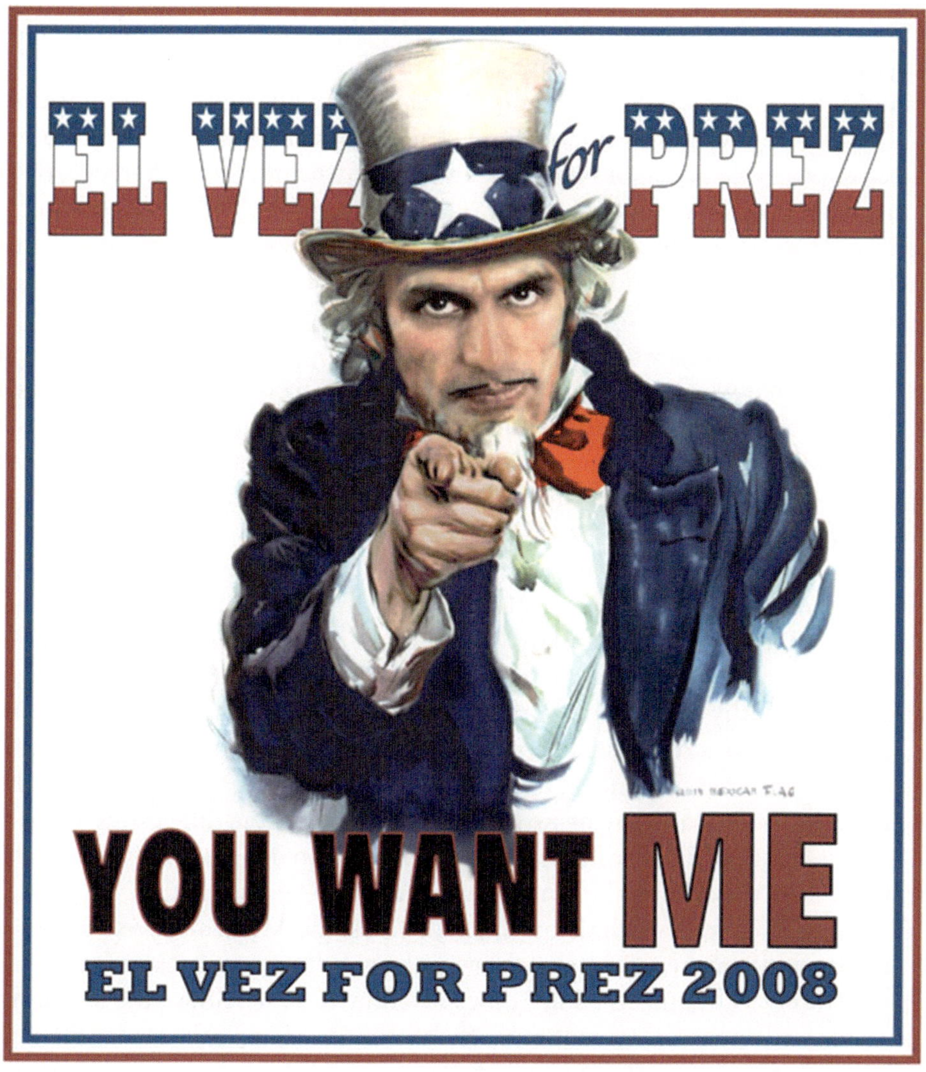

FIGURE 2.1: El Vez for Prez poster, 2008. Courtesy of Robert Lopez's collection.

difference can represent a benevolent, even hopeful wish for new experiences and new knowledges, for interesting and expanding dialogues, for the creation of productive and powerful coalitions. The emotional bridging to another that empathy facilitates, in its most progressive and transformative manifestations, serves as a potent conduit to connection and understanding. El Vez acknowledges this possibility; perhaps what we want from him is his vision of a society in which difference flourishes, where a Mexican Elvis *can* be our national leader, symbolizing the great social strides we have taken together.

And yet that finger scolds us again. By celebrating his appropriation of Uncle Sam as a subversive act of empowerment and holding it up as a marker of our collective progress, actual or potential, are we truly hearing the difference, or are we engaging in a variation of what Laura Edmondson dubs "academic sugarcoating?"[3] El Vez's use of this Ultra-American icon, a stern white nineteenth-century patriarch first popularly adopted during the war of 1812,[4] purposefully recalls an aspect of our national history that many white progressives desperately long to forget: a sustained legacy of the systematic erasure, oppression, and exoticization of difference that we continue to struggle with today. By celebrating this Mexican Elvis Uncle Sam, are we simply sliding difference into the same old American Exceptionalist clothing, soothing ourselves by erasing the racism, but keeping the capitalist, imperialist nationalism that undergirds U.S. power and prominence? Maybe what we really want is for this Uncle Sam El Vez and his discomfiting reminder of our ignoble past and rocky present to recede from view, to assuage our guilt and then disappear. As Sommer asserts, "That is why political philosophy and ethics [...] caution against empathy, which plays treacherously in a subject-centered key that overwhelms unfamiliar voices only to repeat the solitary sounds of the self."[5] Empathy can quickly turn from a desire to understand difference into the need to possess it, to wash it away in a wave of (false) universalism, to force it to say what we want it to mean, to derive pleasure from its strangeness and then discard it. Without really having listened to and learned from differences, empathy can elide it, allowing one the luxury of believing that an imagined they are just like me. Or at least they should be, unless I want them to be different.

Through its linkage with the political process, the Mexican Elvis Uncle Sam image also hints at how contemporary political discourse uses empathy as a power strategy. Organized ruling blocs attempt to rearticulate the social and cultural landscape in emotional and affective terms, evacuating from them the potential for real political engagement. Patrick Anderson describes empathy as functioning as a part of "neoliberalism's economy of affect," in which emotional encounter itself has become a product[6] or as Ventura notes, a way to reinforce and extend neoliberal ideologies as a structure of feeling. Similarly, Lawrence Grossberg submits:

> [P]recisely by repoliticizing and re-ideologizing all of the social relations and cultural practices of everyday life, the new conservatism is effectively depoliticizing a large part of the population. It is creating a "demilitarized zone" within everyday life through a series of "strategies" directed at the national popular.[7]

Thus, when Sarah Palin sneers at the community activism of Barack Obama and applauds herself, on the basis of her "hockeymomdom," for her "real" American political work; or when Mitt Romney suggests at a fundraiser that the "government-dependent" portion of the populace (47%, in his estimate) are somehow not real citizens entitled to the protections and support of the government, or when Donald J. Trump dismisses the votes against him as "rigged" and the result of "fraud" by voters whose votes should not count,[8] these comments in fact erase potent sites of political action (community organizing, government policy, free and fair democratic elections) and politicize emotionally constructed identity positions (hockey mom, makers, patriots) that in fact offer little possibility for involvement. Feeling replaces doing. Tellingly, such rearticulations of the popular require a mode of empathic engagement that turns the public into the Other. In a mirror to the previous example, what we want (or are told to want) in our political candidates is not that they actually be like us, but rather that we consider ourselves to be like them. You want me because you want to believe you are me.

Amid this swirl of meanings, which reading does El Vez want us to take from this image? It's a trick question, of course. In reality, there is no El Vez; there is Robert Lopez, who creates his art not necessarily to persuade his audience, but rather to pose questions. He adamantly proclaims "it's not a crusade,"[9] and he admits that he doesn't have the answers. Rather, for Lopez, the very act of questioning and engaging is the point:

> It's a constant strive, and that's what creative efforts are—to walk through it, to guide through it [...] It's a constant thing. In a way that is a good thing because it will always be to continue to struggle.[10]

El Vez performances such as the El Vez for Prez tour open a forum, a space of world-building in which social realities can be dissected outside of the affective structures that impact current political discourse. More importantly, the tour enacts dialogue rather than absolutist debate. In my analysis of the EV4P poster, I have tried to model the way multiple meanings circulate in his performances, as well as the imagery that supports them. To return to the query, then, which reading is the correct reading? All of them, and countless more, as "readers" themselves multiply. Through El Vez, Lopez allows his audience to engage with the complexities and the contradictions of USAmerican society, becoming active collaborators in the process of world-building through performance.

This chapter interrogates the expansive range of issues that Lopez can explore through El Vez, especially tracking how irony and inauthenticity function in his performances. In it, I first consider two aspects of theatre that are often revered and yet worthy of dissection: empathy and authenticity, both of which are often understood to be experienced through emotional response. I also turn to the way authenticity is understood within rock performance. As I will discuss, Lopez's art overturns a reliance on empathy and authenticity, instead reveling in the ironic and the inauthentic. I will focus on the relationship of Lopez to El Vez in performance, asserting that Lopez's presence is somewhat hidden, while El Vez functions as what Auslander defines as a personage, musical persona, and character, all of which interact with the icon of Elvis. This configuration opens a productive gap between Lopez and El Vez, which allows him to embody the wild inauthenticity of El Vez, and through that, to offer a different form of emotional engagement that is at once destabilizing and connective. By emphasizing ironic engagement over empathetic entrapment and performativity over the real, El Vez shows reimagine relationships between commonly held conceptions of cultural identity. Thus Lopez's use of irony prompts agency on the part of the audience, asking them to become active in the meaning-making of the show and making them co-present contributors to its world-building. That said, El Vez shows are not without emotionally impactful moments.[11] Rather, El Vez's performances disallow the easy equivalencies of empathy in favor of connections that bridge differences rather than elide it. Because these performances do not prescribe a "feeling with" each other as either a starting point or an end goal, El Vez's use of irony expands his message to reach his diverse audience base.

You Want Me: Empathy and Authenticity

Though distinct properties, empathy and authenticity are often used in tandem to describe the emotional response experienced through theatrical performance. Empathy, commonly defined as the ability to understand and share the feelings of another, is a concept that is generally looked at as a public good and as a way to make positive change. Googling "empathy in theatre" yields results that praise theatre's ability to cultivate empathy in its audiences and its artists. A *Los Angeles Times* article penned by three psychology researchers, written in the midst of the pandemic (when theatres were shut down and partisan polarization was high), begins with several quotes from theatre artists that emphasize this linkage, noting that theatre serves as "an empathy gym" that builds the "emotional muscle of empathy." The article details a study that the authors' lab conducted, in which the audiences they surveyed not only demonstrated increased empathy for different social groups but also increased charitable giving.[12] As this article makes clear, we tend to invest a lot in empathy, trusting that the forging of emotional connections in performance will become a catalyst to create change outside of it. Similarly, authenticity usually is deemed an important asset in contemporary performance. Daniel Schulze suggests that "[a]uthenticity today seems to be one of the highest values in society and yet also one of the most elusive ones,"[13] noting that the perceived superficiality of contemporary society perhaps fuels this desire for something that feels true, that feels real. Interestingly, the value of authenticity in theatre—an art that is admittedly fake on some level, where actors pretend to be characters they are not—is highly regarded. Moreover, it is often intertwined with the notion of empathy. Common sense perhaps dictates that authenticity necessarily leads to truth and that empathy is most effectively achieved through truthful representation. But is this accurate? In this section, I will track the complexities that surround the ideals of empathy and authenticity, first in theatre and then in music performance, in order to cast a critical eye upon them, while also tracing how both terms are historically linked with emergent understandings of individuality and individualism.

Empathy as a concept entered the English language in the early twentieth century through the field of psychology.[14] As such, its usage in English is built upon an assumed individual interiority in relation to other psychologically unique individuals. This individualized usage is a departure from empathy's German-language origins, where the term *Einfühlung* reflected one's place within a larger whole; notes Anderson, the empathic was then conceptualized "not as stable experience but rather as subjective quandary."[15] Now gone from contemporary understandings of the term empathy is *Einfühlung's* original potential for destabilizing one's sense of self, both psychically and physiologically, in the empathic encounter with another—what Anderson describes as, "both an undoing and a becoming."[16]

Conceptualizations of empathy in theatre—particularly when empathy is positioned as a mechanism for social change—follow this individualist thrust, where witnessing the experiences of characters onstage purports to make the viewers more compassionate, more understanding, and therefore more likely to take positive action, without much cost to themselves. Not only is such a schema individually edifying in a highly transactional manner (social uplift for the mere price of a theatre ticket), but it also suggests that the labor of social change begins and ends with feeling. As Anderson states, this safely situates empathy "as a model or end-stage of ethical encounter rather than [...] an ethical quandary that we should consider carefully."[17] Moreover, as Lindsay B. Cummings writes, this individual focus actually can prevent us from engaging with the structural contexts of contemporary neoliberalism:

> empathy became the means by which we understood others as psychologically unique beings in the age of bourgeois individualism [...] in this age of late-late capitalism and neoliberalism, this also means empathy risks shifting our focus from systemic conditions toward individual experiences. Empathy tends to focus our attention on a single person, and on our responses to that person, potentially obscuring social, historical, and cultural contexts in the process.[18]

That is, even as it promises the possibility of feeling with another, empathy can in fact act in service to neoliberalism, enforcing our individual separation and atomization and eliding important communal contexts.

Indeed, attempts to foster social action in theatre by "feeling with" often come up short, allowing good feeling and good intent to stand in for ethical engagement and social action. Cummings notes that this can promote "misguided identification, perpetuating an assumption of access to the mind of others, reinforcing power hierarchies, and encouraging an uncritical adoption of others' viewpoints."[19] Scott Magelssen suggests that empathy in this mode can become yet another mode of appropriating the powerless, while Dani Snyder-Young reflects on how empathy can reify power imbalances naturalized by dominant narratives.[20] Nadine George-Graves powerfully notes that, at times, "empathy belies a sick sadistic satisfaction garnered by imagining oneself in other people's suffering—especially black people's suffering producing empathy only with oneself and not the other."[21] Moreover, as Kondo posits, such use of feeling amounts to "affective violence" that drains energy, power, and agency from minoritized subjects.[22] Noting how there can be "willfulness and greed in the guise of embrace," Sommer cautions that "empathic identification violates the other person; and ontological identification eliminates particularity for the sake of unity."[23] In short, empathy can be a power move, a knowledge that possesses.

In contrast, empathy is ethical when it marks the gaps between subjects and acknowledges its limits, functioning as Anderson's undoing and becoming. Sommer asserts that "Discord among culturally and economically disparate subjects reveals the gaps that separate them, which are the space of democratic negotiation. Without gaps, negotiation would be unnecessary. And because of them, listening is not easy."[24] To empathize only with our own self-projections is a failure to listen properly, an inability to expand beyond the subjective self. It prohibits change. Therefore, empathy must be built on careful listening so that these gaps are seen and heard. Finally, ethical empathy also recognizes that "Social differences by their nature are not entirely comprehensible."[25] Thus, ethical empathy sits in the Proehlian gap of knowing and not knowing, acknowledging that some things cannot be fully understood. And El Vez performances, I want to suggest, allow us to experience that kind of expansive, connective emotional response.

Just as with empathy, a review of the concept of authenticity reveals a history that leads from the communal to the individual. Schulze notes that for much of recorded human history, authenticity functioned as a collective understanding in which "one's place in the divine order were foregrounded"[26] and systems of belief and knowledge were reinforced. It offered context for one's place in a larger whole. As concepts of the self and of subjective individuality began to emerge, authenticity no longer referred to collectives, but rather became doubly individuated: authenticity came to refer to singular objects (a play, an artist) that were assessed by an individual, perceived "through emotion and truthfulness rather than rationality and truth."[27] Schulze goes on to trace authenticity's continued evolution through modernity and postmodernity. He posits that authenticity becomes more and more desirable in the face of uncertainty, suggesting that "the concept of authenticity becomes a sort of fetish in a society without reference points."[28] For Schulze, calls for authenticity reveal the instability of the postmodern subject and a longing for something that is assuredly "real." Our desire for authenticity might be "because it carries the promise of some tangible outside and essentialist reality."[29] That is, authenticity seems to offer some sort of certifiable truth in a world without such toeholds.

Though authenticity seeks to provide stability, it is in fact rarely clearly defined. In theatre, authenticity necessarily varies according to genre and performance style; what is deemed authentic in, say, realist theatre, will vary drastically from what is considered authentic within experimental forms, which will vary from modes of performance that fall under the umbrella of performance art. Jessica Chalmers suggests that authenticity is "a moral category having to do with representational purity,"[30] a value judgment subjectively placed upon the art, or upon the artist. E. Patrick Johnson likewise acknowledges that "the pursuit of authenticity is inevitably an emotional and moral one,"[31] especially when it is paired with performance by and about minoritized subjects. Due to this moralizing aspect, authenticity can take on a gatekeeping quality that risks shutting down connections. As Faedra Chatard Carpenter notes, authenticity is often used as a qualitative evaluation—something (or someone reduced to an unthinking something) is deemed good or bad, true or false, authentic or appropriated. She offers a potent advisement:

> it must be noted that *cultural authenticity* is an oxymoron. Cultural practices are not discrete or absolute; they are ever changing and always transforming, consistently affected by the passage of time, as well as inevitable interactions and outside influences. Likewise, racialized associations are temporal, contingent on changing historical circumstances and cultural practices. Therefore, no person or practice can legitimately be designated as culturally authentic, original, or pure in form. What *cultural authenticity* can refer to, however, is how a set of performance strategies—particular to a specific time, place, and socialized group—are used as markers of both inclusion and exclusion.[32]

Recognizing how claims to cultural authenticity can delimit and essentialize artistic expression, Carpenter proposes sincerity as an alternative, one that is especially useful in discussing performance.[33] She notes, "An affirmative judgement of sincerity is about perceiving a connection—about forging a sense of rapport, despite the differences that may exist between subjects."[34] Sincerity, in Carpenter's configuration, avoids the gatekeeping aspect of authenticity, foregrounding instead communication and exchange. Johnson offers a similar assessment of authenticity, even as he recognizes the value it can carry for minoritized subjects, who sometimes take up "authenticating discourse" as a necessary assertion of autonomy and power. He states, "The key here is to be cognizant of the arbitrariness of authenticity, the ways in which it carries with it the dangers of foreclosing the possibilities of cultural exchange and understanding."[35] Johnson stresses that authenticity is malleable, changing, and subjective. And, as with empathy, it can in fact foreclose ethical exchange and engagement.

Thus, while empathy and authenticity are often deemed assets in theatrical performance, they carry their own pitfalls. Moreover, there are other routes to impactful and ethical engagement. Johnson posits that performance and performativity exist as methodologies through which ethical encounters can be enacted. Schulze also suggests that theatre and performance—what he refers to as "live art"[36]—are key sites for unmediated experiences. States Schulze, "there are performances and aesthetic means which induce a visceral understanding and experience of performance [...] However, for obvious reasons, it evades verbal description."[37] Schulze's example resonates with Jill Dolan's theorization of the "utopian performative," the "small but profound moments in which performance calls the attention of the audience in a way that lifts everyone slightly above the present,"[38] allowing them to briefly feel, through affect, a new way of being, a partial understanding of utopia. When Dolan describes how utopian performatives "make spectators ache with desire to capture, somehow, the stunning, nearly prearticulate insights they illuminate,"[39] she speaks to the unmediated affect. Though these moments are necessarily fleeting, they do prompt further intellectualization. Each of these examples illustrates how performance need not rely on empathy and authenticity to be impactful. Moreover, as I will demonstrate, several of these are tactics used by Lopez in his El Vez performances.

Authenticity within musical performance is defined by overlapping, yet slightly different criteria from authenticity in theatre. As is true with theatre, discussions of authenticity carry with them moral judgments about musicians and the music they make, and authenticity is generally viewed as a positive attribute—ideologically, epistemologically, and politically. Like in theatre, understandings of authenticity in music, and indeed authenticity as a value itself, are heavily determined by genre. Indeed, entire genres are often claimed to be more authentic than others; for instance, within pop or dance music, authenticity might not be much of a factor for listeners, yet within such genres (and their various subgenres) as rock, hip hop, and country, authenticity is generally expected but is evaluated differently. And as with theatre, authenticity within musical performance constantly changes.

Just where authenticity in musical performance is found is a matter for some debate. Dario Martinelli reflects on the contemporary discourse, noting that there are generally three forms of usage of the term:

> a common-sensical one, referred to the elements of creativity and originality of the musical work; a marketing one, addressing the (very popular, as we shall see) dichotomy authentic-commercial, where the two features are in inversely proportional relation; and a (sub)cultural one, where given artists or works are "legitimized" within a community, specifically in relation to the degree of musical authenticity exhibited.[40]

Thus, authenticity in music is judged in a variety of ways, including by the quality of the work (its sound, its originality, its difficulty, its value as music), its place in the commercial landscape (and how much commercial motivations seem to factor into the work), and the way it is received by its community. For instance, Simon Frith argues that authenticity is an essential quality, a "feature of the music itself, a perceived quality of sincerity and commitment [...] it is a human as well as a musical judgement."[41] Allan Moore takes the opposite stance, stating, "authenticity does not inhere in any combination of musical sounds. 'Authenticity' is a matter of interpretation which is made and fought for from within a cultural, and, thus, historicised position. It is ascribed, not inscribed."[42] Auslander, whose extensive work on music performance cannot be understated, elucidates in *Liveness: Performance in a Mediatized Culture* what accounts for these competing understandings: whether authenticity is an essentialist concept or an ideological one. Fans and music critics alike tend to view music through an essentialist lens; many believe that they can hear in and through music some sort of truth. Moreover, this essentialized understanding of sound has been used to define the musical genre, linking genre to race in ways that enforce racial division, a topic I revisit in Chapter 4. Yet, Auslander considers music a form of cultural discourse. He notes:

> I treat rock authenticity as an *ideological* concept and as a discursive effect. [...] I will argue that authenticity is not simply present in the music itself and will also emphasize its cultural, rather than ethical, dimension. In other words, I posit that the creation of the effect of authenticity in rock is a matter of culturally determined convention, not an expression of essence.[43]

Auslander cogently identifies the ideological nature of rock authenticity, and he locates its origins in cultural determinations.

One final factor that informs notions of authenticity in rock performance is how it knowingly adopts an oppositional stance, both politically and culturally. In his book *We Gotta Get Out of this Place: Popular Conservatism and*

Postmodern Culture, Grossberg identifies this in its very origins: for youth in the mid-century (to whom Elvis seemed to sing directly), rock functioned as a set of strategies through which they could navigate and critique the social structures of their life, using the concept of authenticity to strike a balance between the optimism of the postwar years and cynicism about living in a nuclear world operating under the logic of the Cold War. Grossberg also notes that wealth had been redistributed and social structures had changed significantly, specifically pointing out how "the move to the suburbs reorganized social space around principles of repetition, marginalization and racism."[44] In the face of such massive changes, authenticity came to matter so much because it proved that rock mattered. This was not mere entertainment; rock provided a public forum and a shared language through which its young fans could grapple with shifting social realities. This oppositional impulse remains embedded in rock authenticity, though the fans, the music, and the specific cultural context it engages with constantly change. Notes Grossberg:

> Rock constantly articulates its own authentic center, which is always on the way to becoming inauthentic [...] rock is constantly seeking to escape its own centeredness, to produce lines of flight which open up new spaces, new possibilities, new centers. Thus, unlike other musical forms, rock's very existence depends upon a certain instability, or, more accurately, a certain mobility in the service of stability. Rock must constantly change to survive, it must seek to reproduce its authenticity in new forms, in new places, in new alliances. It must constantly move from one center to another, transforming what had been authentic into the inauthentic, in order to constantly project its claim to authenticity.[45]

Grossberg thus identifies a tension that underwrites authenticity in rock: rock needs authenticity to remain vital, to stave off co-optation, and to speak in public languages that capture the angst of its fans, but to maintain authenticity, rock must constantly redefine itself.

Of course, social understandings of the authentic also change, as do understandings of what authenticity might still accomplish. Grossberg spends considerable time discussing the impacts of postmodernity on articulations of authenticity within rock performance. He suggests that a postmodern sensibility features "an ironic, knowing distance, coupled with a sense of emotional urgency."[46] Thus irony and inauthenticity become key tactics for speaking truth in a postmodern landscape. As I will discuss in the next section, Lopez uses both of these in his El Vez performances, but I would like to suggest that this is no simple postmodern trick. Rather, Lopez's commitment to ironic performance and inauthenticity allows for creative world-building to occur.

It is vital to recognize the importance of performance in conveying rock authenticity (or, as I will argue, its companion inauthenticity). Auslander suggests that perhaps on its most basic level, live performance authenticates that the musician is indeed capable. Following Theodore Gracyk, he agrees that rock music's primary mode of transmission is through recordings. That is, audiences will likely hear the recorded versions of songs long before they encounter the musicians performing live. States Auslander, "it is only in live performance that the listener can ascertain that a group that looks authentic in photographs, and sounds authentic on records, really *is* authentic in terms of rock ideology."[47] Auslander does not limit the authentication to sound alone; rather, he is keenly interested in how musicians visually perform their engagement with the music, a topic I will discuss in depth in the next section. Keith Negus and Pete Astor take a different stance, suggesting that, while this may be one aspect of authenticity in live performance, it is not the most important. Rather, they point to affect, which emerges through performance. Returning to Frith, they note, "The moment of identification with the sound of a voice, the sense of belonging is formed by music and not in something that is behind it. There is no illusion, no trick. It is what it is."[48] Though many are tempted to name this feeling authenticity, Negus and Astor are content to focus on its impact:

> In the end, what matters is not what authenticity is (a visual representation, a sound, a gesture, a fabricated meaning) but what it does. And, what it does is allow us to express ourselves in specific ways, connect with people in particular places, and explain our understanding of other people [...] what is important is not whether the magic is real or not, but that people experience it. This is the authenticity that both musicians and audiences live their lives by.[49]

They choose to emphasize the social connections that music makes possible and the creative imaginaries that become possible through performance—facets of rock performance that assist in the world-building of El Vez performances.

You May Call Me Bobby, You May Call Me Prez: El Vez as Personage, Performance Persona, Character, and Icon

El Vez's performances sidestep empathy and authenticity, offering instead a different methodology where emotional response is made to prompt active engagement. Several elements contribute to this methodology: the costuming, the music, the celebratory feel of rock performance, all of which I will cover in upcoming chapters. However, here I want to focus on the relationship of Lopez to El Vez.

There exists an ironic distance between the two, heightened by theatricalized inauthenticity throughout. El Vez's embrace of the inauthentic evades a sort of colonizing gaze, just as the ironic displaces the empathic urge and thereby disrupts an urge to "feel with" on the part of the audience.

The particular form of El Vez performances necessitates the careful parsing of just what it is we see when we see El Vez. In his book *In Concert: Performing Musical Persona*, Auslander posits that musical performance is a "socially defined interaction between performers and their audiences," based primarily on frame, genre, and persona.[50] Drawing on Erving Goffman's understanding of social frames, Auslander stresses that frames are collectively defined and serve as a means of making sense of events. This begins with the sound itself, which must be framed as music for us to hear it as music. Genre provides even more crucial information; notes Auslander:

> Genre frames establish expectations concerning what is to happen in a performance, including the coding of the music itself, the assumed shared values that bind audience members to one another and to the performers, what will be seen and heard in the performance (and what will not be), and how the audience will receive and interpret the performance.[51]

I will return to the notion of genre in Chapter 4 to offer a more detailed discussion of how Lopez defies generic boundaries to create a subversive soundscape crucial to his world-building project, but what matters here is that El Vez is largely understood to perform rock music; thus, we expect a certain sound (guitars, bass, drums, and keyboards playing loud and largely up-tempo songs) and a certain performance style (bravado and showy swagger, for instance). Finally, persona points to the identity of the musician in performance. Though Lopez-as-El-Vez troubles the conventions of all three of these criteria, audience expectations are nonetheless informed by the fact that El Vez primarily plays rock shows in rock clubs.

As the title of his book suggests, Auslander is most interested in analyzing musical personae, even suggesting that "What musicians perform first and foremost is not music, but their own identities as musicians, their musical personae," in which the "musical work and its execution" contribute to the overall performance, but are not primary.[52] I do not go quite so far as Auslander in discounting the musical work; rather, I maintain that sound and music, along with costuming, props, merchandise, and persona all contribute significantly to the meaning-making and world-building of an El Vez show. However, Auslander's emphasis on persona helps to unpack the relationship between Lopez and El Vez.

Auslander posits that musical performance combines "three signifieds: the real person, the performance persona, and the character [of the song lyrics]."[53]

Auslander further elaborates to include David Graver's concept of personage as a more nuanced understanding of "real person"; personage is not simply the real person, but rather is a "liminal phenomenon that mediates between" the real person and the performance persona, a representation of the self that emerges within the discursive domain of performance.[54] Having established that we never fully have access to the real person, but only glimpse it through the personage, Auslander goes on to emphasize the importance of the performance persona, which he asserts is:

> the single most important aspect of the performer's part in that process. The persona is of key importance because it is the signified to which the audience has the most direct and sustained access, not only through audio recordings, videos, and live performances, but also through the various other circumstances and media in which popular musicians present themselves publicly.[55]

Audiences generally negotiate these multiple signifieds with relative ease, though in music performance they often assume the distance between the real person/personage and the persona to be closer than, say, an actor on stage playing a role.[56]

The model that Auslander lays out works differently for an artist like Lopez when he performs as El Vez. For one, Lopez adopts a highly theatrical and inauthentic persona in El Vez, though this is not wholly unheard of in rock performances. Indeed, glam rock, a genre that emerged in the early 1970s, and which Lopez very much cites in his performances as El Vez, embraced a spectacular approach to music performance; glam rockers such as T. Rex, The New York Dolls, Gary Glitter, and David Bowie dressed outrageously, wore outlandish makeup, and defied gender codes. In his book *Performing Glam Rock: Gender and Theatricality in Popular Music*, Auslander describes glam rocks' embrace of spectacle and inauthenticity as a "profound challenge to the 1960s counterculture" that preceded it.[57] He tracks how the psychedelic rock of the counterculture eschewed ocularity, instead favoring antitheatrical performance as evidence of its authenticity. In contrast, "By insisting that the figure performing the music was fabricated from makeup, costume, and pose, all of which were subject to change at any moment, glam rockers insisted on the constructedness of their performing identities and implicitly denied their authenticity."[58] That is, the performativity of glam rock denounced authenticity—or at least the kind of antiocular authenticity of psychedelic rock—as an ideal to be upheld in rock performance. In fact, Lopez's adoption of the El Vez persona is not unlike Bowie's use of the Ziggy Stardust persona early in his glam rock days. El Vez and Ziggy are both fictional entities created by the artists who perform them, and these fictionalized personas "became the actor who impersonated the characters delineated in the songs [...] Revealed on stage, the 'real person' who portrayed the characters in the recordings turned out not to be a real person at all."[59] And yet there are key differences between their two approaches. For one, Bowie only performed as Ziggy Stardust from 1972 to 1973 before he retired the persona and moved onto others. Even as he adopted the persona of Ziggy Stardust, Bowie was known to be the real person behind him.[60] In contrast, Lopez has embodied El Vez for decades, so much so that the persona seems to eclipse the real person, making El Vez the personage we see in performance.[61] Moreover, unlike in glam rock, where inauthenticity repudiated the values of psychedelic rock and the hippie counterculture, Lopez uses irony and inauthenticity to voice subversive and sophisticated social, cultural, and political critiques and to activate his audience to participate in world-building.[62]

Lopez, the real person, is the artist, present in the aesthetic choices made in curating the show: the theme, the song selection, the lyrical revisions, the musical mash-ups, and the overall dramaturgical arc. But in performance, Lopez recedes, effectively disappearing into both the personage and persona of El Vez. Importantly, Lopez maintains a disidentificatory engagement with El Vez that opens up a gap between the two of them, through which he both signals El Vez's inauthenticity while also convincingly embodying him. The two are drastically different, yet deeply intertwined. Lopez is gay, El Vez is straight; Lopez is a former punk rocker, El Vez is an entertainer who functions "like a jukebox exploded,"[63] Lopez a complex human being, and El Vez a conduit through which he can speak. Most striking is the distinct way they each approach the world. While he admits that "there is the romance of optimism in Robert Lopez" that comes out in his performance of The Mexican Elvis, Lopez asserts that he is a pessimist, and he is very much a contrarian.[64] In comparison, El Vez is earnest and positive in all that he does. Perhaps the greatest irony of an El Vez show is that El Vez himself is completely unironic. Lopez notes:

> I guess El Vez doesn't see it as art as opposed to this is my life and this is my cause and this is what I'm telling you. And then Robert Lopez would say the art of, "Okay well is it that? Or am I making fun of that?" Robert Lopez is more prone to juxtapositions that might occur in the performance as opposed to El Vez, who will live it.[65]

Thus, Lopez constructs irony in the juxtaposition of El Vez's pure belief and his refusal of it. Though he fills in El Vez with details from his own experiences, there remains a distance between the two of them (so much so that Lopez almost always refers to El Vez in the third person), which provides a productive gap between the ideas and images he presents to us and how we choose to interpret them.

The audience does not need to know Lopez's biography to intuit this gap. Linda Hutcheon posits that irony involves "an oscillating yet simultaneous perception of plural and different meanings,"[66] which Lopez makes clear through his embodiment of El Vez. Carefully constructed to be the ultimate fake, the personage of El Vez comes complete with an infectiously positive personality and an impossibly absurd history. He was born in East L.A. on the Cinco de Mayo, the Fourth of July, or Christmas Day, depending on what time of the year you see him; his mother named him El Vez; and he was destined to grow up to become the best Mexican Elvis President Preacher Revolutionary in all the world, a true King. This signals to the audience that a playful irony is in use, making a multiplicity of meanings possible. Not surprisingly, he is biggest when onstage, dancing, tearing off his costumes, and flirting with the Lovely Elvettes and his audience. Yet, the El Vez persona also appears on other public sites—at the merch table after the show, in interviews, and (especially in the 1990s) on television and in print. Furthermore, the El Vez persona will interact with and often align with the characters of the songs.[67] Though we know the songs to be based on pre-existing hits made famous by Elvis and others, it is easy to read the revisions as El Vez's, as if they are telling his story. Lopez so effectively embodies El Vez that you are tempted to believe in him. This, too, is tactical; Lopez says, "I want fans to believe El Vez lives 100% in his own world and life that is always wonderful."[68] The effect of such details is to situate El Vez as the impersonator who through his inauthenticity achieves authenticity, the fake that becomes real, the trickster who speaks the truth. Notes Lopez, borrowing from Courtney Love:

> i am heralding the un-authentic
> the impersonator
> the fake
> impersonate so real
> so real i am beyond fake.[69]

Of course, there is always an impulse to look behind the curtain in an attempt to fix the real, which I link back to a desire for the believed toehold of authenticity. Lopez certainly has observed this inclination among his fans, who will ask, "Do you really love Elvis? Are you really a Mexican activist? Are you really this? Are you really that?"[70] Perhaps because he so effectively signals El Vez's inauthenticity on stage while at the same time convincingly embodying him, fans desire to glimpse the real person, to know who Lopez is and what he thinks. In fact, Lopez-as-El-Vez includes in his banter biographical details (many false, but some true) along with references to details from the tour and other such tidbits. And audience members likely discern Lopez's Elvis fandom along with his general political stance through the show content. Hutcheon reminds us that "irony is simultaneously disguise and communication."[71] So too is El Vez—a personage and a performance persona that simultaneously obscures Lopez and creates a platform from which he can speak.

Moreover, with El Vez, there is a further layer that informs an audience's understanding of the three signifieds of personage, persona, and character: El Vez's relationship to Elvis. El Vez activates Elvis, critiquing the status quo The King is seen to represent and harnessing the many discourses attached to Elvis as a pop culture idol. As discussed in the previous chapter, Lopez locates the character of El Vez in the iconicity of Elvis, who, though instantly recognizable, lacks any sort of fixed position in the web of meaning. Elvis is everywhere, and because he is everywhere, he is effectively nowhere. Sideburns, jumpsuits, showmanship—Elvis conjured in three brushstrokes, decades of USAmerican culture signified in an efficient, instantly recognizable package. It is significant that Lopez uses the terrain of pop culture as the site of his social and political critique. To return to Grossberg's analysis, popular conservativism seeks to "restructure people's investments in the sites of the popular."[72] That is, it mobilizes people's affective investments in the symbology of pop culture to strip them of political agency. In contrast, Lopez picks up the most sacred of pop culture icons in order to inject thought back into the emotional pull of Elvis.

Lopez's ironic placement of his performance persona in conversation with the Elvis icon also pushes against essentialist discourses from both the dominant and the minoritized positions. Notes Habell-Pallán:

> To incorporate the iconography of Elvis (as a supreme icon of Americana) into the milieu of Chicano culture disrupts the demand of Chicano nationalism for a return to an uncorrupted mythic indigenous past [...] it transforms the dominant culture's imposition of social codes that attempt to define "Mexican immigrant" or "Mexican American" identity and place in society, as well as subaltern demands to reduce Chicana and Chicano identity to an essentialized, fixed form. His aesthetic of resistance disrupts both the dominant and the subaltern dictates for strict, unyielding definitions of identity, sexuality, and citizenship and suggests that breaking with Chicano nationalism does not signify a break with Chicano politics.[73]

Habell-Pallán points out the "doubled-edged" thrust of the critique at the heart of the El Vez project. Not only does his use of Elvis disrupt white supremacist tropes, but it also allows for multiple embodiments of Chicanx subjectivity. It acknowledges the diversity that exists within groups of people. Lopez concurs:

> I have always known this, [...] but there's no one Chicano manifesto, no one Chicano state of mind and one person can't be a spokesman for, even a movement because within a movement there is so many other ends to it [...] And I have always been comfortable with that, so the idea of me having to speak for all isn't an issue for me.[74]

Indeed, Lopez rejects essentialist notions that would have him speak as one, for all.

Like Saldívar and Habell-Pallán, I contend that the gap between Lopez and El Vez enacts a productive ironic distance within El Vez's performances. However, that is not the only reading available. Calafell similarly identifies the gap between Lopez and El Vez, discussing the tensions at play in Lopez's project while sharing the critiques that her students often raise:

> After viewing the documentary *El Rey de Rock 'N Roll*, two Chicanas from California vehemently criticized Lopez/El Vez, questioning Lopez's authenticity to tell the stories he tells when he performs as El Vez. They wondered aloud how a punk rock kid can embody the story of a *cholo* in the barrio. They argued he was embodying Conquergood's critique of the infatuation of the enthusiast who enters with an anthropological gaze of superficiality. Is there a sense of privilege in being able to perform and walk away from that socially maligned identity, while others cannot? Other students have questioned the audience for whom El Vez was performing, arguing he was embodying modern-day minstrelsy. Some students have felt he was a misogynist. Overwhelmingly, every semester students question whether the progressive and political lyrics that El Vez sings are enough. What if the audience cannot critically interpret or unpack the embodiment? I remind the students of El Vez's pointed commentary between his songs and his manipulation of popular culture and visuals to make critiques. [...] Does the fact that the students are not seeing El Vez in the actual state of performance, but simply through reproductions on video tape and compact disc, affect their reading? Are they missing the affective political charge of El Vez and his music?[75]

Calafell notes that she takes her students' concerns seriously, and rightly so. As articulated above, her students touch on the way we often understand performance, both theatrical and musical: through the lenses of empathy and authenticity that leans towards realism, coupled with an expectation of seriousness rather than humor or irony, and with emphasis on the text (both the song lyrics and his spoken commentary) as the primary location of meaning. Audience expectations and ability are raised with concern; students worry the audience will miss the point. Finally, though Calafell gestures toward a more robust understanding of performance, suggesting that live performance perhaps carries more affective power than is captured in various recordings, she also goes on in the chapter to question his tactics.

Muñoz notes that disidentificatory performance exists at a point of collision. Building on the ideas of political theorist William E. Connolly, Muñoz sets aside the "stale essentialism versus antiessentialism debates that surround stories of self-formation," to instead consider how "fixed dispositions clash against socially constituted definitions."[76] That is, Muñoz acknowledges that there are aspects of identity that are more or less fixed—the way we see ourselves and are read racially, our gender identity, our sexual orientation—but he moves away from rigidly enforcing such identity markers. He continues:

> This collision is precisely the moment of negotiation when hybrid, racially predicated, and deviantly gendered identities arrive at representation. In doing so, a representational contract is broken; the queer and the colored come into perception and the social order receives a jolt that may reverberate loudly and widely, or in less dramatic, yet locally indispensable ways.[77]

I want to suggest that the questions and critiques that Calafell and her students raise in fact mark the jolt of the collision that Muñoz describes, the moment "where the discourses of essentialism and constructivism short-circuit."[78]

Lopez favors inauthenticity, theatricality, and ironic distance, making these the conceptual foundation of the entire El Vez performance event. He sets his sights on social meanings that circulate in popular discourse, using performance to highlight instability and in-betweenness rather than fixity. Indeed, through performance; he at once *is* and *is not*. For example, Lopez's first El Vez business card (Figure 2.2),

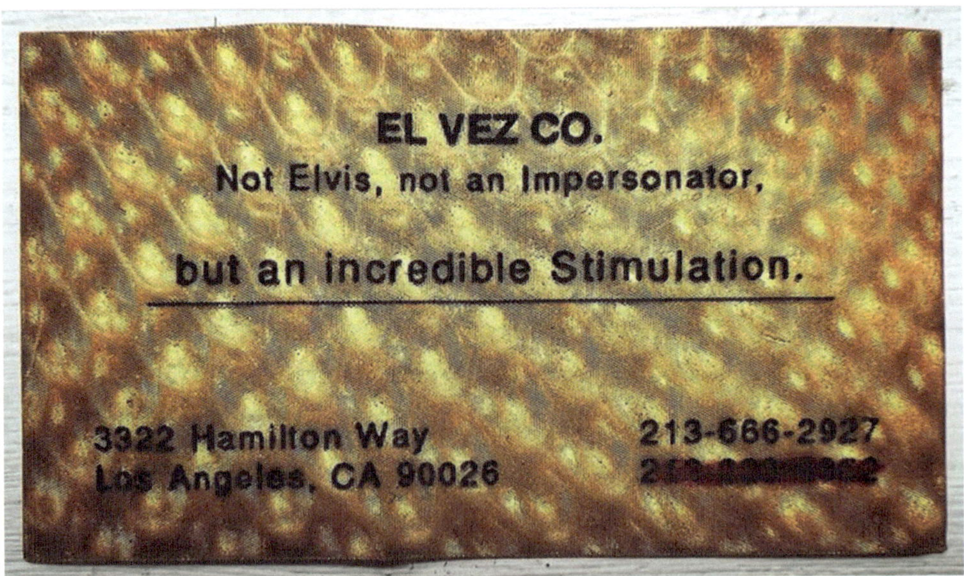

FIGURE 2.2: El Vez's first business card, 1989. Courtesy of Robert Lopez's collection (also available on his Instagram).

which he had made for his second appearance at Memphis' Weep Week in 1989, signals his willingness to exist in disruption: "Not Elvis, not an Impersonator, but an incredible Stimulation."[79] It is an apt description, capturing the uniqueness of the art he creates and the humor and showmanship with which he presents it. Auslander suggests that musical performance is made legible through social frames—frames that Lopez scrambles and exploits. The card both claims and denies the social frame of Elvis Impersonator, demonstrating the way that Lopez speaks a certain truth through the inauthentic persona of El Vez. El Vez may be an impersonator (indeed, he is fond of saying that he is the greatest Mexican Elvis Impersonator there is), but Lopez is not; he is an artist who makes use of Elvis in subversive and provocative ways.

Lopez's use of ironic distance and inauthenticity contributes to the world-building of his shows. Through El Vez, Lopez can voice strong political statements, using irony, quick pacing, and the El Vez sense of humor to sidestep the polemics that shut down discourse. By using irony as a discursive strategy in performance, Lopez can offer critique and prompt affective responses without relying on empathy as the mode of connection. This is because, as Hutcheon notes, "irony has an evaluative edge and manages to provoke emotional responses in those who 'get' it and those who don't, as well as in its targets and in what some people call its 'victims'"[80] For instance, the 2008 El Vez for Prez show was highly critical of the Bush Administration.[81] Structured as a Town Hall Forum, El Vez as a candidate fielded questions "from the audience" (these were pre-written prompts read by the Lovely Elvettes), to which he then responded with song. Several pieces took on the Bush Administration's full embrace of the War on Terror, and the domestic policies and international actions taken under this aegis. Lopez-as-El-Vez sang of immigration rights, critiqued the ongoing creep of Christian rhetoric into matters of state, enacted a burlesque "Stripping of Our Civil Liber-Tease" to protest the Patriot Act, tore up posters of George W. Bush in an homage to Sinead O'Connor's controversial *Saturday Night Live* appearance, and proclaimed Bush to be a perverse clown, noting "Our tragedy has been your comedy." Clearly, these serious iterations have an edge—they voiced opposition to specific policies and affirmed a progressive political stance. Yet, these more pointed statements were paired with observations about his "political platform shoes" ("looks like a pump, feels like a sneaker"); his big, impressive inaugural balls (or, in a car-themed song, his fuzzy dice and hydraulics, delivered with some pelvic thrusts); and how, in his tiger-striped bell-bottomed jumpsuit, he is King of the Jungle ("I feel grrreat!"). Hutcheon suggests, "Irony rarely involves a simple decoding of a single inverted message [...] it is more often a semantically complex process of relating, differentiating, and combining said and unsaid meanings—and doing so with some evaluative edge."[82] This is especially true with El Vez. What he presents may be meant as a genuine critique or it may be nothing more than a stupid joke; consequently, nothing should be taken at face value, and nothing should be unquestioningly believed in. His rapid-fire barrage of ideas and sentiments requires active decoding from the audience. In the open forum of Lopez's construction, strong statements are freed from didacticism.

That an El Vez show centers entertainment and is steeped in humor and pop culture references further add to his ability to dig into contentious political and social issues. In her book *Satire and Dissent: Interventions in Contemporary Political Debate*, Amber Day considers the seeming upswing of irony, parody, and satire since the 1990s (which, perhaps not surprisingly, coincides almost directly with Lopez's invention of El Vez). Day stresses that, as public discourse itself has become more spectacularized (through the 24/7 news cycle, the rise of political punditry to new heights, and the increased marketing and packaging of political issues and identities, for example), ironic performances "have become complexly intertwined with serious political dialogue."[83] Far from lessening the impact of such speech, Day argues, the overlap of ironic speech, pop culture, entertainment, and real political content in fact broadens engagement. Day notes, "Much of that communication occurs not as serious, rational argument, but in every other register of exchange, including sarcasm, irony, parody, and satire, all of which afford the opportunity to say things one otherwise might not in 'serious debate'"[84] The performance persona of El Vez broadens not only what can be said but also who can hear it. Due to things including the novelty of the name, his clear linkage to Elvis, and the fact that he often plays in festival lineups and at public events, El Vez shows often attract a diverse audience who may or may not know what to expect.

Musical performance is a social event that is understood through human interpretation, and in performance Lopez remains open to the possibilities that emerge as the audience reacts to his songs and banter. Auslander suggests that "the musical event is produced through interaction between two groups, performers and audience, who must arrive at a mutually satisfactory modus vivendi for the duration of the interaction."[85] And yet there are times in El Vez shows where the meanings become rather publicly contested. Lopez's engagement with the audience can be described as "improvocation"—a combination of improvisation and provocation.[86] Though El Vez shows feature a dramaturgical arc that is thoughtfully planned in advance, he remains open to audience response. Lopez does not shy away from negative reactions, which often arise semi-simultaneously from opposite sides of an issue. For example, Lopez recounts an EV4P performance at Seattle's Seafair in 2008 where audience members visibly contested his message.[87] Seafair celebrates the maritime history of Seattle, and "was designed to attract tourists and showcase marine events in keeping with Seattle's history as the 'boating capital of the world.'"[88] With a naval base nearby, many audience members are military personnel and their families. The show opened with Lopez-as-El-Vez singing his version of "God Bless America." Dressed in a bell-bottomed Uncle Sam suit, he sang the first verse of the song as originally written, asking the audience to join in. During this initial verse, a group of teenaged girls approached the stage and gave him the thumbs down, shouting what Lopez recalls as something to the effect of, "We don't like America. We don't like America. Boo!" Lopez's rewritten second verse undercuts the sunny patriotism of the first:

This mess América
We need help from above (or below!)
We're in trouble
Tensions double
For the weak and the meek and the poor
From Afghanistan
To Iraq-Iran
Not to mention
Troubles at home
This mess América
We reap what's sown
God bless América
My home sweet home.[89]

At this point, the teenaged girls were assuaged by his more critical tone, but a group of young military men came forward to voice their outrage. They booed and swore at El Vez, and when he entered the audience to shake hands with his constituents, they refused to do so, standing erect and holding their military IDs in his face. Lopez describes how, "at the end of the song, I lay down dead on the stage, and they were at eye level with me, flipping me off. And it was exciting to me."[90] As Lopez describes it, his message was perhaps more nuanced than either of the protesting groups received:

> I'm dressed like Uncle Sam singing God Bless America and they [the teenaged girls] were giving me the thumbs down [...] I wanted to stop and say, "That's not what this is about, it's not, you know, 'America love it or leave it,' I mean, 'My country right or wrong.'" But I didn't have space between my lyrics to tell the little girls that. And then to make the military boys mad. I was saying, "Well you have to think, 'Support the U.S. Troops,' but your government's not supporting you. Think how hard it is to get treatment for medical stuff after and all the red tape and, you know, reenacting, you know, your contracts when you are just about done. You call that support?"[91]

And yet what matters most, suggests Lopez, is that the audience is encouraged to be a part of the meaning-making. Summarizes Lopez, "It's a symposium of ideas under the Elvis frame. To make them think is the most important thing."[92]

Similarly, I was witness to two other striking (and opposing) moments of response at a free public Cinco de Mayo show held outside the El Vez Restaurant[93] in Philadelphia, PA in 2013, celebrating the restaurant's tenth anniversary. The restaurant hosted a free, public, day-long block party in the street, with plenty of drinks available. As I recall, it was a party that reflected the USAmerican engagement with this holiday—an excuse to get drunk, possibly while wearing a ridiculous sombrero. As part of his set, El Vez performed his "Lordy Miss Lupe," a take on "Lawdy Miss Clawdy" blended with a dash of Toni Basil and "Little Latin Lupe Lu."[94] The medley rather faithfully (if irreverently) recounts the story of Juan Diego encountering the Virgen de Guadalupe:

> Oh well, Lordy, Lordy, Lordy Miss Lupe
> Well, you sure look good to me
> Whatcha doin' in the desert now
> I don't believe what I see
> You've got roses growing from stone, yeah
> And you say you got a message for me
> You want to build a little church here
> So everybody can see.[95]

As further detailed in Chapter 3, the performance also uses some sequined stage magic to re-enact the miracle of La Virgen's image imprinted on Juan Diego's cloak. Leading into this song, Lopez-as-El-Vez pokes fun at the ubiquity of this sacred figure, showing a "photograph" of La Virgen depicted on a decorative silk scarf.[96] At this particular performance, some older Latina women near the front of the stage evidently grew upset with the depiction, yanking the scarf out of his hands and attempting to make off with it. Lopez-as-El-Vez was able to quickly recover it, and he wagged a finger at the women with a playful mocking tone, but it made for a surprising moment of attempted intervention enacting a complaint over his irreverent depiction of La Virgen. Later in this same show, a group of college-aged white men started chanting "USA! USA!" in response to some of Lopez-as-El-Vez's songs and commentary, which I read as irritation with the injection of political and cultural content that challenged their white privilege and their colonialist engagement with Cinco de Mayo.

A final example of responses to Lopez's improvocations can be heard on his 2002 album *Sno-Way José*, which features a live recording of "Brown Christmas."[97] The track was recorded at the Trocadero in Philadelphia on December 7, 2001—Pearl

Harbor Day—as part of the Merry MeX-Mas tour. More potently, the United States was still reeling from the terrorist attacks of September 11 and had launched Operation Enduring Freedom, a bombing campaign against the Taliban in Afghanistan, in October. Just two days prior to the Trocadero show, the Bonn Agreement and United Nations Security Council Resolution 1383 installed Hamid Karzai as the Interim Administration Head in Afghanistan, with the assistance of an American-led UN Peacekeeping Force in what would become the longest war in our nation's history.[98] Lopez recounts that he had created a video for this tour, and the Trocadero—"a great theatre"—had a large video screen available for use. "Brown Christmas" was the encore. The recorded track begins with the crowd chanting "El Vez! El Vez!" while cheering and clapping, awaiting his return to the stage. The crowd settles as the Memphis Mariachis take the stage, and begin the song with the opening licks of the Beach Boys' "California Girls." This segues upward into the start of "Brown Christmas"; as it does, the crowd cheers and applauds loudly, making clear that El Vez has walked on stage. He begins to sing the verse, and cheers accentuate key phrases of the song. However, after the first few lines, the crowd gets strangely quiet. There are still some isolated screams, but there is also a discernable rumble of dissent, which even turns to boos and a few USA! chants. Says Lopez, "At the lead, the screen came down, and it started off with a montage of Pearl Harbor images, and then that week's news [footage] of Afghanistan."[99] With particular emphasis, Lopez continues, "The audience was *audibly* against it. [...] They wanted a Christmas set"[100] At 2:34 into the track, with the line, "And so this is Christmas / And what have you done," the song transitions into "Happy Xmas (War is Over)," and you can hear the crowd begin to shift again. Now understanding the references and the purpose of the video, a portion of the crowd begins to applaud. Not long after, a woman yells, "Take your pants off!" and Lopez knew he had them (or at least most of them) back. The track ends with many cheers, peppered with some chants of USA!, the Lovely Elvettes singing, "Everybody wants to rule the world," and Estefan Bravo, a roadie for the tour who assisted with calling the video projection, shouting for a black out. As the band plays the final notes—a lick from The Beatles' "Something" into the final chords, the audience again cheers and applauds. The track ends with the sound man saying, "That's it. It's over." Says Lopez, "It's my favorite [...] To me it's a nice, live, up and down, what a show should be, [plus] the drama of us working." Indeed, it's quite a roller coaster—"Which is always the hopeful attempt,"[101] affirms Lopez. The track charts the highs and lows of the audience, who turn from pro to con to pro in under five minutes. Jokes Lopez, "Now that's entertainment!"[102]

I bring up these anecdotes to illustrate the way that El Vez's performances can prompt negative responses, often from multiple opposing positions or beliefs. Steeped in improvocation, El Vez's performances make visible Muñoz's collisions of meaning. And while each of these anecdotal examples reveals differing audience expectations and alignments, they also suggest a high level of critical engagement in the midst of the frenetic and festive energy of a rock concert. Interestingly, the first two moments occurred at very public events at which El Vez performed as part of a larger celebration or festival, events played to an extremely broad audience who may have arrived at the event with little to no knowledge of El Vez at all. However, the third example happened at a ticketed El Vez show where he was the headliner, and where he had recently, movingly played just days after September 11. Perhaps these moments signaled a misalignment between audience expectations of the musical event and Lopez's improvocations—that is if people arrived expecting "pure" entertainment or kitsch and were taken aback by the political commentary. They might also point to audience hopes or expectations about what a Mexican Elvis might say and do, or what positions he might hold in the wake of a national tragedy. These moments might also make visible the presence of different social groupings among the audience. Hutcheon points to the way that "discursive communities"—groups that share social, historical, cultural, and/or political context—factor into the deployment and decoding of irony. Indeed, Hutcheon argues that these discursive communities make irony possible, and they also reveal irony's emotional capacity. As Hutcheon notes, "Those who might not attribute irony where it was intended (or where others did) risk exclusion and embarrassment. In other words, even the simplest social dimensions of irony frequently involve an affective component."[103] Because irony must be unpacked, it spurs an intellectual engagement with the content; however, there is also an emotional aspect to it that centers around whether one is in on the joke—or perhaps is the butt of it.

Given El Vez's engagement with divisive issues surrounding race and ethnicity, gender identity and expression, sexual orientation, religion, and politics, an additional reason why these moments prompted strong responses may be because they caused audience members to become acutely aware of their own positionalities in relation to the ideas that El Vez expresses. Here it is useful to consider what feminist theorist Donna J. Haraway describes as situated knowledges. Haraway, disavowing the value of "objectivity" by pointing out that it is generally reserved for those who occupy positions of power and privilege, instead argues for "embodied objectivity that accommodates paradoxical and critical [...] projects."[104] According to Haraway, "Feminist objectivity is about limited location and situated knowledge, not about transcendence and splitting of subject and object. It allows us to become answerable for what we learn how to see."[105] That is, we should recognize the embodied positions we occupy, which are necessarily shaped by Muñoz's fixed dispositions. And yet, situated knowledges can be at times uncomfortable. Moreover, situated knowledges offer "a practice of objectivity that privileges contestation, deconstruction, passionate construction, webbed connections, and hope for transformation of systems of knowledge and ways of seeing."[106] These anecdotes highlight moments of contestation that may lead us to better ways of seeing, and of being in community together.

Of course, in working through my analysis of these anecdotal moments, and of El Vez's performances overall, I need to take into account my own positionality as an older, educated, middle-class, cis-het white woman, which impacts my own embodied vision of El Vez. As Haraway asserts, "The split and contradictory self is the one who can interrogate positionings and be accountable, the one who can construct and join rational conversations and fantastic imaginings that change history."[107] Thus, I add my analysis to an ongoing dialogue with other scholars, so that our different positionalities will allow us, collectively, to stitch together "the connections and unexpected openings situated knowledges make possible."[108] Undoubtedly, my white privilege impacts how I experience and interpret El Vez shows, particularly the personage and performance persona of El Vez and the ideals he presents.

For instance, Calafell critiques "the 'contradictions' of the public performance of El Vez and the ways that Robert Lopez's backstage performances disidentify with the potentially problematic parts of El Vez's performance,"[109] particularly his use of stereotype and excess and his seeming embrace of the logic of the American Dream. She notes, "El Vez, through his accent, costumes, dancing, and hyper-heterosexuality, performs and the ideal exotic Other to be gazed upon and consumed, but in the hope that in that consumption, politics will also be consumed."[110] While she appreciates how this campy performance allows him to interject political commentary into the shows, Calafell questions whether the excess in which El Vez revels might overshadow the critiques embedded in performance and in Lopez's offstage discourses. I contend that because Lopez willingly inhabits these stereotyped performances and is the author of it, he thwarts its limitations. Through his embodiment of stereotypes, he interrogates the way such representations are used to enforce political and cultural hierarchy. This is particularly pronounced in his banter around his songs about immigration such as "Immigration Time." We hear him differently with an accent than we would without it, just as this is complicated by the flashy costumes he wears and the sexy persona he performs.[111] The accent reinforces the story he tells as the character of this song—that he is an eager immigrant to the United States who intends to achieve the American Dream. By positioning himself as the thickly accented *Mexican* Elvis, he purposefully marks the difference in a way that mirrors negative portrayals of undocumented workers as uneducated aliens. As Sommer reminds us, the use of the performed accent can be understood as a powerful endorsement of difference, as "our accents safeguard American diversity from the meanness of one standard sound."[112] In this, he enacts what Cornel West dubs the new cultural politics of difference:

> The new cultural politics of difference are neither simply oppositional in contesting the mainstream (or *male*stream) for inclusion, nor transgressive in the avant-garde sense of shocking conventional bourgeois audiences. Rather, they are distinct articulations of talented (and usually privileged) contributors to culture who desire to align themselves with demoralized, demobilized, depoliticized, and disorganized people in order to empower and enable social action and, if possible, to enlist collective insurgency for the expansion of freedom, democracy, and individuality.[113]

Through his accent and other visual markers, Lopez calls on Otherness in order to better align himself with the disenfranchised so that he can sing their stories from the Elvis platform he has established. The accent helps him to disrupt the construction of immigrants as invaders, criminals, and pollutants. El Vez as a character is desirable and enchanting—like the Uncle Sam poster says, we do want him. And he, in turn, gives himself to us.

Calafell's critiques in part stem from a concern about how audience members might incorrectly read his performance, as well as from a frank awareness of the power dynamics at play in the realm of stereotype. She asks "whether all audiences are prepared, willing, and able to make these [resistive] readings [...] beyond the kitsch factor that is so often desired and consumed."[114] Or, to use Hutcheon's framework, Calafell questions if audience members are of the requisite discursive community to accurately decode the irony within the performance. And if not, what are the risks of that? Hutcheon stresses that we each exist in many discursive communities; "This overlapping is the condition that makes irony possible, even though the sharing will inevitably always be partial, incomplete, fragmentary."[115] Thus, it is likely that audiences are able to decode at least some of the ironies within an El Vez performance. And even if there are missteps, Lopez contends that only adds to the fun. Hutcheon goes on to stress how irony in fact depends on the agency of both ironist and interpreter; both are vital to the meaning-making. As I will return to at the conclusion of this chapter, that agency is key to the world-building that occurs.

Because the ideas Lopez-as-El-Vez puts forth must be decoded, he activates his audience members to produce specific meanings that relate to their own situated identifications. Auslander stresses that both performers and audience participate in meaning-making, to which I add their engagement in world-building, arguing that audiences become co-creators of the musical event and that they become invested in that creation. I want to suggest that these improvocations make visible the kinds of misalignments and collisions of meaning that in fact are vital to more democratic ways of being. As described above, these can sometimes be strongly felt and hotly contested, and they may align or conflict with Lopez's own personal beliefs. Truly, Lopez welcomes these sorts of responses and takes it as evidence that he is accomplishing his artistic goals; he states:

> You know, my full intent is never really fully understood by the people. But enough to jar them, in a good way or a bad way, is good for me [...] when someone says something, pro or against, it always is good to me because that means it struck a nerve enough about them to make a reaction.[116]

The gaps Lopez opens between enunciations of cultural differences disrupt discourses of hegemony. They productively destabilize meaning, perhaps offering a return to the conception of *Einfühlung*, an undoing and a becoming, or perhaps just making visible the short-circuiting that disidentificatory performance makes possible.

We Can Go on Together: An Anti-Assimilationist American Dream

El Vez's song "Immigration Time," a revision of Elvis's "Suspicious Minds," is replete with images of the American Dream, aspirational and material. He sings of Lady Liberty, the promised land, green cards, gold cards, and the Melting Pot. A standard in his repertoire, "Immigration Time" is often in rotation, and certainly is included in his El Vez for Prez tours (in much the same way that immigration is a perennial campaign topic, though there seems to be little political will to actually address the issue through legislation or executive action). Seeing him singing the song, perhaps wearing a red white and blue jumpsuit to fully embody the icon, asks us to reconsider what constitutes the American Dream (Figure 2.3).

Calafell offers a potent critique of Lopez's use of the American Dream in conceptualizing El Vez, questioning if it can be reconciled with a Chicanx consciousness. She highlights how Lopez embraces his Chicano identity and makes use of Chicanx ideology and iconography in his performances. Yet, she also notes how Lopez, in different interviews, slips into rags-to-riches rhetoric, linking that to Elvis's own narrative while also asserting that such a pathway should be open to everyone. This reliance on a bootstraps narrative, Calafell suggests, downplays the impact of racial politics and oppression; it not only overlooks the way that white privilege factored into Elvis's superstardom but also elides the everyday workings of white supremacy culture and "the material benefits of whiteness, because not all can pass or choose to pass."[117] Moreover, because Chicanx identity is often theorized as inhabiting a borderland consciousness, Calafell notes that:

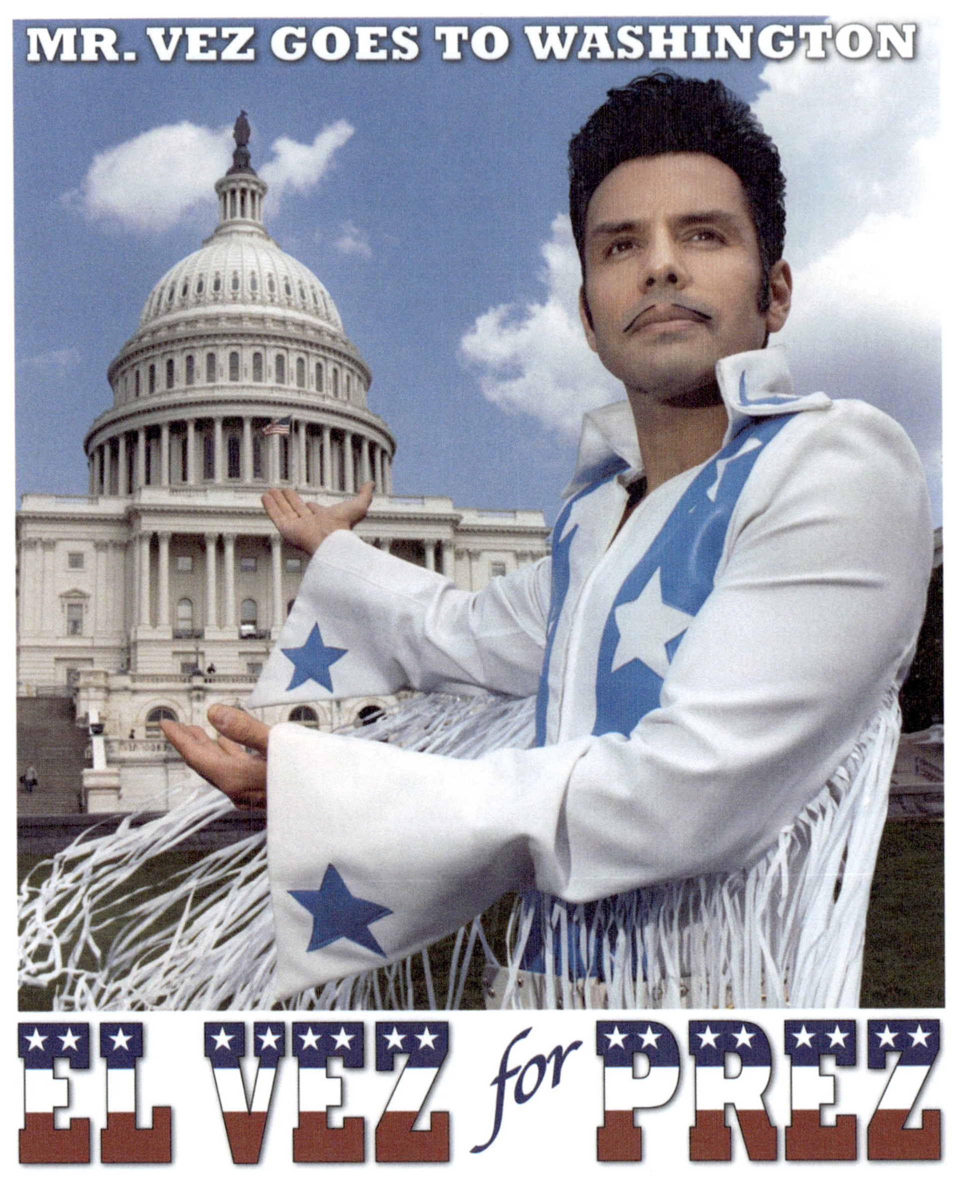

FIGURE 2.3: Wearing his Evel Knievel jumpsuit, El Vez poses in front of the U.S. Capitol in the "Mr. Vez goes to Washington" EV4P publicity postcard, *c.*2004. Photograph by Randall Michelson. Courtesy of the author's collection.

> [T]o ascribe to this identity is to place oneself on the borderlands as being neither Mexican nor U.S. American, rather as existing in (an)other space. The American Dream is antithetical to a Chicano/a politic because of its uncritical, unconditional assimilationist tendencies.[118]

Rather than aspiring to assimilate to a universal whiteness (one that has never been universally available to BIPOC individuals), a Chicanx consciousness embraces its hybridity.

Though Lopez certainly does play with the rhetoric of the American Dream, I suggest that he does so not to assimilate difference to the Dream, but rather to build a world in which difference can flourish. As he often says, he picks from popular culture and narrative tropes so that he can "put a mustache on it, and flip it to my purposes."[119] Through the distance he constructs between himself as an artist and El Vez as persona, he is able to craft an event that revels in the multiplicity that irony enables. As Hutcheon notes:

> [I]ronic meaning is simultaneously double (or multiple), and that therefore you don't actually have to reject a "literal" meaning in order to get at what is usually called the "ironic" or "real" meaning of the utterance [...] the said and the unsaid together make up that third meaning [...] the ironic meaning.[120]

We can take in what El Vez says and sings, and we can listen through the ironic distance to find a third meaning. One way of locating this unsaid meaning is to look for a Gatesian "signal difference." In "Immigration Time," I hear it in the chorus. The Elvis original depicts the crippling suspicion that ends a relationship, where the lovers can't go on together. El Vez, in contrast, posits immigration as a positive beginning, proclaiming that "We *can* go on together / It's Immigration Time / And we *can* build our dreams / It's Immigration Time."[121] To me, this expresses a desire to revel in difference rather than in assimilation, and to build an imagined social space out of that difference. While I don't want to hinge the entirety of my interpretation of El Vez on four short lines of one song, I call this example up to demonstrate how we might hear the polyvalence in his performances, where we might imagine a different social space, or a different American Dream—the Graciasland Dream—even if at the same time we may acknowledge its seeming impossibility.

I propose that the ironic and wildly inauthentic musical persona Lopez-As-El-Vez enacts makes possible an ethical act of co-creation on the part of the audience; indeed, it is key to his world-building. Through his embodiment of *El Rey*, Lopez constructs not only a flamboyant and engaging character but also the meeting ground in which the wildly inauthentic figure of El Vez comes together with his audience. His playfully named Graciasland becomes a site of connection in which all are welcome, but in which audience members remain individuals steeped in their own situated knowledges. In this utopic space, notions of cultural, social, and individual identities open up, enabling alliances to form across lines of difference within the audience itself. Though one fan might enjoy the amazing musicality of his shows and another his expression of Chicanx pride, what matters is that they stand side by side to dance and sing along with *El Rey*. As Lopez notes, El Vez creates multiple access points to and through his performance, thereby expanding the reach of his message to an audience. He becomes a node around which webs of relation form:

> A great thing about El Vez is that it's a very inclusive, party idea, very "the world is one" [...] Act globally, think Elvisly! And it's really trying to connect the millions and millions of dots that is life, politics, [society ...] And to say, this reading means this way, but this reading means another way.[122]

Because he avoids empathic conflation, each dot remains grounded in its unique specificity, and each audience member is activated to decode his message as they do.

Hutcheon makes clear that irony is transideological—it can be used to express liberal views or conservative views, it can work to subvert or inscribe power, and it can operate in any sort of political order. And yet she notes that "In a more democratic situation, where different positions or 'truths' theoretically coexist and are valued, irony is actually even riskier—though less materially dangerous."[123] Misinterpretation, Hutcheon suggests, is always possible when engaged in an ironic mode; there is no guarantee that the ironist's intent will be realized; she notes, "Risks like these, though, are part of the double bind of democratic discourse."[124] So what is gained from using an ironic mode? There are two things that I want to uplift from Hutcheon's robust analysis: irony is evaluative, and irony is linked to community. Day expands on this notion even further, noting that because irony is linked to discursive community, ironic communication is particularly adept at making "members feel as if they are actively part of a community. [...] it then sets out to *convince* the world that such a public exists, while making a case for the importance of its outlook."[125] Irony emerges from shared, often overlapping discursive communities, just as it affirms those communities.

As I have argued throughout this chapter, the relationship of Lopez to El Vez is built on ironic distance and inauthenticity. It should be noted, however, that Lopez himself slightly reframes these terms. Unsurprisingly, he is opposed to any idea of authenticity that is rigidly enforced, slyly asking, "Isn't that how terrible nationalism starts?"[126] To Lopez, if authenticity is to be found, it is found by being present in the moment of performance, and in following through his improvocations to see how they unfold. He firmly locates his embodiment of El Vez in longstanding entertainment traditions, naming specifically Mojo Nixon, David Lee Roth, Sammy Davis, Jr., Johnny Rotten, as well as vaudeville:

> What I feel I do is vaudeville, in a sense. [...] It's vaudevillian in the sense of we don't know what we're doing, but with our information of the past of how to entertain, or watching others entertain, we are live in this moment of authenticity because we both don't know what's going on. But something's happening right here. [...] [It's] being a student of showbiz and [knowing] how to keep a ball rolling and keeping it real in the authentic of the moment of "We don't know what we're doing, but we're going to go there together. And that's what you are experiencing with me now, via my live show." [...] It's a vaudeville idea [...] of reading the room, commenting on the room, making a connection with the past or with what's coming up in the show that we're doing. How to linearly connect things, comment on them, connect and comment, and then flip it with something that you weren't thinking of, an absurd part.[127]

He also stresses the importance of entertainment and enthusiasm in his performance of El Vez, to which Lopez is careful to add, "But, you still have to do it with sincerity."[128] This echoes Carpenter's intervention into authenticity: sincerity that leads to connection. Or, in Lopez's case, sincerity that leads to audience activation, engagement, and world-building. He playfully says, "Hence El Vez, is 'Oh, I'll make you angry, and make someone else happy with that anger.' Or, 'I'm just talking about America!'"[129] It is improvocation, grounded in "an appreciation of the here and now, but you have to know what your hand of cards is."[130]

I see in this Lopez's consideration of presence, entertainment, enthusiasm, and sincerity both a respect for the audience and an awareness as a performer. After 30+ years onstage, Lopez knows performance history, he knows the cards he holds, and he knows how to structure a show to please an audience while also keeping himself present in it. He even describes how he would keep himself engaged when on the extended tours of the 1990s:

> The whole idea was I still probably early in the game, but I'm so tired of doing this, and so in my lack of enthusiasm for that [...] I'd taken all the hits—I took like ten songs that everybody wanted to hear—and packed them into one song and gave them this great medley of all the things, and I did all the costume changes, like four costumes in one long song. "Okay, I got all that all out of the way, now I can go on to do what I want to do."[131]

Lopez balances the expectations of the audience with his own artistic aims, trusting his artistic voice and the ELVIS/MEXICAN frame he has created. This allows the content of the show to evolve with him, as he continually (re)making meaning out of his past canon. In conceiving of his different shows, he begins by acknowledging:

> This is where I am right now, this is how it is right now. And that might be personal, that might be reflective of where society is right now [since] society inspires and bothers me a lot. So that is my authentic expression of my personal. [...] As an artist I think [the question], "How do I deal with this?" is a wonderful chore and a pleasure.[132]

Thus at the core of the work is an artistic questioning.

Though the relationship between Lopez and El Vez may operate through irony, and much of the stage banter must be interpreted by the audience to make sense of it, the enthusiasm and sincerity of the performance and the creativity of the questions that prompt it are perceptible. And perhaps, this is what we truly want from our Mexican Elvis Uncle Sam—someone to pose difficult questions in a way that interweaves irony, inauthenticity, entertainment, and art; questions that we are then forced to answer. The next chapter discusses how the costumes and spectacle dramaturgically anchor this ironic performance, interacting with the music to make meaning. It also touches on the vital role that merch plays in allowing the audience member continued access to the performance long after they have gone home. These elements add further complexity to the performances Lopez crafts, aiding in the world-building of an inclusive social space.

NOTES

1. I initially drafted portions of this chapter as a conference paper in 2008, when Barack Obama faced John McCain in the election. At the time—during the Great Recession, coming off of years of war in Iraq and Afghanistan and the broader War on Terror, and with birtherism and other such racist tropes at play among a portion of the electorate—the election seemed to carry great stakes. Much of the work on this book has spanned an even more eventful portion of our history: I wrote another draft as the House Select Committee to Investigate the January 6th Attack on the U.S. Capitol had begun, and continued to expand and revise it as indictments against Donald J. Trump were raised and trial dates set, and am making final edits in late October 2024, just days before the election. If democracy was endangered in 2008, it is arguably much more so today.
2. Doris Sommer, *Proceed with Caution, When Engaged by Minority Writing in the Americas* (Cambridge, MA: Harvard University Press, 1999), 3.
3. Laura Edmondson, "Of Sugarcoating and Hope," *TDR: The Drama Review* 51, no. 2 (Summer 2007): 7. Edmondson touches on theatre scholarship's penchant for focusing on the possibility of transcendence and transformation that performance can make tangible. While she asserts that it is useful and necessary to uplift hope, resistance, and resilience in

the face of oppression, she cautions against doing so in order to soothe the discomfort of seeing how one may be complicit in that oppression. This brief essay resonates with some of the critiques of empathy that are raised in this chapter.

4. The "I Want You" poster that Lopez parodies was painted by James Montgomery Flagg in 1917 to recruit soldiers to enlist to fight in World War I.
5. Sommer, *Proceed with Caution,* 3.
6. Anderson credits Akiko Takeyama's concept of "affect economy" in shaping his thinking. Patrick Anderson, "I Feel For You," in *Neoliberalism and Global Theatres: Performance Permutations*, edited by Lara D. Nielson and Patricia Ybarra (New York: Palgrave Macmillan, 2012), 87.
7. Lawrence Grossberg, *We Gotta Get Out of This Place: Popular Conservatism and Postmodern Culture* (New York: Routledge, 1992), 259.
8. Each of these are emblematic examples from past presidential election cycles in which Republican candidates seemed to impugn the basic workings of democracy in different ways. I do not mean to suggest that Democratic candidates are above reproach; they, too, are worthy of criticism, especially in their adoption of neoliberal policies and their subservience to the donor class. That said, there has been extensive coverage of the authoritarian leanings of the current Republican party, with many scholars, journalists, and pundits noting that 2020 in fact is best understood as an attempted coup. The fact that the Big Lie has not just persisted within the party but indeed has flourished suggests that democracy is in a precarious position right now, especially as Trump continues to make claims of election fraud, suggesting that the only way Kamala Harris can win is by cheating.
9. Lopez, email to author, September 29, 2005.
10. Lopez, personal interview, August 27, 2008.
11. For example, my article "'And I say who has ever ever seen this place?': Feeling Change at the Performances of El Vez, The Mexican Elvis," published in *Theatre Annual*, examines how moments of powerful affect bolster and uplift the audience in moments of social turmoil.
12. Steve Rathje, Leor Hackel, and Jamil Zaki, "Op-Ed: Why Theater Makes Us Better People. Bring It Back," *Los Angeles Times*, May 2, 2021, accessed June 22, 2022, https://www.latimes.com/opinion/story/2021-05-02/theater-empathy-live-performance-psychology. They note that the San Francisco Playhouse prominently displays a plaque that names itself "an empathy gym," and they cite Oscar Eustis, artistic director of the Public Theater, who asserts that theatre is essential to democracy because it builds the "emotional muscle of empathy."
13. Daniel Schulze, *Authenticity in Contemporary Theatre and Performance: Make It Real* (London: Bloomsbury, 2017), 29.
14. Lindsay B. Cummings offers a succinct summary of the history of the term empathy and its travels from the German-language concept of in her book *Empathy as Dialogue in Theatre and Performance*, as does Patrick Anderson in his article "I Feel For You," cited above.
15. Anderson, "I Feel For You," 85.

16. Anderson, "I Feel For You," 86.
17. Anderson, "I Feel For You," 87.
18. Lindsay B. Cummings, *Empathy as Dialogue in Theatre and Performance* (London: Palgrave Macmillan, 2016), 15.
19. Cummings, *Empathy as Dialogue*, 13.
20. Scott Magelssen, "Why Do They Think This Is Okay?: Critiquing Performance as a Means for Change," and Dani Snyder-Young "Despite Artists' Intentions, Emancipated Spectatorship Reinforces Audience Members' Existing Attitudes and Beliefs." Both of these essays are found in Stephani E. Woodson and Tamara Underiner's edited collection, *Theatre, Performance, and Change* (Cham: Palgrave Macmillan, 2018).
21. Nadine George-Graves, "An Environment of Cascading Consequences," in *Theatre, Performance, and Change* (Cham: Palgrave Macmillan, 2018), 101.
22. Kondo, *Worldmaking*, 21.
23. Sommer, *Proceed with Caution*, 27.
24. Sommer, *Proceed with Caution*, 2.
25. Sommer, *Proceed with Caution*, 27.
26. Schulze, *Make It Real*, 16. Schulze traces this back to the ancient Greeks, and notes that, though the ancient gods were replaced with the tenets of Christianity, this reinforcement of the social order through authenticity persisted at least through the Renaissance. Fractures in the divine order could be seen emerging in the Renaissance, which continued through the Enlightenment and Romanticism, at which point concepts of individuality became prominent.
27. Schulze, *Make It Real*, 21.
28. Schulze, *Make It Real*, 28.
29. Schulze, *Make It Real*, 6.
30. Jessica Chalmers, "Marina Abramović and the Re-performance of Authenticity," *Journal of Dramatic Theory and Criticism* 22, no. 2 (Spring 2008): 23.
31. E. Patrick Johnson, *Appropriating Blackness: Performance and the Politics of Authenticity* (Durham, NC: Duke University Press, 2003), 2.
32. Faedra Chatard Carpenter, *Coloring Whiteness: Acts of Critique in Black Performance* (Ann Arbor, MI: University of Michigan Press, 2014), 204, original emphasis. It is worth noting that while Carpenter's book covers all kinds of performance—theatrical, political, popular, comedic, and aural—this topic emerges in the chapter "'Sounding Off on Sounding White': Aural Whiteness, Linguistic Whiteface, and the Economics of Opportunity," in which she focus on the voice and vocalics.
33. Lopez also uses this terminology, as I will describe later in this chapter.
34. Carpenter *Coloring Whiteness*, 205.
35. Johnson, *Appropriating Blackness*, 3. Johnson offers a nuanced discussion of appropriation and authenticity, and acknowledges how false claims to authenticity have been used to author oppressive and false representations of Blackness in service to a white supremacist system of power. Moreover, this essentialized understanding of race authored by whiteness

can be appropriated and manipulated for cultural and economic capital. He states, "I do not wish to place a value judgment on the notion of authenticity, for there are ways in which authenticating discourse enables marginalized people to counter oppressive representations of themselves." Rather, he argues that performance itself offers the possibility to form an understanding of authenticity's value.

36. Schulze, *Make It Real*, 59.
37. Schulze, *Make It Real*, 37. A key exploration of Schulze's study considers how, though authenticity seems to stand in opposition to artificiality and mediation, it paradoxically must be marked and conceptualized through language, which, some scholars suggest, renders it inauthentic. Thus, he is especially interested in unmediated performance, as a means out of this bind.
38. Jill Dolan, *Utopia in Performance: Finding Hope at the Theater* (Ann Arbor, MI: University of Michigan Press, 2005), 5.
39. Dolan, *Utopia in Performance*, 8.
40. Dario Martinelli, *Authenticity, Performance and Other Double-Edged Words* (Helsinki: Unweb Publications, 2010), 11. Martinelli credits this basic framework to Roy Shakur.
41. Simon Frith, *Performing Rites: On the Value of Popular Music* (Cambridge, MA: Harvard University Press, 1996), 71.
42. Allan Moore, "Authenticity as Authentication," *Popular Music* 21, no. 2 (2002): 210.
43. Philip Auslander, *Liveness: Performance in a Mediatized Culture* (London: Routledge, 1999), 70, original emphasis.
44. Grossberg, *We Gotta Get*, 201.
45. Grossberg, *We Gotta Get*, 208–09.
46. Grossberg, *We Gotta Get*, 212.
47. Auslander, *Liveness*, 78, original emphasis.
48. Keith Negus and Pete Astor, "Authenticity, Empathy, and the Creative Imagination," *Rock Music Studies* 9, no. 2 (2022): 164.
49. Negus and Astor, 170–71.
50. Philip Auslander, *In Concert: Performing Musical Persona* (Ann Arbor, MI: University of Michigan Press, 2021), 2–3.
51. Auslander, *In Concert*, 9–10.
52. Auslander, *In Concert*, 88.
53. Auslander, *In Concert*, 33–34.
54. Auslander, *In Concert*, 88.
55. Auslander, *In Concert*, 36.
56. Frame and genre play into this understanding as well. Auslander suggests that audience might expect a more authentic persona from a singer/songwriter such as Taylor Swift than they would of the band Kiss, decked out in full hair, makeup, and costumes. Similarly, frame and genre might impact the way the audience understands the character of the song. An artist like Swift is known to write songs drawn from her own life, so again we see a

compressed distance between her personage, persona, and characters that we would not read in a song like David Bowie's "Space Oddity."

57. Philip Auslander, *Performing Glam Rock: Gender and Theatricality in Popular Music* (Ann Arbor, MI: University of Michigan Press, 2006), 66. Auslander begins the book by dissecting the same Phil Ochs concert that I mention in Chapter 1, suggesting that Ochs, by self-consciously donning an Elvis costume, bucked the ideal of authenticity as it was upheld by the counterculture. Says Auslander, "his visual performance was not secondary to his aural one," 19.
58. Auslander, *Performing Glam Rock*, 66.
59. Auslander, *Performing Glam Rock*, 120.
60. Though *The Rise and Fall of Ziggy Stardust and the Spiders From Mars* (1972) was his breakthrough album, Bowie had already released singles under the names Davy Jones and David Bowie. Moreover, the *Ziggy Stardust* album cover bears Bowie's name.
61. This is further enhanced by the fact that he is often billed and interviewed as El Vez. When he worked at Teatro ZinZanni, for example, usually he was listed in programs as El Vez, or as El Vez with his name in parentheses.
62. This is not to suggest that glam rock songs did not also issue social and cultural critiques. Rather, I am simply considering Auslander's assertion that the theatricality of glam rock was in conversation with the rock musicians that preceded it.
63. Lopez coined this phrase early in his career and has used it in many press releases and interviews.
64. Lopez, personal interview, August 27, 2008. For evidence of his contrarian tendencies, see his Foreword, which begins "wrong wrong wrong."
65. Lopez, personal interview, August 27, 2008.
66. Linda Hutcheon, *Irony's Edge: The Theory and Politics of Irony* (London: Routledge, 1994), 66.
67. For example, El Vez assumes the character of a newly arrived immigrant in "Immigration Time" and of a Latinx everyman in "Takin' Care of Business."
68. Lopez, email to author, September 29, 2005.
69. Lopez, email to author, September 29, 2005.
70. Lopez, interview with author, May 22, 2018.
71. Hutcheon, *Irony's Edge*, 95.
72. Grossberg, *We Gotta Get*, 256.
73. Habell-Pallán, *Loca Motion*, 189.
74. Lopez, interview with author, May 22, 2018.
75. Calafell, "My Love/Hate," 73–74, original emphasis.
76. Muñoz, *Disidentifications*, 6.
77. Muñoz, *Disidentifications*, 6.
78. Muñoz, *Disidentifications*, 6.
79. Robert Lopez [@mr.robertlopez], post, *Instagram*, June 1, 2022.

80. Hutcheon, *Irony's Edge*, 2.
81. All descriptions and citations are taken from the author's field notes, El Vez for Prez, Los Angeles: Key Club, August 23, 2008.
82. Hutcheon, *Irony's Edge*, 89.
83. Amber Day, *Satire and Dissent: Interventions in Contemporary Political Debate* (Bloomington, IN: Indiana University Press, 2011), 3.
84. Day, *Satire and Dissent,* 20.
85. Auslander, *In Concert*, 94–95.
86. I *wish* I had coined this term, but all credit goes to my dear friend and mentor Tamara Underiner, who invented the term as I was talking through initial drafts of this chapter with her.
87. Lopez shared this story when I interviewed him following his Los Angeles El Vez for Prez performance in 2008, cited below.
88. "History," accessed January 30, 2023, https://www.seafair.org/history.
89. Field notes, El Vez for Prez, Los Angeles, Key Club, August 23, 2008.
90. Lopez, interview with author, May 22, 2008.
91. Lopez, interview with author, May 22, 2008.
92. Lopez, interview with author, May 22, 2008.
93. Because Lopez had been performing as El Vez long before the restaurants came into being, he has a licensing agreement with the three El Vez restaurants, and has performed at and DJed events there.
94. "Lawdy Miss Clawdy" was written and first recorded by Lloyd Price in 1952. Elvis recorded his version in 1956 and also performed a signature acoustic version of it during his '68 Comeback Special. El Vez shows move from this depiction of La Nuestra Señora into a bridge inspired by "Hey Mickey," with the Lovely Elvettes singing "Oh Lupe You're So Fine," and then into a fast-paced rock version of The Righteous Brothers "Little Latin Lupe Lu."
95. El Vez lyrics transcribed from *How Great Thou Art: The Greatest Hits of El Vez*, Sympathy for the Record Industry, 1994.
96. In a live recording on the *Sno Way José* album, Lopez-as-El-Vez introduces the song while covering an Elvettes costume change by sharing with the audience some air freshener and making a visual joke on its packaging. He says, "We got this at a truck store—a truck stop in Northern California and it's called 'Our Lady of Guadalupe Spray' and they promised I could bring the Elvettes back to life with this 20% free extra spray. So I'm going to try it right now." As the audience laughs, he sprays the spray, quipping, "Smells like virgin!" He goes on to say, "And it works!" as the Elvettes return to the stage to begin the song.
97. El Vez, "Brown Christmas," *Sno-Way José: An El Vez Christmas Album*, Graciasland Records, 2002. All audio descriptions are taken from this live recording. The narrative of the event was told to me by Lopez on March 4, 2024. I also describe a live performance of this song at the 2016 Merry MeX-Mas in Chapter 4.
98. Council of Foreign Relations, "The U.S. War in Afghanistan, 1999–2021," accessed April 12, 2024, https://www.cfr.org/timeline/us-war-afghanistan.

99. Since video projection was not always available at the tour venues, it had to be cued by the roadie for the people working the sound and lights.
100. Lopez, interview with author, March 4, 2024, original emphasis.
101. Lopez, text to author, April 12, 2024.
102. Lopez, interview with author, March 4, 2024.
103. Hutcheon, *Irony's Edge*, 15.
104. Donna J. Haraway, "Situated Knowledges: The Science Question in Feminism and the Privilege of Partial Perspective," *Feminist Studies* 14, no. 3 (Autumn 1988): 581.
105. Haraway, "Situated Knowledges," 583.
106. Haraway, "Situated Knowledges," 585.
107. Haraway, "Situated Knowledges," 586.
108. Haraway, "Situated Knowledges," 590.
109. Calafell, "My Love/Hate," 76.
110. Calafell, "My Love/Hate," 80.
111. I talk more about the accent in Chapter 4.
112. Sommer, *Proceed with Caution*, 2.
113. Cornel West, "The New Cultural Politics of Difference," *October* 53 (1990): 94, original emphasis.
114. Calafell, "My Love/Hate," 78.
115. Hutcheon, *Irony's Edge*, 92.
116. Lopez, interview with author, May 22, 2008.
117. Calafell, "My Love/Hate," 82–83.
118. Calafell, "My Love/Hate," 83.
119. Lopez, interview with author, July 10, 2022.
120. Hutcheon, *Irony's Edge*, 60.
121. El Vez, "Immigration Time," *Graciasland*, Sympathy for the Record Industry, 1994, emphasis added.
122. Lopez, interview with author, May 22, 2008.
123. Hutcheon, *Irony's Edge*, 16.
124. Hutcheon, *Irony's Edge*, 16.
125. Day, *Satire and Dissent*, 16, original emphasis.
126. Lopez, interview with author, July 10, 2022.
127. Lopez, interview with author, March 4, 2024.
128. Lopez, interview with author, March 4, 2024.
129. Lopez, interview with author, March 4, 2024.
130. Lopez, interview with author, March 4, 2024.
131. Lopez, interview with author, July 10, 2022.
132. Lopez, interview with author, July 20, 2022.

3

He with the Shiniest Pants Wins: Costumes and Merch

I'm kneeling on the cement floor, which is painted a lovely gold with just the right amount of metallic flake in it to capture the eye before becoming garish. Down the hall from me is a wall filled with thrift store paintings of clowns (very garish! but also part hilarious, part poignant, and part terrifying, depending on your relationship with clowns). To my right is the Elvis guest bedroom, where I've nestled into satin sheets and laid my head upon Elvis's visage on the pillowcase, taking care to sleep turned away from the disturbing WowWee Alive singing Elvis bust that sits atop a dresser. And to my left is the closet, overflowing with El Vez costumes. The floor is cold and the damp September Seattle air settles a chill into my bones; the mustiness of the Pacific Northwest stuffs up my nose and makes me sneeze. I am surrounded by costume pieces as I pick my way through the closet in the basement of Lopez's house, diligently cataloging the different pieces so that I can get a sense of this material aspect of El Vez's performances. I find a small blue suitcase of mid-century design—one of many Lopez owns. It evokes the exuberance of early air travel, when owning matching luggage pieces of all sizes was de rigeour for intrepid travelers. I open it and audibly gasp: it contains the El Vez boxing kit worn in the album art for *Boxing with God* and during The Gospel Show tour (Figure 3.1).

Carefully removing the items from the suitcase, I am struck by the emotional impact these costume pieces have on me. There is a white satin boxing robe; white satin shorts, trimmed with black satin and equipped with Velcro side panels so they can be torn away to reveal another costume piece underneath (gold lamé hotpants, I presume); and most importantly, one set of Mexican flag-adorned boxing gloves. Perhaps I'm inspired by the album title, but the boxing kit feels almost sacred to me—it evokes complicated feelings as it transports me back in time to a show I never saw live. Playfully dubbed "A Judeo-Christian, Zen Buddhist, Krishna-Consciousness, Jewish, Santeria, Aztec Sacrifice, Religious experience!"[1] The Gospel Show grapples with the role of religion in modern life and considers the tensions that surround religious freedom within our contemporary

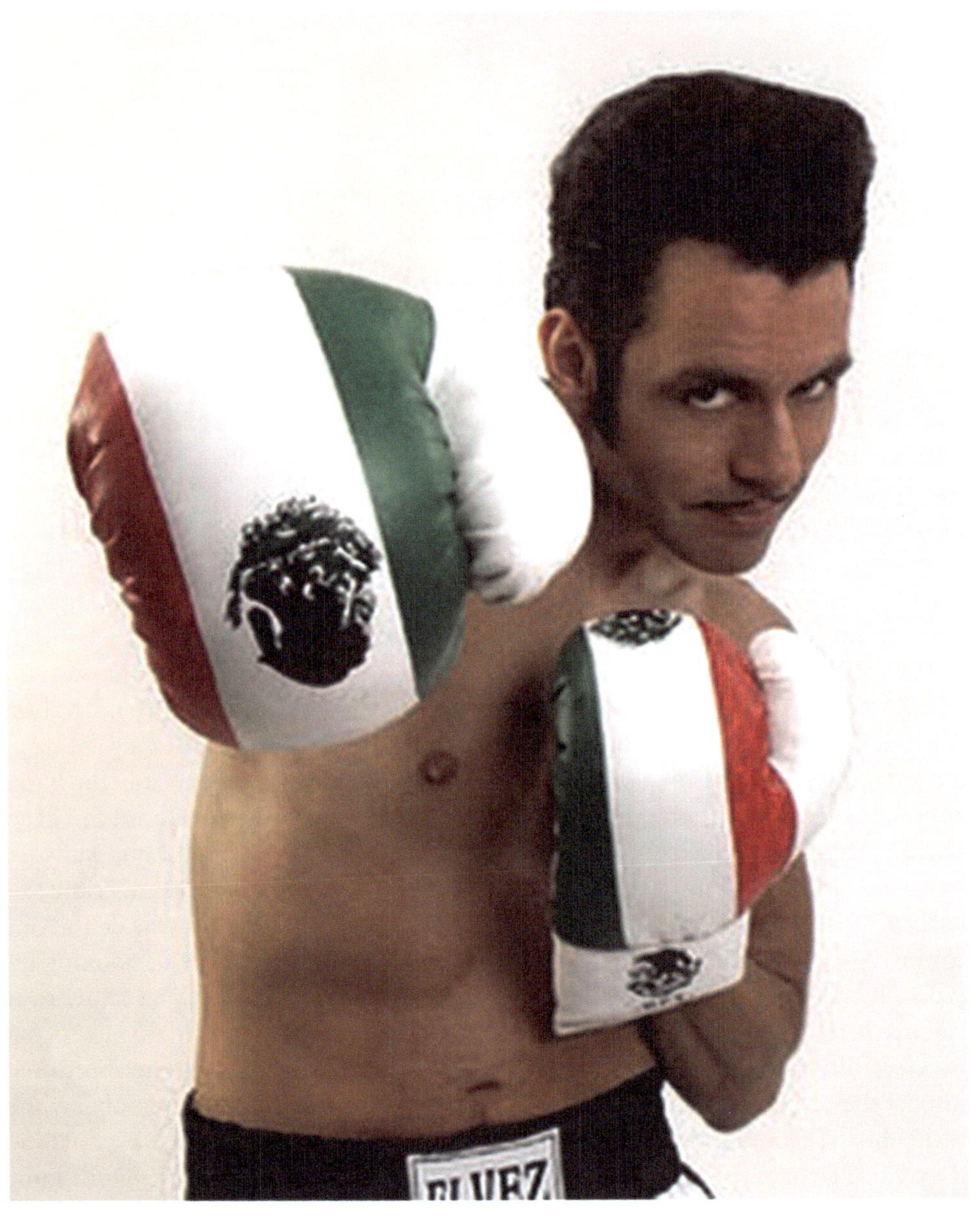

FIGURE 3.1: El Vez dons his Mexican flag boxing gloves in publicity images for his *Boxing with God* album, *c.*1999. Photograph by Randall Michelson.

pluralistic democracy. Though there have been several different iterations of the show, my mind immediately conjures up the version that toured in the Fall of 2001. As guitarist Pierre Smith recounts, they had played Dallas the night of September 10, and woke up the next day to the dreadful images of planes flying into the World Trade Center. They were scheduled to play in Austin that night, September 11:

> The promoter said the show had sold out so he still expected and encouraged us to show up. We did [...] and then continued the rest of the tour: New Orleans, Atlanta, then the Black Cat in DC on the 14th which took us past the still smoldering Pentagon with the crowd at the show chanting "Thank you, thank you, thank you!" after the last encore. Dante, the promoter there, said that people were grateful because so many bands touring with trailers went home while bands flying were stuck. Next came the Trocadero in Philly and Maxwell's in Hoboken followed by the 17th and 18th at the Mercury Lounge in Manhattan. Houston street had just been opened to regular traffic that day. There was a pall, literal and figurative. It didn't seem real. The rest of that tour, which ended at the Troub[adour, in Los Angeles] in mid October, was a dreamscape of hand painted signs hung on freeway overpasses, strangers being particularly nice with one another, well attended shows despite the new reality, and the eerie sense that everything had changed and nothing would be the same again.[2]

Or, as Lopez quipped on Instagram, "this was 9–11 week [...] a real what the 'hell' am I doing? Talking 'bout 'heaven'?"[3] Holding these costume pieces allows me to imagine what it was to be in the audience at that time, when our nation's collective emotions were raw. I imagine The Gospel Show as providing through its art a palpable sense of salvation. If world-building creates temporary social spaces that re-imagine society, how powerful must it have been in 2001 to come together as a community, to participate in a show that questions the role of religion in our lives, to imagine other ways of being, and to be present in a messy mix of grieving and celebration in a moment of national uncertainty.

Or at least that's what I imagine. I am writing, now, over ten years after the weekend I spent up to my ears in El Vez costumes, envisioning a show I didn't see that happened some ten years prior to that, undertaking time travel initiated by the objects that surrounded me.[4] And yet while I can only imagine these moments, the costume pieces I held delicately in my hands (Why delicately? They're boxing gloves! And why did I treat them with such care and reverence? I could have slipped my hands into them and taken them for a test jab! Why didn't I?) were physically there, actively participating in the world-building of El Vez by contributing to the fantastic spectacle of his performances while dramaturgically reinforcing the ideas he presents.

The previous chapter discussed Lopez's reliance on irony and inauthenticity as crucial modes of audience engagement that enable his world-building. Even though, as Lopez puts it, El Vez "is not based on a r[obert] logic,"[5] in performance, Lopez as artist recedes behind El Vez as both personage and performance persona to enact an ironic gap between these two figures. Costumes both mark that gap and mask it, simultaneously contributing to the appearance of the ironic, inauthentic, and theatrical while also enabling an audience's willingness to believe El Vez to be real. El Vez's costumes are outrageous, so there is no doubt that they are costumes, just as there is no doubt that El Vez is a performed persona; but somehow they also seem real, as if El Vez truly does only wear sparkly suits and tear-away pants and runs for president and serves as a religious leader. Using Aoife Monks's thoughtful analysis of the bridging work that costumes do, in this chapter I consider how costumes support Lopez's highly inauthentic impersonation, and open up further pathways of thinking about the relationship of Lopez to El Vez. Unlike a more standard theatrical character, no one else can really embody the character of El Vez. El Vez depends on Lopez's body, El Vez is built on that body, but El Vez is not really that body. Indeed, costumes are tricky like that—which is what makes them so much fun to think about.

I begin by analyzing costuming's role in crafting the El Vez persona and dissect the various ways that costumes collaborate with Lopez and the other performers to create meaning in his shows and to contribute to the world-building of his art. I also consider what Monks refers to as bodies-in-process to consider all that we see in looking at El Vez. I analyze how select costume items function more obviously as costumes, taking on a different role in the storytelling of an El Vez performance. Finally, I discuss how costumes function dramaturgically, charting a course through the performance and supporting the narrative arc of the show. This chapter also considers how the stuff of El Vez contributes to meaning-making and world-building through performance, as it also adds to the audience experience. Like fans after a show, at the end of the chapter, I will spend some time at the El Vez merch table. I use a thing-centric approach to examine how the items for sale augment the work of the costumes, allowing the show to live on in the minds of the audience. Equally as important, the purchase of these items grants audience members access to the man himself—after every show, El Vez greets his public, talking briefly with his fans while signing their merchandise. These items go on to perform as mementos of the live performance event, especially when they are further resingularized with the addition of his autograph. Irreverently tapping into multiple discourses of Catholicism, Latinidad, celebrity, and Elvisness, these items become, quite literally, performance remains that might be carefully preserved so as to exist as tangible memorials, objects through which the world-building of the show might live on. At the same time, they provide a much-needed revenue stream to support Lopez's work as a touring musician.

Never, Ever Touch the Shoes of El Vez: Costuming El Rey

The performances of El Vez, The Mexican Elvis make extensive use of costumes, and the costumes perform important labor. As Lopez notes, costumes do a lot:

> That's the art thing of it. They have to represent Mexico, represent Elvis, represent Vegas, represent sex, represent an Aztec god, represent angelic qualities, represent heaven, represent hell, represent the devil. So there's that, on top of durability and costs.[6]

Iconographically, they insert El Vez into the ELVIS/MEXICAN frame Lopez employs. The gold lamé, bell-bottomed jumpsuits, tight pants, and lounge jackets all reference Elvis at different points of his career, while the mariachi suits and Mexican flags clearly link to the Mexican and Chicanx culture from which Lopez offers his social and cultural critiques. Costumes also add an element of surprise, anticipation, and entertainment to his shows. El Vez shows feature multiple costume changes—usually between 5 and 15. Sometimes these happen offstage, while the Memphis Mariachis play an instrumental piece: El Vez might dash off, possibly with the Lovely Elvettes, who also change clothes to coincide with the outfits of El Vez. Other times, El Vez performs his costume changes center stage; he might shed his own tear-away pants, or have his costume ripped off of him by the Elvettes, or he might perform a shadowy burlesque behind a screen that is backlit to reveal his silhouette as he strips down. All of this keeps the audience engaged and on its toes, wondering what will come next. Because of the vital functions these costumes perform, costumes and costume changes are integral to the performance event, enhancing the show by providing it with outrageous spectacle. The sparkle and swagger of his costuming supports the fantasy of the performance. We believe he really is a Mexican Elvis, and really is a rock star, because his costumes so capture our imagination.

El Vez's costumes are the flashiest, but the Lovely Elvettes and the Memphis Mariachis are also costumed. Though the performers have changed over the years, the Elvette stage names remain constant (themselves a kind of costume), as do many of their pieces. Whether it be their hot pants, their short skirts and dresses, or their form-fitting jumpsuits, the Elvette costumes visibly link them to El Vez, display their sexy bodies, and contribute to the over-the-top performativity of the event. The costumes of the Memphis Mariachis are much more subtle and subdued than those of El Vez and the Lovely Elvettes (though they have appeared onstage in Santa suits and, in Spain, in *capriote* attire).[7] As is usual for many rock performances, their dress reads more as clothing than as costumes, wearing, say, dark pants and white button-down shirts. That they are coordinated, however, sets them apart from the audience and hearkens to their supportive role in the show.

They might also have playful pieces that link to the theme of the show: Santa hats and ribbon ties at MeX-Mas time or straw boater hats with red, white, and blue bands for El Vez for Prez.

As Aoife Monks notes in her 2010 study *The Actor in Costume*, there is an inherent "porousness between actors and their costumes and between life and performance," which is worth unpacking.[8] With costuming, the real and the unreal butt up against each other. There are real bodies dressed in real material formed into real outfits; yet these exist to support the fantasy of the performance. Costumes mediate the relationship between the performer and the imaginative, as well as the relationship between the performer and the audience. Costumes also produce the body—or several bodies—that are active in performance. Monks offers a definition of costuming that points to the way the body of the performer collaborates with the costume, each with their own level of agency: "Costume is that which is perceptually indistinct from the actor's body, and yet something that can be removed. Costume is a body that can be taken off."[9] She emphasizes how the materiality of costumes and the bodies they clothe open up new ways of thinking about theatrical looking on the part of the audience, which contributes to the world-building of the show. Monks suggests that we practice "viewing costume like a kaleidoscope, with the same ingredients creating new effects and outcomes depending on how it is viewed."[10] She posits that costuming produces different bodies-in-process made visible through a deep consideration of the (literally) material items that clothe the body during a show.

Through a discussion of the bodies-in process, Monks charts the complexity of the relationship between the performer's body and costumes and notes the rapidity with which our vision can shift. Borrowing from such theorists as Bert O. States, David Graver, and Michael Quinn, Monks defines bodies-in-process and offers how the concept allows us to more deeply analyze performance:

> The borders between the actor and the costume are unclear. The costume is the spectator's means to access the actor's body, and is also a means for the actor to access the world of the performance. When spectators watch an actor in performance they might imagine they see only one figure, but if they were to relax their eyes slightly, this single figure would blur into multiple ones, all of whom are doing a different job in performance, all of whom are a product of the performance. These blurred and multiple figures might even suggest that the actor's body is a composite of many bodies. Using the word "body" suggests that we need to approach the actor not as a given, real object, but as a process: a series of practices that are ongoing.[11]

Monks offer several examples of the different bodies-in-process available to the audience, including the aesthetic body, the historical body, the character's body, the working body, and the self-expressive body. These different categories can help us to pinpoint the way we perceive body, personage, persona, and costume in different moments of an El Vez show. We see El Vez, but we might also see Elvis, Elvis impersonators as a category, Lopez-as-El-Vez, and even Lopez himself. We might see Chicanx, Mexican, and Latinx imagery and references; we might see stereotype; or we might see a productive tension between these. We definitely see an excellent group of musicians performing a complex rock show augmented by spectacle. Throughout, illusion and theatricality mix with the real to produce meaning and to contribute to world-building, with costuming functioning as a bridge between what is imaginatively constructed and what is real. Using this framework, I will analyze key costuming moments that occur in El Vez performances.

Aesthetic, character, and historical bodies function semiotically as signs to be read within the world of the performance. In El Vez's shows, these are linked to the performance persona as well as to the histories that inform him. Borrowing from The King's iconography, El Vez's costumes first situate him in the realm of Elvis impersonator. There is a familiar silhouette to many of his pieces (indeed, google "Elvis impersonator" and nearly every image features someone in a bedazzled jumpsuit), even as these pieces are also highly customized, form-fitted, and made for Lopez alone. He often pairs these with accessories directly linked to Elvis, such as his Flying Eagle belts and gold sunglasses. Lopez even has replica costume pieces—which he jokes are his own "authentic reinterpretive reproductions"[12]—that are recognizable to die-hard fans, such as the white suit that Elvis wore in his '68 Comeback Special, though of course Lopez's white suits (he has two) feature tear-away pants.[13] Lopez's costume collection also includes several pairs of skinny tear-away pants, made of thin materials and built to be nestled under each other to perform multiple costume changes in a row while still allowing him to dance and perform. Many of his costume pieces include Mexican iconography, especially La Virgen de Guadalupe. His favorite pieces are the mariachi suits—he owns several, including the gold lamé suit that was displayed in the Smithsonian (Figures 3.2 and 3.3), several black and white versions (one with pants and one with shorts, both with rhinestones added by Lopez), a white and gold suit, and one that displays the Mexican flag.[14] States Lopez:

> I really like the mariachi outfits. They were custom, so they're made for me and they get the idea across and it's still wrong. They don't read strictly Elvis, but [they don't] read traditional mariachi. [...] When they can be breakaway, which is always hard because of the structure of the mariachi side panels—that's another story! But the mariachi to me, I enjoy the most. I mean the jumpsuit is the traditional, that's an obvious as opposed to the mariachi, which is not as obvious and it's presented in a new way.[15]

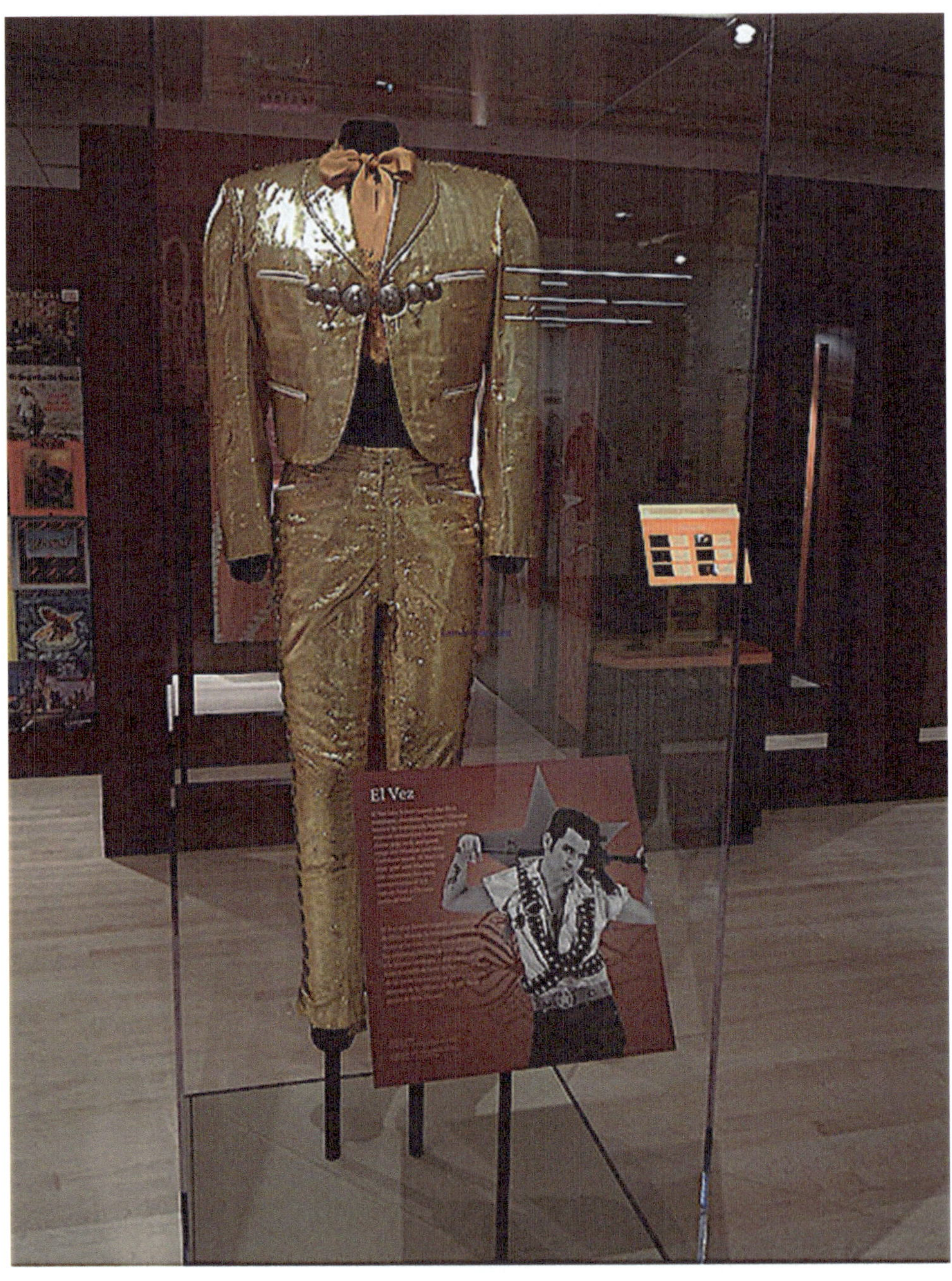

FIGURE 3.2: El Vez's gold lamé mariachi suit on display as part of the American Sabor: Latinos in U.S. Popular Music museum exhibit, *c.*2011–15. Courtesy of Robert Lopez's collection.

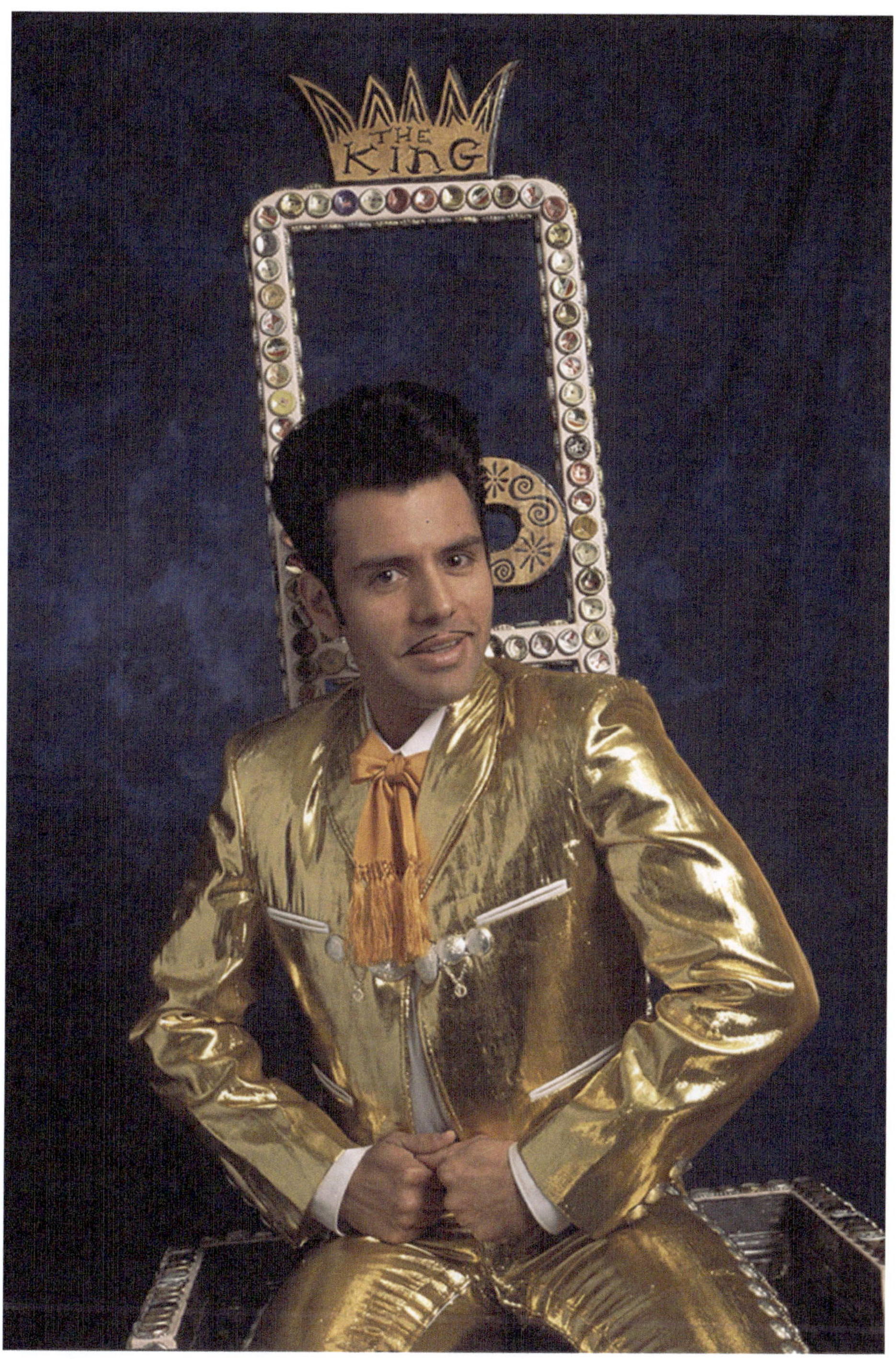

FIGURE 3.3: El Vez sits in his throne (crafted by Jon Bok), resplendant in gold lamé, *c.*1990. Photograph by Marcus Cuff. Courtesy of Robert Lopez's collection.

El Vez's costumes visually elevate him above his audience, drawing attention to him as he performs the outsized role of a rock star. As we take in these costumes, we view the aesthetic and historical body, using codes, conventions, and social knowledge to decode their meanings. We may also view what Monks describes as the character's body (though I will use a persona to be consistent with my terminology in the previous chapter), which Monks asserts "is central to the fabric of illusion woven on the stage [...] costume is expected to appear to disappear, to become so fused with the reality of the character that it appears as inevitability."[16] This body asks us to see these items not as Lopez's work clothes, but as El Vez's regular clothing.

In contrast, the working, sensate, and self-expressive bodies align more with the personage than the persona. The working body is that which comes into view as Lopez-as-El-Vez sings and dances. The audience hears his voice and watches the physicality of his performance, evidenced, say, by his sweat and his heavy breathing. Monks note that "many costumes are meant to foreground the performers' work,"[17] and El Vez's form-fitting jumpsuits, which show off his body and can be unzipped down to the belt around his waist so he can wipe the sweat from his chest—a performative gesture that not only links him to Elvis but also is a necessity in his highly physical performance—indeed foreground Lopez's working body. Witnessing the working body also allows the audience to imagine the sensate body, which refers to the sensations the performer experiences onstage while wearing the costume. For instance, when El Vez is swathed in black vinyl trimmed with white fur for his Merry MeX-Mas show, we can imagine the heat he feels under the lights and the tight feel of his costume on his skin.

The self-expressive body, in which the physical body of the performer or personage competes with the performance persona, can emerge through costuming as well. Notes Monks, "costume that foregrounds the self-expressive body often functions as decoration, and inevitably extends to the display of the actor's body itself as a source of visual pleasure, framing, emphasizing, and revealing it in ways that we can admire."[18] For example, Lopez-as-El-Vez performs a reverse strip tease to his song "Quetzalcoatl," his version of the Elvis hit "Heartbreak Hotel." Meaning is made through a collaboration of the music, the costuming, and the body. Through its lyrics as well as the performance, the song interrogates how we eroticize the racial and cultural Other as it offers a view of the Conquest in which Cortez is not the hero. Lopez-as-El-Vez begins the song wearing only gold lamé hot pants. How he gets stripped down may vary: the Lovely Elvettes may remove his previous costume piece by piece, or, as in the Gospel Show in Madrid detailed below, he may tear off his clothes himself, starting with his shirt on the first line of the song, "Pues when I was an Aztec" and his pants on the second "Before the Empire fell," holding for applause in between both lines. The Lovely Elvettes then proceed to dress him in an Aztec warrior's costume piece by piece as he sings an irreverent song about the feathered god: "He was an Aztec, baby / He might have been Jesus. / He was an Aztec who could fly." Once they wrap the loincloth around his waist—which has a decorative front piece that hangs to his knees—he swings it back and forth between his legs in a phallic display. Last comes the feathered headdress. His costume complete, Lopez-as-El-Vez will often strike a challenging yoga pose and quip about how yoga is key to his longevity as an Elvis impersonator. The bodies here are blurred—it is Lopez who does yoga every day, it is El Vez who impersonates, and the Aztec-inspired figure before us is perhaps a combination of both.

El Vez's undressing somewhat sidesteps objectification: after all, he controls the strip, he is the one who offers his body to the audience in a pop culture introduction to the Aztec god Quetzalcoatl. Yet, there is an element of exoticization that he plays with. His performance calls out how the brown body can be made erotic, noble, and ahistoric, reduced to an object of titillation and consumption. Obviously, this is a burlesque, both in form and in intent. Yet, his unadorned body is made more desirable not through the reveal (as in the case with typical burlesque), but by layering the costume pieces that signify the Aztec past upon him. The result is an insightful commentary on the processes of exoticization, and costuming and its interactions with bodies-in-process are key to the meaning-making of this moment. Moreover, the costume is very Vegas in its look: though it is reminiscent of Aztec regalia, it is also obviously inauthentic, with gold lamé and satin materials and chunky plastic beading. As such, it fits into the tacky aesthetic we often associate with Vegas Elvis, along with the showgirls, the sexiness, and the visual spectacle of Sin City. It thus also speaks to commodification enabled by colonization: once-sacred regalia, divorced from its religious context, available for purchase at your local mercado.[19] Of course, music contributes to the meaning-making of this moment as well: we cannot hear the melody of "Quetzalcoatl" without hearing the Elvis original, a lament about having been left by a lover; the song thus encourages the audience to understand the Conquest as heartbreak. The lyrics also conflate ancient Aztec and Christian theology, deifying Quetzalcoatl and marking equivalencies between the Aztec beliefs and the dominant Christian position. Combined with the costuming, the song offers a pre-Columbian imagining: Lopez-as-El-Vez transforms into a sort of glamorous Aztec avatar before our eyes, highlighting what he introduces as the "First religion in North America."[20] We see the aesthetic body in reading this costume as Aztec, decoding the iconography alongside the guidance of the lyrics; we also know the costume to be unmistakably El Vez's, as it features gold lamé, beads, and feathers. Interestingly, when we consider the persona, we read this costume not as clothing, but as a costume that El Vez wears. We can also see past the costume to view Lopez's working, self-expressive, and sensate bodies; we can marvel at his balance and flexibility and the focus he might feel in this pose in the midst of a raucous show. Finally, it reveals another body-in-process, one not discussed by Monks in her book on costuming: the aging body.[21] Lopez and his band mates have been at it for a long time, and accordingly, they have aged over their decades of touring. Yet, they still get out there and put on an amazing show. U.S. society may favor youth, but there is something powerful in seeing these bodies onstage—wearing revealing clothing and looking extremely fit and sexy, while still also looking their age—as they absolutely rock an incredibly physical act.

In gazing at these multiple bodies, this reverse strip tease also subverts the very act of looking that the audience is involved in. As Monks notes, "The theatricality of striptease reveals how theatre's investment in pleasure is inherently concerned with power, and shows us that the act of looking is not neutral."[22] Striptease invites the audience to gaze on the body as an aesthetic object. Usually, that stripping body is gendered young and female, while the voyeuristic gaze of the audience is gendered male. Lopez-as-El-Vez instead objectifies his own body, putting it on display to be consumed by his audience. This moment subverts the gendered gaze: it is Lopez-as-El-Vez—a man now in his sixties (and looking great)—that the audience devours. It also queers traditional masculinity. As Habell-Pallán notes, "At the climax of the song, the El Vettes crown El Vez with a colorful feathered headdress. Any pretense of hetereosexual masculinity evaporates at that instance"[23] (Figure 3.4).

Perhaps the most potent, yet least-lasting costume piece is El Vez's mustache, drawn on with a Sharpie before each show and refreshed throughout as he sweats

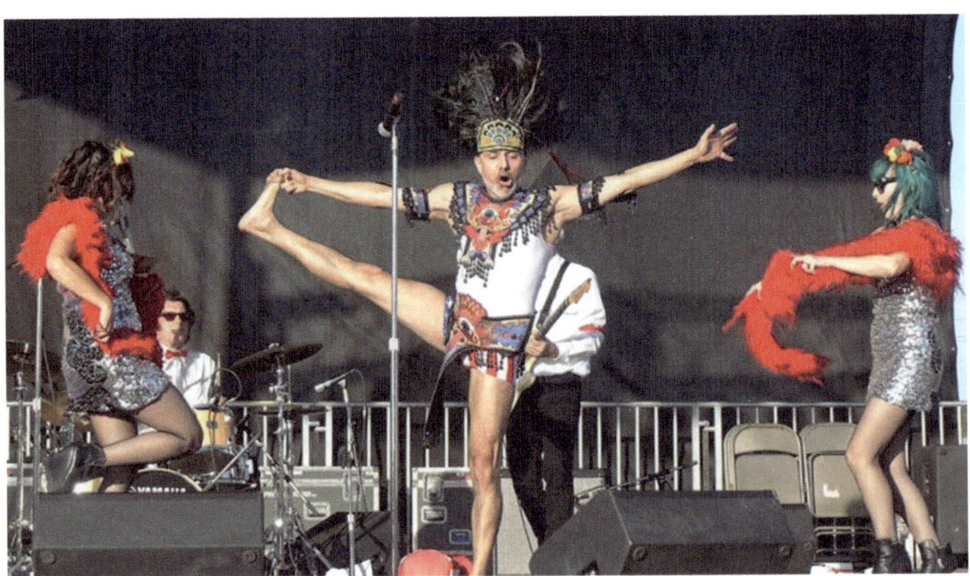

FIGURE 3.4: The self-expressive body of Lopez holding a yoga pose on stage, flanked by the Lovely Elvettes Priscillita (Crissy Guerrero) and Lisa María (Pinky Turzo), 2016. Photograph by Taggy Lee Mermis Bowers.

it off. Though impermanent, the mustache was a constant for many years.[24] Lopez recalls, "the mustache was the mask, and I like that it was the mask, and the simplest mask. [...] It was a mask underlining and camp underlining and sexuality underlining—underlining my nose!" He also notes that the mustache alluded to many icons, again stressing the multiplicity of meanings that circulate in and through El Vez, "it was referencing the mustaches of Charlie Chaplin, Cantinflas, John Waters, Suave Clark Gable [...] all those things at the same time."[25] The costumes may have changed, with certain outfits linked to different tours, but the mustache is visible in nearly every publicity photo, album cover, and performance. Moreover, the mustache serves as a metaphor for his art. Not only is he introduced as "The Man, The Myth, The Mustache!"[26] but Lopez also frequently uses this phrase to describe his process. He likens his work to the Duchampian readymade with a key revision: "I put a mustache on it."[27] Sometimes this is literally true – he used to sell as merch small busts of Elvis, mustachioed and signed by El Vez (Figure 3.5 a and b). As a costume piece, the mustache compresses the gap between persona and personage; it encourages a commingling of inside and outside that enacts a rather fleeting dance between ink and artist. As a costume piece, the mustache is extremely porous; it sits atop his skin until it is secreted off, sinking into his skin until it is sweated out over the course of the performance. Lopez also notes that at the start of his career, the mustache, coupled with the accent, allowed him to fully embody the persona of El Vez. Lopez recalls how he relied on the mustache, and how it occasionally led to some comic misunderstandings:

> In the early days it was a very strong thing, and the funny thing is having to touch it up every quarter of the show. It was such a funny thing, like don't let the mask fall! Or is it falling on purpose or exactly? Or the energy wipes it away. And that just underlines the campiness. I remember these French boys—we did a residency in Paris once—and every time I would go off the stage to fix my nose, they thought I was doing cocaine. Well, actually, I'm getting high on the Sharpie perfumes.[28]

So completely did the mustache blend with his body, that many audience members (and, evidently, French stagehands) did not realize that it was fake; thus it was present and invisible at the same time.

I want to return briefly to those pieces that clearly function as costumes for El Vez in the shows. I have already described the Quetzalcoatl costume, and there are several other costume pieces that do heavy storytelling work through their operation. Lopez has a piñata costume that literally transforms El Vez into a brutalized plaything, rendering him objectified and abused. In a performance at California Plaza in 2007, for example, El Vez entered the stage as the piñata, only to have the Elvettes beat him with nightsticks. After being beaten, El Vez then did a quick

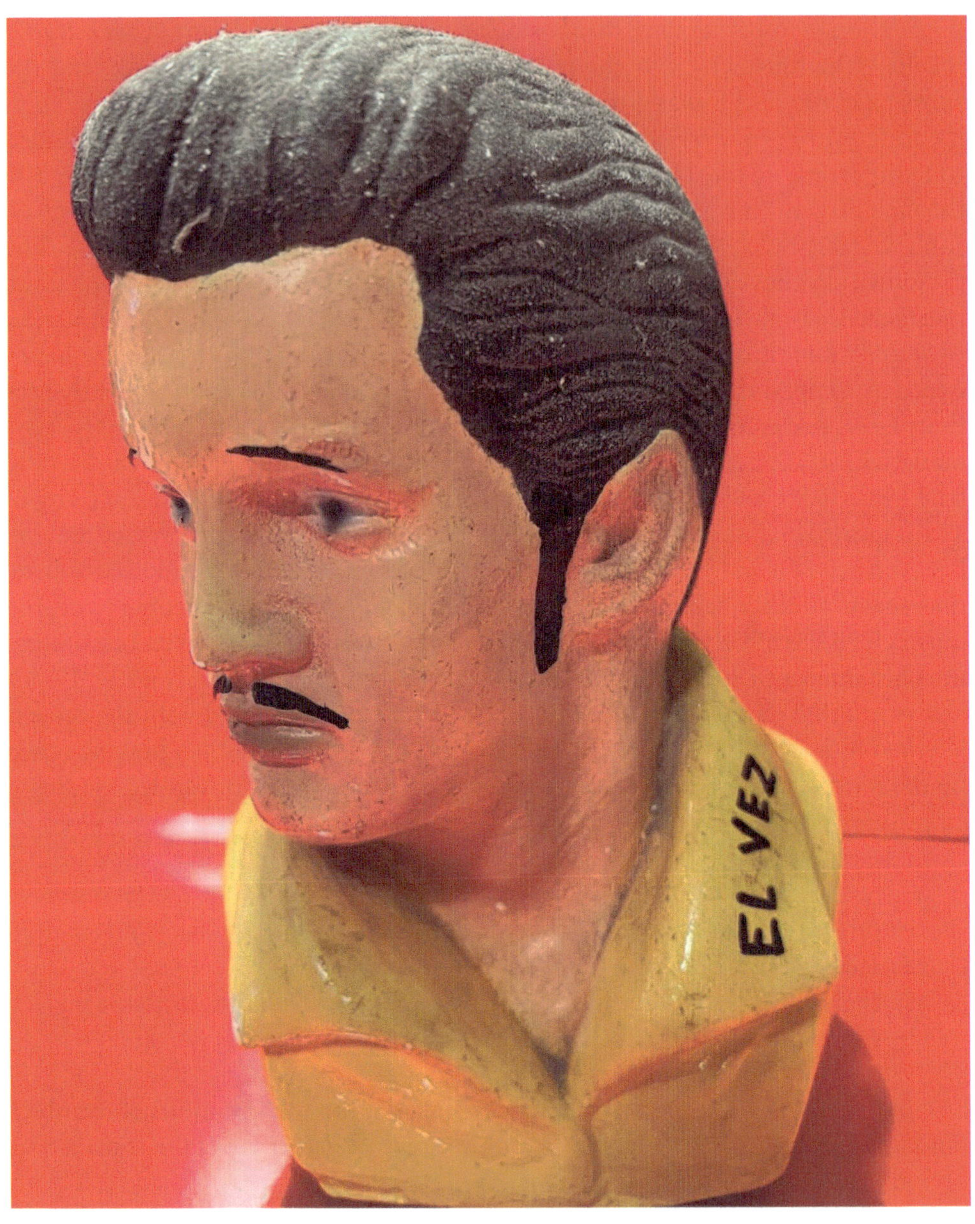

FIGURE 3.5a–b: El Vez puts a mustache on an Elvis bust to sell as merch, *c*.1990. Courtesy of Robert Lopez's collection [also available on his Instagram].

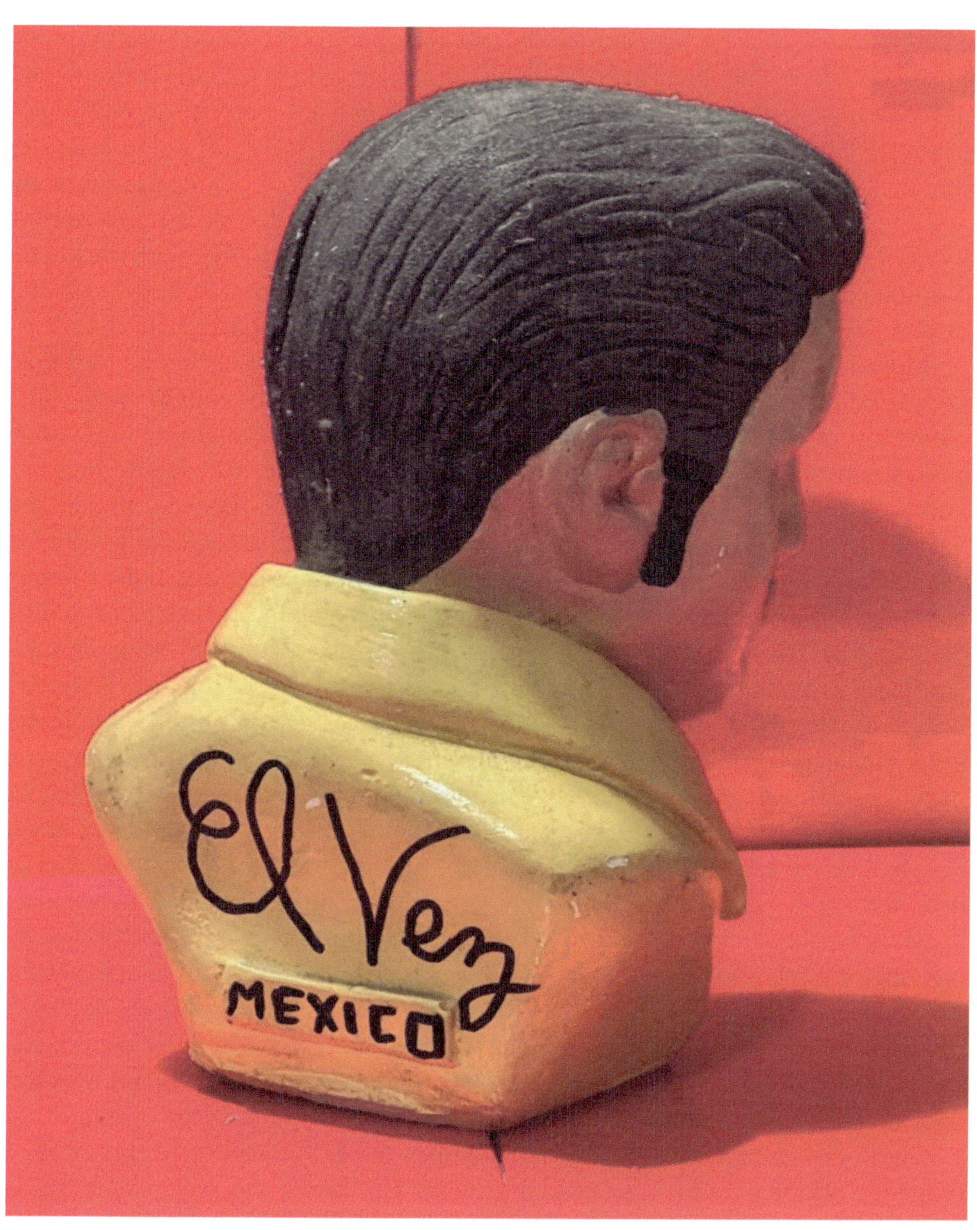

FIGURE 3.5a–b: (*Continued*)

change into a police officer's uniform and returned to the scene to subdue the Elvettes.[29] When they shied away from him, he assured them that the police would never beat anyone—a powerful moment that referenced a recent slew of police beatings that had made the news in L.A., part of a long legacy of police brutality that includes such highly publicized events as the LAPD's attack of Rodney King and the Rampart Scandal. He has similarly used the police uniform to put his work in conversation with the Black Lives Matter movement. Through the piñata costume, it becomes clear how BIPOC individuals are viewed with distrust and disdain, as criminals to be subdued or as playthings for violence.

Most interesting to me, however, is the costume piece that tells the story of Juan Diego and La Virgen de Guadalupe. This piece nearly vibrates with its agency and autonomy, for, unlike all of the other costumes mentioned, it costumes an (un)witting audience member,[30] one who may or may not be Latinx, and who may or may not know the story of La Virgen. The song teaches its audience about La Virgen and the sainted Aztec. As mentioned in the previous chapter, El Vez begins by singing what he calls a "light blues—more like a periwinkle" (because "Latinos are a happy people"), belting out his song "Lordy Miss Lupe," to the tune of Elvis's blues cover "Lawdy Miss Clawdy." During the song, he and the Elvettes perform with the audience member a mini-pageant, which rather faithfully re-enacts the story of La Virgen's miracle as it has been passed down through Mexican culture. The drama culminates in La Virgen giving Juan Diego roses to present to church officials, which emblazon her image on his serape. In El Vez's version of this sacred event, the audience member is dressed in a plain serape and handed a bouquet of fake roses which El Vez or the Lovely Elvettes will roll up in the front of the garment for the audience member to hold until, with some theatre magic (and Velcro), the serape is unfurled to reveal an image of La Virgen that is as sequined as an Elvis jumpsuit, a conflation of grandiose religious style and Vegas tackiness. More importantly, the reveal punctuates the closing line of the song, "You are La Nuestra Señora / And you're brown like me." Thus, El Vez enacts a final Chicanx mode of being: sanctification, beatification, and salvation. Latinidad becomes a vehicle for redemption, which El Vez grants to everyone, including the audience member who briefly becomes Juan Diego onstage.

The bodies-in-process and costumes of Lopez and El Vez are imperceptibly intertwined, working in tandem to make meaning. This raises a provocative question around this performance persona. Can there be another El Vez—an El Vez impersonator?—or is El Vez specifically tied to the particular body of Lopez?[31] Does that make El Vez more than a persona? Is it this direct linkage of Lopez to El Vez that tricks the audience into conflating them, and believing them to be real? And how much of this relates to costume? Monks argues that "costuming is indistinguishable from the actor, indeed, it makes the actor's body possible, and is fundamental to the relationship between the actor and the audience."[32] Costumes fully bring El

Vez into being and they contribute to the world-building of the performance event. Coincidentally, El Vez has dabbled in impersonators: early in his career, as he was gaining visibility, he appeared on NBC's "To Tell the Truth" (episode no. 167 in 1991) with two other men—dressed in Lopez's costumes. The celebrity judges David Niven, Jr., Dr. Ruth Westheimer, John Callahan, and Kitty Carlisle were asked to determine which one was the real El Vez. Lopez shared, "I remember the point where I hesitated with an answer, but it was an actual hesitation. And they took that hesitation as, 'I don't know what I'm doing, I'm just pretending I'm El Vez.'"[33] even though he was giving a real answer. So, at least in this instance, the costumes really did do the work: the real clothes of El Vez successfully hid the fake bodies of the others, including the man the panel of judges deemed to be the "real" El Vez.[34] The appearance netted Lopez $1000 in prize money, the ability to say he has El Vez impersonators, and a polka-dotted tie (stolen from Alex Trebek).[35]

I have spoken about how costuming collaborates with Lopez to create El Vez onstage, but I have said little about the materiality of these costumes when they are not on display in his performances. On tour, everything that goes into making El Vez, save Lopez's body, travels in one or two large suitcases.[36] Costumes, props, shoes, Sharpies—on one MeX-Mas tour I observed closely, over 25 pieces just for El Vez—each of which requires careful attention. The costumes must be hung in relative order before the show and the props carefully laid out on a table. Due to the quick costume changes, the dressing room after a show is a mess, with costume pieces strewn all over the floor by the garment rack. They must be collected and repacked. Back in his hotel, costumes are wiped down and hung to dry because, as Lopez has noted in interviews, "Vinyl doesn't let you breathe."[37] Indeed, in my experience, they are heavy with sweat and wet to the touch. Thus, the costumes carry a degree of intimacy—in wearing these pieces, the fabric touched his skin as the sweat soaked the material, and those traces remain. Yet, they also require care and attention. After hanging overnight, they will again be placed in the suitcase and put in the back of the van for the drive to the next city.[38] Lopez later launders the costumes and stores them.[39]

Another important element of costumes is the design. The choice of fabric, the silhouette, and the overall look help to create El Vez. Aly Renee Amidei states, "The costume designer curates the visual external body for the character while the actor gives life to its heart, mind, and the physical body in motion."[40] In the world of El Vez, the designer and performer are one: Lopez himself. Lopez sources and purchases the material for his costumes, often from the Fashion District in downtown L.A., where there are several stores that sell bulk fabric. He also envisions the look. Once designed, he hires a tailor to build the pieces. Lopez has worked with several tailors who have custom-made the majority of his costumes over the course of his career: he first worked with a Mexican woman in Downey; he also worked with Bobbie Kaminski, who made several of his original jumpsuits (Kaminski worked at Soap

Plant, and also designed and built stage attire for Cheap Trick and other bands);[41] Lopez later went to Je T'aime on Hollywood Boulevard, where he worked with a Persian man who primarily made stripper clothes.[42] In 2012, each custom-made outfit cost approximately $150 to construct, which included two fittings. Lopez also purchases off-the-rack items (mostly club wear), which might be modified and used in performance.[43] Belts are also custom-made, based off of Elvis. When I cataloged his costumes in September 2012, he had over 260 pieces on hand. Thus, his costumes represent a considerable financial investment. Indeed, when I asked Lopez about the kind of thinking that goes into his costume design, he did not hesitate with his answer:

> Economic. [...] What can I do in my limited budget? I guess during my heyday, when I was getting things made, it was nice. I would still have to think wear and tear, how is this going to last? And I know the fabric—if I'm rubbing on the floor, or breaking away—how it's going to tear every day from that point. It's going to become weak, sweat holding, because on a tour, you don't have time to get them dry cleaned. Is hand washing going to make the colors fade? Durability. Stinkability. Stage appearance, how the light will hit it. Comfort is usually the last thing that I get to think about. [...] I have to think about so many different things. I had sequined jumpsuits made, but you can't put them on a hanger because the weight of it will make it hang and it will stretch it. There's so many stupid things you have to think about with the costumes![44]

Given the investment, El Vez costumes have come to represent his artistic history. Indeed, he has had several pieces from the start, including his black and white mariachi suit. As both a scholar and a fan, the elation I felt when I came across certain pieces—his Rock and Revolution camouflage bell-bottomed jumpsuit; his *Boxing with God* shorts, cape, and Mexican flag boxing gloves described above; his gold lamé mariachi suit; an original Elvette bustier with tiny sombreros over the breasts; and his first custom costume piece, a painted jean jacket made in 1988—was palpable.

The jean jacket, made by artist Vicki Berndt, is in fact the first costume piece Lopez ever commissioned, specifically for his debut. Lopez had shown her work La Luz de Jesus, including at The Elvis Show; she makes jackets, votive candles, and portraits, often blending religious iconography with secular themes.[45] As noted in Chapter 1, he paired the jacket with gold lamé jeans and a sombrero for his first trip to Memphis in 1988. Lopez states:

> That was the first show I did. But I had the jacket made for the show, so I invested into it, but I hadn't become El Vez yet. [...] It's funny to think, before I had even done it, I paid. And I think I only paid like $150 [...] which is a good investment, but the idea that I would invest that much money into a show I hadn't done yet.[46]

It was a fairly high price for a joke, a performance that he thought would be a one-off. A close reading of the jacket provides many insights (Figure 3.6). It exemplifies the mixing that takes place in an El Vez performance: earnest sincerity and ironic flippancy, deep critical thought and irreverent humor, political incisiveness and pop culture superficiality, intellect and entertainment, Mexican and American, El Vez and Elvis—all with a kitschy veneer. These contradictions exist side-by-side, literally next to and on top of each other, emphasizing the multiplicity of identity positions we all occupy. The jacket also reveals Lopez's process in creating El Vez: he takes something that already exists—a jean jacket or an Elvis song—and then layers his own ideas, influences, and interpretations (and his face) on top of it, thereby making something new, something unique. Additionally, the jacket underscores the DIY aesthetic that grounds Lopez's approach to his art. Though it emphasizes spectacle, it does so through the ironic reuse of everyday items paired with interpretive artistry.

In cataloging the costumes, I was also struck by how their materiality might affect Lopez's performances. For instance, the Smithsonian suit was extremely

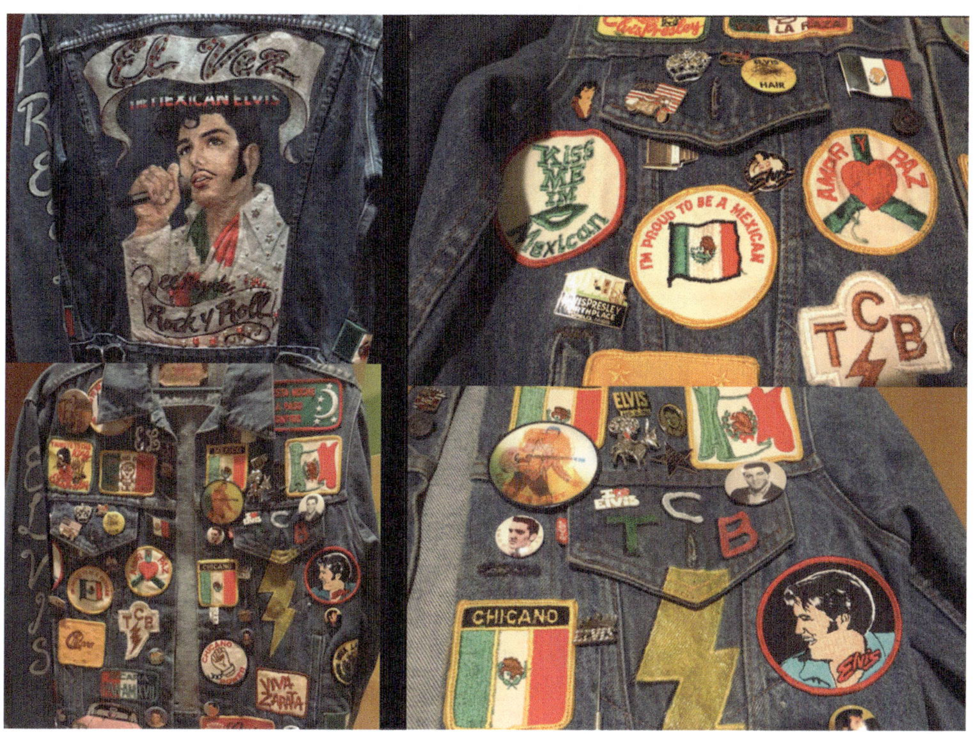

FIGURE 3.6: Detail of Lopez's first commissioned El Vez piece: the jean jacket he wore to Weep Week in 1988. Photograph by author, 2012.

heavy, weighed down by the shield-like button-and-chain adornments up its legs. A poinsettia jumpsuit made from stiff plasticized material could stand on its own and clearly would cause Lopez to sweat profusely. Yet as he notes, comfort is his last priority. Indeed, going through the costumes made clear just how physically demanding Lopez's performances of El Vez must be. This strain, in fact, is evident on the costume pieces, which display wear and tear not noticeable onstage. Missing sequins, sweat stains, tears in the armpits and crotch, and holes in the knees speak to his physicality in performance. In fact, he shared that he is considering having a jumpsuit made from the material in Mexican floor cloths, only half-joking when he described how he would use this in performance:

> I want to make a jumpsuit out of that and roll on the floor, showing I'm a human mop. And I'm thinking, "Oh , the durability would be so good!" I mean, getting used is the idea, so to rub on the floor, which is the duty of that fabric, is not having to be precious about it, as with a lamé or a sequined something.[47]

Finally, when the costumes get too worn, he moves them from the closet to the merch table, cutting them into small pieces and selling them as relics. This move again links him to Elvis, or more precisely to Colonel Tom Parker, who had Elvis's old clothing cut into swatches and placed in small envelopes that read "Something from ELVIS' wardrobe for you," that he sold with B-sides in 1971.[48]

Costumes play an active role in El Vez's performances, contributing to the world-building of the shows. Costumes bring El Vez into being, allowing him to seem incredibly real, despite his clear inauthenticity. Costumes simultaneously link El Vez to Elvis and outdo him, out-spectacle-ing The King of Spectacle. They also hide the body of Lopez behind the personage and persona of El Vez, reinforcing the illusion that El Vez lives onstage and off, while also helping to reveal the different bodies-in-process that exist during performance. Finally, costumes offer new imaginings of Chicanx history, displaying the multiple modes of cultural being offered in the United States. They also assert their own materiality and carry their own histories. As I will discuss in the next section, there is another way that costumes function in El Vez's performances: they provide dramaturgical structure while also creating specific meaning in performance.

Son of a Lad from Spain?: Costumes as Dramaturgy in the Gospel Show in Madrid

Though I have never seen it live, I do have the video *The Gospel Show in Madrid* from 2007.[49] Like the album *Boxing with God,* this show grapples with religion, both in the historic past of the Mexican Conquest and in the contemporary moment. While some songs draw connections between religions, marking similarities between, say, the Aztecs and the Hindus, most of the performance points out hypocrisies and contradictions contained within all religious systems. Lopez-as-El-Vez sings about conflicts that flare up between religions; devastation for which religion has no adequate answers; the way religion has been used to justify warfare, exclusion, and empire; and the doubts these produce. In performance, the various iterations of The Gospel Show follow a general arc, aided by the dramaturgical assistance of his costuming. El Vez arrives on stage a true believer, faces temptation and sin, suffers a moment of doubt, yet returns to grace, a bit wiser and bearing a simple, divine message: Peace, Love, and El Vez. The encore is fashioned as a sort of afterlife to the show, in which El Vez and the audience arise to Heaven. In this section, I offer a detailed analysis of how the costumes work to reinforce the loose narrative arc of this two-hour-long show, tracking El Vez's journey from innocence to experience.

Lopez specifically chooses costume pieces to offer a rich bed of allusion to the audience. Take, for instance, the opening of the show. A Lovely Elvette is already onstage, wearing a blue gospel choir robe and playing a tambourine. The band, dressed in black trousers, white short-sleeved shirts, and black ties, don the dress requirements of male missionaries from The Church of Jesus Christ of Latter-Day Saints. El Vez reinforces this allusion by introducing them as the Mormon Mariachis. Though subtle, their costumes reinforce the playful juxtaposition of religious practice at the heart of The Gospel Show. El Vez, who enters to the gospel song "Where Could I Go But to the Lord," rewriting the final line to sing, "Where could I go but to El Vez," wears his '68 Comeback Special white suit with a red necktie, red suspenders, and a red liner.[50] The suit sparks a number of references. It calls up Elvis and his love of gospel music, which confounded some fans because gospel seemed to contradict his connection to gritty rock and roll and to confuse his image as a sex symbol. The suit also evokes the stereotype of the Bible Banging Preacher, suggesting a visual linkage to the Evangelical South. Additionally, it recalls the message of peace and love embedded in the song "If I Can Dream," with which Elvis ended the Comeback Special while costumed in the white suit. ("If I Can Dream" was written in response to the assassinations of MLK and Bobby Kennedy; Parker was against including it, but Elvis defied him and sang it as the closer.) More broadly, white signifies purity of faith, even as the red might connote temptation (especially when Lopez-as-El-Vez opens the coat to reveal the red lining).

This particular iteration of The Gospel Show was unique in that only one Elvette, Lysa María (performed by accomplished musician Lysa Flore, who blends her actual name with her stage name to perform as Lysa María) was able to tour with the ensemble. Usually when El Vez tours, he includes 2–4 Lovely Elvettes as backing vocalists. In all of his shows, Lopez is careful not to make the Elvettes seem subservient to El Vez;

this dates back to his early punk days when the bands were highly inclusive, mixing "boys & girls, Queer and Straight [...] part of our original '76 Punk Rock roots."[51] Within the fiction of the show, the Lovely Elvettes adore him, but as performers, they are his equals. However, with only one Elvette, Lysa María risked being read as disempowered and beholden to El Vez. Acutely aware of this possibility, Lopez rewrote their relationship to make them siblings. In his introduction of her, he first stresses that "You know, every great man, there is a great woman behind them,"[52] and quips "Ella es mi hermana, de veras. Es como Jack White and Meg [of The White Stripes]. Solamente Morenos."[53] This relational shift both elevates Lysa María to equal status and shuts down the notion that they are a couple (and allows for a funny joke to boot). He continues this move away from her objectification, using costumes to simultaneously make another joke and to pose a strong statement about the display of female bodies onstage. Every musician who performs with El Vez is given a personal introduction and a few bars in the spotlight. The Mariachis back Lysa María's introduction with a sexy riff, which she couples with an equally sexy dance. Rather than stripping to something more revealing, however, as it appears she will do as she begins to unzip her robe, she instead removes one choir robe only to reveal a second. It is red, perhaps connoting a more lustful choir girl, but she remains covered for the time being. In fact, it is El Vez who is first to undress, in his song "Quetzalcoatl," described above.

A brief survey of the rest of the show reveals the additional purposes that costumes serve: they cover quick changes, up the excitement of the show, make political points, reach out to the audience, and provide context. The costuming for "Quetzalcoatl" only lives in one song and El Vez quickly exits the stage. Having performed his own strip tease, it is now Lysa María's turn to cut loose (and to cover El Vez's costume change). The Mariachis sing about her to the tune of "Devil with the Blue Dress" she struts her stuff and removes her robe to reveal—what else—a blue dress. This moment is so on the nose that it is not only funny, but it also ups the energy and signals that things are about to get a bit wilder. Enter El Vez, in a skin-tight red patent leather bell-bottomed jumpsuit. He carries a pitchfork, and the band breaks into "Sympathy for the Devil." It would appear that El Vez has already crossed over to the dark side, but it turns out that he is not the devil in this equation, despite the red suit. A roadie darts onstage wearing a George W. Bush mask, and El Vez chases him off, with a bit of banter deriding the then-president. Not only does this bit cover Lysa María's costume change—she returns to the stage clad in a tight red patent leather dress to match El Vez[54]—but it also makes the point that yesterday's Spain is today's United States. The previous song recalled the Conquest, while this interlude condemns the warmongering of the United States. Though it may lack subtlety, the bit is well received by the audience, who shout their approval at the lampooning of an imperial president. This brief interlude also paves the way for El Vez to return to songs about immigration and colonization, and for his audience to hear them slightly differently, not as a condemnation of the past, but as continuing problems to be addressed. It would seem that the devil his costume signifies is the violence of oppression and conquest, whether it be that of present-day USAmerica or fifteenth-century Spain. The contextualization it provides allows the audience into the performance by signaling an awareness of the complexity of international politics.

Having confronted the devil in the form of imperialism, El Vez changes into what he calls his "traje de luz," a rhinestone-studded jumpsuit. He dubs himself "A matador for El Señor"; and questions God for having unleashed the horrors of the world, especially the AIDS crisis.[55] He asks, "¿Es un chiste? ¿Que hace hombre?"[56] He brings up the ongoing tensions in the Middle East, saying, "Israel, chill. Hamas, no más." The Mormon Mariachis launch into a surf-style mash-up of "Miserlou" and "Hava Nagila" to cover yet another costume change, which brings Lysa María and El Vez to the stage in gold for a rowdy set of songs that speak to dreams of prosperity, lust (for Christ), and war.[57] From there, the show takes a more pensive turn, as the band plays the melody to U2's "I Still Haven't Found What I'm Looking For," and El Vez and Lysa María enter dressed in black for "un momento de duda." El Vez even declares to God, "If you exist, strike me down... y nada."[58] This moment of doubt is short-lived, however. He covers another costume change with the introduction of the Mormon Mariachis and returns to the stage, redeemed, with faith renewed, in a white choir robe. He sings the gospel classic, "How Great Though Art," before shedding the robe to reveal his Evel Knievel jumpsuit, white with blue starred stripes and long fringe.[59] No rock show is complete without an encore, and the entire ensemble returns wearing a T-shirt with a giant El Vez face on it (available for sale at the merch table) and black pants. El Vez wears the same, only with red vinyl pants and angel wings.[60]

Lopez thinks carefully about costuming and costume changes, putting them to use in his performances to make meaning in multiple ways. A close reading of his costumes makes clear how they reinforce the dramaturgical arc of the performance. Though I have detailed one performance captured on video, all of his shows feature a narrative arc—he may fall from grace, he may celebrate the holidays while revealing their darker underside, or he may be assassinated as he runs for president, but he returns to the stage redeemed, enlightened, or reborn, and costume changes are key to marking these transitions.

Buy Some Elvis and You'll Feel Good, Buy Some El Vez and You'll Feel Even Better!: El Vez Merchandise[61]

After experiencing an El Vez show, excited audience members line up to peruse the memorabilia for sale, perhaps selecting something to purchase and bring home.

Shortly after the encore, El Vez will arrive, ready to chat with his fans and to sign the items they buy. Lopez-as-El-Vez will wear a new costume that more closely resembles regular street wear—say a modified El Vez T-shirt and vinyl pants. Lopez curates these outfits just as carefully as he does the rest of his costumes, making sure to exude rock star cool and to be recognizably El Vez, while also getting out of his sweat-drenched costume. In fact, he has done this since his earliest time performing as El Vez—in an Instagram post documenting his return to Memphis in 1989, he notes that he wears, "my favorite vintage shirt w/stripes of pale pink black and grey. [...] I like that even then I had the notion to wear a 'post show' out fit."[62]

I have been on both sides of the merch table and can recall my excitement when I spoke briefly with El Vez after the first show I attended.[63] Plus I own a lot of El Vez merch, which I have lifted, organized, carried, cataloged, stored, displayed, worn, and moved across the country more than once. In this section, I want to consider the materiality of all this stuff, by which I mean not simply their physical form, but also the histories and knowledges embedded therein. It is easy to look past what they *are* in order to discuss what they *mean*, that is, to fall into the all-too-common tendency to privilege representation over materiality without recognizing that the physical conveys meaning on its own. Elizabeth Edwards and Janice Hart theorize objects as "important bridges between mental and physical worlds." They continue, "Objects [...] are therefore not just stage settings for human actions and meanings, but integral to them," noting how we must view objects not as inert matter, but as "social actors" that impact social meaning.[64] Physical material is dynamic. Here, I will consider this El Vez stuff as matter whose very form impacts human interaction, in order to consider how these objects participate in meaning-making and even impose "their force as sensuous presence"[65] to assert agency through their vital materiality. These things play an integral role in the creation of El Vez and they actively collaborate with him and contribute to the world-building of his shows. Moreover, these things continue to perform long after El Vez (and his audience) has left the building. Because they travel home with the purchaser, they allow the show, the ideas it circulates, and the progressive social space it engenders, to live on.

Using a thing-centric approach, this section explores the complicated relationship between El Vez, the stuff he sells, and the way that stuff sells him. By focusing almost exclusively on some of the specialty items available for sale at his performances, I dissect how these things skillfully promote El Vez long after the show is over. Their materiality allows them to tap into multiple discourses of Elvisness, Catholicism, Latinidad, and celebrity to prompt remembrance, mourning, veneration, and intimacy. By doing a close reading of these things through the lens of my own scholarship and fandom, I discuss how they operate as highly charged souvenirs and relics. Following Diana Coole and Samantha Frost, I emphasize "materialization as a complex, pluralistic, relatively open process" and insist "that humans, including theorists themselves, be recognized as thoroughly immersed within materiality's productive contingencies."[66] Thus, much of this section documents my interactions with these items and the personal meanings these interactions create. As in the previous chapter, I explore how the presence of these things points to the gap that exists between the artistry of Lopez and the persona of El Vez, helping to constitute the persona of El Vez through the corporeality of Lopez. By examining the interplay of these three categories—things, artist, persona—I reveal how the vital materiality of these performing objects both enacts and commemorates the labor of performance that brings the persona into being, while simultaneously masking that labor.

In rock vernacular, items sold at concerts are referred to as merch—short for merchandise—stressing their function and value as commodities. Merch signifies goods produced specifically to be sold: objects that exist, first and foremost, for the purpose of raising revenue that immediately goes directly to the performers. This terminology squarely places the merch table in the business end of rock performance.[67] Arjun Appadurai reminds us to look beyond a traditional matrix of economic exchange, urging us "to follow the things themselves, for their meanings are inscribed in their forms, their uses, their trajectories."[68] Many of the items for sale at El Vez's merch table, such as T-shirts or CDs, are fairly standard, with recognizable forms and uses: one wears a shirt (maybe even with the same design worn by El Vez!), displaying one's appreciation for El Vez and one's concert attendance; one listens to a CD, perhaps even dances or sings along with it, thereby recalling, extending, and embodying the concert once again.

More interesting, however, are the specialty items El Vez has on offer (Figure 3.7).[69] Though these now exist as commodities, their materiality features a more complicated history: they once performed alongside and with Lopez-as-El-Vez. Because of this proximity *before* they were put on sale, as merch they possess what Jane Bennett describes as "the strange ability of ordinary, man-made items to exceed their status as objects and to manifest traces of independence or aliveness, constituting the outside of our own experience."[70] Their exteriority becomes an epistemological limit that butts up against our own, which "gives voice to a vitality intrinsic materiality."[71] As I will discuss further, part of these objects' allure derives from their closeness to El Vez. They possess an intimacy with El Vez that the fan at the merch table cannot personally achieve, but can approximate through his or her purchase. Through their material histories, these items mark the limits of self and others (fan and star) as they also bridge that divide.

As noted, as a scholar and a fan of El Vez, I own several of his specialty items—all that I could get my hands on, in fact.[72] Though they comprise a body of study

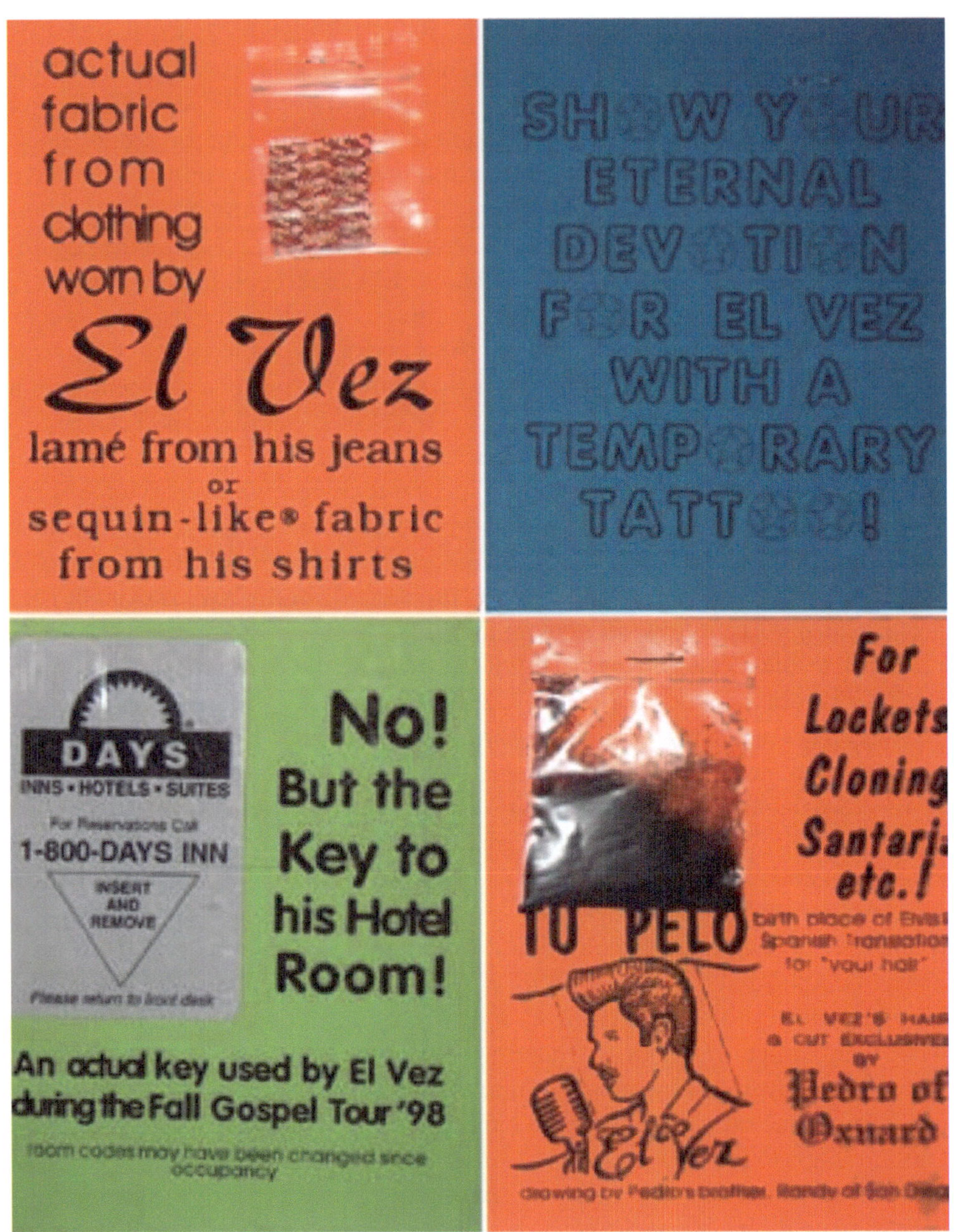

Figure 3.7: El Vez speciality items from the author's collection, 2003–12. Photograph by author, 2023.

to me as a scholar, and as a fan they function as memorabilia. Depending on the lens through which I view them, these objects operate differently for me: archive, commodity, souvenir, relic. My collection includes two temporary tattoo cards—one intact, one missing the tattoo and signed "Karen / Love Me / El Vez" where the tattoo had been; his hotel room key from The Gospel Tour; fabric from his clothing; and his hair, which in reference to Elvis's birthplace, he identifies as "Tu Pelo," (Your Hair), rather than "Mi Pelo" (My Hair) or "El Pelo de El Vez" (El Vez's Hair), thereby transferring ownership of the hair to the purchaser both physically and linguistically. Each of these specialty items is stapled or glued to colorful light cardstock with text printed on them. Their construction reveals the DIY aesthetic that runs through El Vez's performance: they are somewhat off-kilter and unevenly cut and clearly rather cheaply produced. However, that they are irregular and inexpensively made adds to their mystique; one can imagine El Vez, or someone closely affiliated with him, cutting the cards by hand and stapling the specialty items to them after printing them at home or at a copy shop.[73]

It is worth noting that though the commodity potential remains latent in these specialty items once they leave the merch table, they rarely re-enter the commodity phase. There are two official channels through which one can purchase El Vez merch: at a show or through his website.[74] Of course, there are other ways of acquiring things: eBay and Craigslist, for example. And there is no shortage of El Vez items available there.[75] Yet, it is the more recognizable items—CDs, DVDs, publicity photos, and concert posters—that are normally up for sale. It may be that fans like me are unwilling to sell the specialty items because they continue to hold meaning for them. Or perhaps these items have been discarded. Though I saved my used temporary tattoo card, it is likely that others applied the tattoo and disposed of the card. If we engage with the materiality of the specialty items, even more possibilities emerge. Without a personal connection to them—the memory of an El Vez show and the continued pleasure the memory brings—these items easily become junk. Hotel key cards, worn-out clothing, and hair trimmings are essentially garbage. It is through his placement of these items on the card and the card on the merch table that Lopez converts the throwaway into the readymade, even though they can easily revert back to detritus. Even his signature, which appears to singularize the objects by making them highly unique, misleads a bit; El Vez signs *everything*, staying at the merch table every night until his last fan has seen him, and he has done so for his entire career.[76] Though his signature points to signs of exclusivity that circulate within fan culture—autographs gain value the more difficult they are to obtain—it in fact exists as so much ink on ephemera. These specialty items, complete with his signature, reveal through their materiality a rich interplay of ideas. They are commodities, but simultaneously more-than- and less-than-commodities, the excess paradoxically produced by the evident worthlessness of the assembled materials and signs.

Significantly, it is the autographed card with its missing tattoo (my first purchase, bought in Minneapolis after the 2002 Merry MeX-Mas show) that functions most powerfully as a souvenir for me, perhaps because embedded in it is a sense of loss. Susan Stewart's study of the souvenir discusses how physical items act as stand-ins for absent objects, people, or periods. Notes Stewart, "whether the souvenir is a material sample or not, it will still exist as a sample of the now-distanced experience, an experience which the object can only evoke and resonate to, and can never entirely recoup."[77] Souvenirs denote something as being worthy of remembrance while also acknowledging that the souvenir is only a meager substitution for the original. As they pay homage to the importance of that which is no longer wholly there—an item, an individual, or an experience—souvenirs mark their present incompleteness:

> In fact, if it could recoup the experience, it would erase its own partiality, that partiality which is the very source of its power. Second the souvenir must remain impoverished and partial so that it can be supplemented by a narrative discourse, a narrative discourse which articulates the play of desire.[78]

Thus, souvenirs necessarily operate as fragments, attempting to fill the void of a lost experience through their partial physicality and narrative bolster.

The missing tattoo, its materiality supplanted by an autograph and a staple hole in the paper, visibly and powerfully marks loss. After purchasing it, I immediately applied the tattoo to my neck in the bathroom of the performance venue, First Avenue, thereby performing as the card instructed: "Show your eternal devotion for El Vez with a temporary tattoo!" In a co-scripted collaboration between it and me, that particular tattoo moved from waxy paper to my skin, where its image sat until I later scrubbed the adhesive away. It is gone, dissolved, and run down the shower drain. Only when I became serious about studying El Vez did I purchase a replacement, as I amassed an archive to interrogate.[79]

But of course, it isn't really the tattoo I recall in looking at this thing nor its passing that I mourn. Rather, this thing—or this thing with a crucial thing missing—recalls my initial encounter with El Vez, a record that also marks my current distance from it. As Stewart notes, in an exchange economy, "the search for authentic experience and, correlatively, the search for the authentic object become critical [...] 'Authentic' experience becomes both elusive and allusive as it is placed beyond the horizon of present lived experience."[80] The souvenir, as an object, functions as a surrogate for the memory of the lived, embodied experience, the being in the here and now of performance, to use Lopez's words; or, to follow the thrust of this book, it conjures a feeling of existing in the progressive social space engendered through the world-building of performance. The materiality of this particular item, with its absent tattoo, staple hole, and signature, reveals "the capacity of objects to serve as traces of authentic experiences."[81] In a highly personalized interaction between this object and myself, I can recall a wholly irretrievable encounter. Only during that first concert was I *just* a fan, experiencing El Vez as the majority of his first-time audience members do. Holding it today, I recall the excitement I felt during the show; I recall waiting in line to buy the tattoo and get it signed; I recall applying the tattoo before going to a raucous party, where I flounced around, thrusting my neck in the faces of my friends and colleagues so that they could witness my just-discovered undying love of El Vez.[82] It represents the loss of the purity of that first encounter, which is why I have not thrown it away as the useless piece of paper it could appear to be. The absence of the tattoo also marks my lack of critical distance in that first encounter—I *used* the item as it was intended!—just as my retention of the card perhaps signals that I knew, even then, that this thing was meaningful, even if I could not possibly foresee how El Vez scholarship would or could become my career.

Yet as I look at this card now, I recognize that this thing is at once more real and more staged than any of the other El Vez items I own. It represents my unmediated first encounter with El Vez; I was simply another fan in the mass of strangers crowding the merch table, thrilled by the performance event I had just witnessed and wanting to know more. As I nostalgically look back at it, that night carries with it a sense of purity. And yet I know that my encounter with El Vez was also staged; I interacted with the El Vez personage and persona, not with the artist.[83] The "Love Me" autograph was one of any number of set catchy, Elvis-themed phrases signed by El Vez to his memorabilia, a signature that had no real relation to me as an individual. That this item provokes such opposing thoughts and emotions in me speaks to its power and its function as a souvenir. Following Stewart, this souvenir is overfilled with meaning through the multiple narratives I attach to it, which help to locate the desire it articulates for me. It also speaks to the active role that merch—especially these specialty items—can play in world-building, because they activate the imagination and agency of the audience members, and make them co-collaborators in the creation of that shared social space. Without my personal story, the card with the missing tattoo is simply an autographed piece of colored cardstock with a funny joke written on it. Working in collaboration with my narrative, the card recounts an originary experience of excitement and critical innocence.

The used tattoo card points to the different positions it occupies. At the moment of financial exchange, it performed as a commodity whose consumption was fueled by individual desire. Its application to my body allowed me to display my fandom to others, to visibly continue my participation in the community of El Vez fans after the show had ended. In this, Appadurai reminds us that, "consumption is eminently social, relational, and active rather than private, atomic, or passive."[84] Having used the object as intended, my narrative, prompted by the staple hole and the embodied history to which it grants me access, gives this dynamic thing significance as a souvenir, making it a marker of something more personal. As Stewart notes, a narrative affixed to a souvenir "is a narrative of interiority and authenticity. It is not a narrative of the object; it is a narrative of the possessor."[85] So for me, this thing holds within it a tension: the tension between the social act of consumption, the shared social space of performance, and the private act of memory. It points to both a communal experience and a highly individualized reverie.

In contrast, the hotel key, fabric, and hair proclaim a differently invested materiality that, in partnership with their respective inscribed narratives and the multiple social and cultural discourses referenced by them, enables these things to exceed the level of souvenir and approach that of relic. Through their materiality, they reference Catholicism, which continues to dominate the Mexican and Chicanx culture in which El Vez is steeped. In the Catholic faith, first-class relics include physical remains of a venerated person and second-class relics feature items the venerated person used frequently or wore. All three of these things, then, function as relics in the veneration of El Vez. The fabric swatch most overtly ties to Catholic theology through the joke inscribed on the card: "Touch the Hem of the Garment...Now own it!" Referencing the Gospel of Luke, this fabric playfully aligns with the healing powers of Jesus (and, as noted earlier, to Colonel Tom Parker's merchandising scheme). The El Vez relic is not about healing, however, but rather about the participatory fandom of consumer culture in general, Elvis fanaticism in particular, with El Vez layered on top. A second quality all three of these items share is a high degree of durability. Catholic relics most commonly include teeth, bones, and hair, as these obdurate things will not erode. Christiane Holm notes, "separated hair can last forever whereas the body will not. Moreover, the separated hair will no longer grow, it embodies as materialized time an epoch that is absolutely past."[86] So too do these specialty items seem to freeze time through their lastingness.

The provenance of these relics, clearly marked on two of the cards, records what Holm calls, "the very moment when its natural status was transformed into a cultural status, and when the present presence of the body is anticipated as a future absence."[87] The details provided by the copy authenticate their linkage to El Vez. The key card dates from The Gospel Show Tour in Fall 1998, four years prior to my first encounter with El Vez and eight years before my purchase of it. The hair is even older; according to the card: "This hair has been cut by El Vez's personal hairdresser Pedro of Oxnard during the year of 1995."[88] Identifying his hairdresser as "Pedro of Oxnard" plays with place-name designation common in

Medieval literature, further stressing the relic-like nature of the thing along with the now-anachronistic custom of saving hair. The card emphasizes the idea of origins, mentioning the birthplace of Elvis and the place-name of the haircutter to prove that the hair is/was El Vez's.

In addition to authenticating these items, the inscribed narrative affixes both legibility and desirability to them. The only item that might be instantly recognizable in its own materiality is the fabric, had a fan seen him perform in the costume piece now parceled off for sale. The key card and the hair, however, require further explication for them to have value and meaning; like a souvenir, they rely on a story to make them complete. Crucially, El Vez, and not the fan, provides the story, which titillates by emphasizing how the materiality of these things closely interacted with the corporeality of his body. He held the key in his hand; it opened the door to the room where he slept, showered, and dressed. The fabric came even closer; it touched his skin and perhaps absorbed his sweat, traces of which might still be embedded in the sample. Closest of all is the hair, an item that literally grew from him, a thing that only becomes out-side in the act of its cutting. An element of the erotic adheres to each entity, linked as they are to the intimate space of his body. The narrative affixed to the things further enhances this erotic play. The key card flirts, "The key to El Vez's heart!?!" and playfully asserts that one might find emotional and physical intimacy through it. Meanwhile, the hair mentions, "Lockets, Cloning, Santaria," suggesting that El Vez is already a beloved, absent lover. However, as the narrative on the cards asserts a former proximity to El Vez, it simultaneously marks the fan's unresolvable distance from him. The *things* experienced intimate moments with El Vez; they now serve as proxy to experiences the fan never enjoyed. He or she did not travel with El Vez to the Days Inn or Oxnard, and can only fantastically imagine having been there through the materiality of these things.

There is, of course, a further complication to this account that stresses physical proximity to El Vez. The body that held the key card, wore the clothing, and grew and styled the hair was not that of El Vez, but rather Robert Lopez. Thus, the materiality of these things extracted out of the performance context absents El Vez from them. As discussed in the previous chapter, the act of performing allows Lopez to masquerade as El Vez, but El Vez "exists" only through performance, thus his presence is bound by its temporal limits. Though he seems real, El Vez in fact has no materiality. He is pure personage and persona, a mélange of references in shiny pants.

It always comes back to the pants. Can El Vez truly live onstage without his tear-away gold lamé and his bell bottoms, or do these objects actively transform the artist Lopez into the character El Vez? I turn once again to the fabric swatch, which suggests how the vital materiality of things collaborates with the human. The copy reads: "actual fabric from clothing worn by El Vez." This label hints toward the complexity of this interchange between object, artist, personage, and persona.

Unlike the other relics, this thing speaks the truth: though the body that wears the costume is Lopez's, the act of wearing the clothes creates El Vez. That is to say, the materiality of the costume sits upon the corporeality of Lopez's body, where, as an actant, it works with Lopez to constitute El Vez, who actually wears the clothes. The fabric swatch thus commemorates El Vez's performance, yet also obscures the labor of Lopez. There is also the Sharpie; for many years, before heading to the merch table to greet his fans, Lopez would reapply the mustache, potentially using the same Sharpie on his upper lip that he would use to sign autographs. The ink that is impermanent on his skin becomes permanent on paper, potentially laced with his sweat. Thus, the autograph might (invisibly) possess the intimacy that the specialty items promise. Through these different materialities of costume and ink put to body and paper, the gap between the character and artist is insurmountable and yet bridged.

Even though it is easy to fall into the privileging of the representational over the material, clearly I intuited the importance of these physical things. For if meaning were truly abstracted from the material, why continue to criss-cross the country with all this El Vez stuff? These items make tangible my ongoing intellectual and personal relationships with El Vez and Lopez. They provoke emotional responses: laughter, reverie, fandom, and the occasional groan in response to their silly puns. They grant me access to histories that predate me, allow me to relive long-past personal experiences, and open up new possibilities in my current work. Thus, it is with some frequency that I pull out my merch—especially the specialty items—to interact with these things, to hold them in my hands, to recall through them my earlier El Vez memories as I more deeply analyze his performances.

Dancing Around in Gold Lamé Hot Pants: There Is Nothing Real About It!

So there you have it
El Vez, This is Your Life
You are King of all you parlay
And the world is the same
You haven't changed it a bit
They didn't buy your revolution
They didn't want your religion
They didn't vote you as el Presidente

El Vez,
You're a 43 year-old man who still dyes his hair black,
Dancing around in gold lamé hot pants

Pretending he is Elvis
You are just an impersonator
There is nothing real about it![89]

—El Vez, "The End of the CD"

The closing track of the CD *God Save the King: 25 Years of El Vez*, released in 2013 to celebrate The Mexican Elvis's "Silver Jubilee," features a self-reflective El Vez speaking over an acoustic guitar that softly strums Elvis's "Love Me Tender." As Lopez explains in the liner notes, this track was originally used in 2003 as a "pre-recorded monologue that played while i got into my last and final costume change" in El Vez's one-man show *Around the World in 80 Minutes (Or Less)*.[90] The monologue references several El Vez tours and the albums they promoted: Rock & Revolution, The Gospel Show, and his multiple EV4P tours. In marking these tours, it also calls attention to the different theatrical conceits that undergird them: that El Vez was indeed leading a revolution, preaching a new religion, and running for elected office. The monologue specifically mentions costuming of different sorts—hair dye, gold lamé hot pants—and the impersonation that these costumes help make possible as they bring forth the persona of El Vez, the fantasies he creates, and the worlds that he builds. That it was recorded to fill time during a costume change further gilds the lily as it both marks the theatrics of an El Vez show and masks them. Finally, the monologue calls attention to the fiction—"There is nothing real about it!"—yet covers the labor of the performer by allowing time to pass seamlessly as he changes clothes.

This chapter has considered the vital work that costuming undertakes in the performances of El Vez, allowing Lopez to inhabit the performance persona in a way that somehow seems real, both because of and despite the glitz and the gold lamé. Costuming collaborates with the different bodies in process that make up a performance, making meaning and providing dramaturgical structure to the show. Yet, there is a final way that costumes work in the performances of El Vez: they allow Lopez to speak his radical vision and, through world-building, engender an ephemeral space of belonging and inclusion for all. El Vez states this towards the end of "The End of the CD":

I wanted to share my dream.
I wanted to make the world a little bit smaller
Then my pride could be your pride
To show you that your world is my world
I wanted to be King
But I wanted to show you
You could be King.

And here, somewhat shockingly, the accent vanishes and he speaks in a lower register—Lopez interrupts El Vez.

> I just wanted to be real
> To show you where I come from
> To show you what I think about
> To show you the real me
> By using the disguise of a mustache.
> Someone you could really love
> I just wanted to be loved, is that so wrong?
> So love me tender
> Love me long
> Why can't we all just get along?

Costuming helps to create El Vez's dream and El Vez's world, and the spectacle of it invites us to find our own place in it, to collaborate with El Vez to build a progressive social space. Costuming also makes meaning through performance, hinting at what the "real" Lopez thinks about and believes. The disguise allows us to intuit the artist behind it. As I will argue in the next chapter, music and sound are even more important to the world-building of El Vez performances. The use of the accent, stage banter, lyrical rewrites, and, most importantly, the juxtaposition of different genres, styles, and samples within the songs and over the course of the performance overturn the way we often think about music and authenticity. Indeed, it is through the music itself that Lopez gives us a taste of what "getting along" looks and feels like, by building a world in which disparate sounds and ideas can interact.

NOTES

1. This phrase, coined by Lopez, appears on T-shirts sold as merch during the tour.
2. Pierre Smith, Facebook post, September 11, 2020.
3. Robert Lopez [@mr.robertlopez], post, *Instagram*, March 9, 2023.
4. I was able to catalog Lopez's closet in September 2012.
5. Lopez, text to author, September 13, 2013.
6. Lopez, interview with author, July 16, 2023.
7. The *capriote* attire is specific to the Spanish Catholic tradition. Once linked to the Inquisition, they are now generally worn during the Easter Holy Week. They feature large conical pointed silk hoods that look like (and were perhaps appropriated by) Ku Klux Klan hoods, which explains why they are only worn when El Vez performs in Spain.

8. Aiofe Monks, *The Actor in Costume* (London: Palgrave Macmillan, 2010): 3. Monks repeatedly uses the term actor, as her analysis is rooted in a more traditional theatrical setting. However, her use of actor applies incredibly well to Lopez as a performer, with the main difference being that El Vez shows do not rely as heavily on fictional narrative as does a typical playtext. Thus, throughout this section, I often use the term performer where Monks might use actor.
9. Monks, *Costume,*11.
10. Monks, *Costume,* 11.
11. Monks, *Costume,* 20.
12. Lopez, interview with author, March 4, 2024.
13. In fact, he made use of the tear-away pants when he officiated my wedding. After declaring my husband and I legally married ("by the power of Elvis love"), he ripped off his pants to start the celebration off right.
14. Lopez says there are others that are only used for photos; they are not really stage-ready in terms of the movement he needs to be able to do in them. Lopez, interview with author, March 4, 2024. The Mexican flag mariachi suit is my personal favorite.
15. Lopez, interview with author, July 16, 2023.
16. Monks, *Costume*, 23.
17. Monks, *Costume*, 21.
18. Monks, *Costume*, 23.
19. While out and about in Mexico City, Lopez and I priced several versions of the "Quetzalcoatl" costume at a mercado. That they are readily available for the Mexican public to purchase brings up interesting questions of authenticity. They are not authentic to the Aztec past, but they are common items, perhaps making them authentic to modern Mexican pop culture. I was prompted to consider the ramifications of these issues when a Native scholar reminded me of the way that the word "costume" can negatively impact Indigenous people, whose attire and regalia have been appropriated throughout the history of settler colonialism. I would like to believe that the obvious, showy inauthenticity of the costume signals its distance from more sacred regalia, but there is no doubt that the costume calls up the history of colonization throughout the Americas.
20. He says this, in Spanish, in the Gospel Show in Madrid video detailed below.
21. I thank the participants in a Critical Response Process workshop at Arizona State University for raising this idea.
22. Monks, *Costume*, 106.
23. Habell-Pallán, *Loca Motion*, 200.
24. The Rock & Revolution tour was the only one from the early portion of his career that did not feature the thin black mustache. Lopez grew his facial hair out and sported a goatee. Only recently has he stopped dying his hair black and has he replaced the Sharpie moustache with his own graying facial hair.
25. Lopez, interview with author, July 16, 2023.

26. As I note in my article "Profiling El Vez, The Mexican Elvis: A Dramaturgical Methodology to *Make the Dream Real*," published in *Pamiętnik Teatralny*, this offstage announcer is actually Lopez, speaking in his unaccented voice.
27. Lopez, interview with author, May 19, 2018.
28. Lopez, interview with author, July 16, 2023.
29. Lopez recalls that he was wearing part of the police costume under the piñata, and then he had to do a tricky exit to make this bit work. "I had crawl underneath the bandstand where the drums were and get out and come around the other way to make an entrance as a cop." Lopez, interview with author, March 4, 2024.
30. Sometimes this person will be in on the joke—a roadie, a friend of the band, etc.—and sometimes it will really be a person plucked from the audience.
31. Thanks to Tom Lynch for suggesting this idea to me. As he notes in a voicemail message, "Hamlet is a character, but a million people could play Hamlet, right? And we don't necessarily think of him as real then; he's just a character [...] Could anybody other than Robert play—be El Vez? And if not, then he's something more than a character, right? [...] He's a character tied to an individual, a particular individual." Tom Lynch, voicemail to author, December 12, 2012.
32. Monks, *Costume*, 12.
33. Lopez first shared this story on Instagram on April 20, 2023, and then gave me more details later. Lopez, interview with author, March 4, 2024.
34. It should be noted that the contestants were only interviewed by the panelists; they did not sing or otherwise perform as part of the judged contest (though El Vez and the Lovely Elvettes did perform a snippet of "Está Bien Mamacita" after the judges had wagered their guesses). In watching the episode, which can be viewed on the El Vez YouTube channel, it is striking to note that Lopez is the only one to speak in an accent. It seems that at least one of the judges, Kitty Carlisle, seemed to think he did not speak much English. https://www.youtube.com/watch?v=FNnELVMhBrE, accessed April 20, 2023.
35. Lopez took a black tie with white polka dots on it, which he would wear during his Little Richards performances. Trebek was sponsored by Hugo Boss; recalls Lopez, "He had boxes of unopened clothes. And I go, 'Surely, he won't miss one little tie.'" Lopez, interview with author, March 4, 2024.
36. Additional band costumes may require another duffel bag, as was the case with the Santa suits and hats on the MeX-Mas tour I observed in 2012. Each Elvette also maintains a medium-sized show suitcase.
37. Lopez quoted in Brad Kutner, "El Vez Is Like a Jukebox Exploding in Your Face," RVAmag.com, August 15, 2013, accessed September 27, 2013, https://rvamag.com/music/el-vez-is-like-a-jukebox-exploding-in-your-face.html.
38. I was able to travel with Lopez and the band from Milwaukee to Minneapolis to Chicago during the 2012 Christmas show and observe their backstage/offstage activity. At First Avenue in Minneapolis and the Double Door in Chicago, I set up the costume rack with

Lopez's assistance and helped collect the costumes later. Normally either he or his tour manager will tend to the costumes.

39. Active Elvettes maintain their own costume storage, though Lopez does have some of their items as well. Before he moved to Seattle, Lopez had a small Tiki Hut in the back of his property that he used for storage. In Seattle, he had ample space, with most of the costumes stored in his downstairs closet. Now that he has moved to Mexico, Lopez has several costumes there, but space considerations have forced him to whittle down what he has access to. The rest are in storage. Lopez, interview with author, March 4, 2024.
40. Aly Renee Amidei, "Where'd I Put My Character? The Costume as Character Body and Essential Costuming for the Ensemble Actor," *Theatre Symposium* 26 (2018): 50.
41. Lopez, interview with author, March 4, 2024.
42. Costume pieces made for his Teatro Zinzanni performances are property of the theatre and do not leave the premises. Lopez, interview with author, September 13, 2013.
43. In 2022, Lopez did a El Vez tour in Spain, working with Spanish musicians and Elvettes. His luggage got lost for several days when he traveled to Europe, and so he had to purchase whatever he could find to perform in (the brown suit he wore on the plane wouldn't cut it for a Merry MeX-Mas show). This included some ugly sweaters and other holiday attire. Lopez, interview with author, December 21, 2022.
44. Lopez, interview with author, July 16, 2023.
45. Berndt's work can be viewed at https://vickiberndt.com/blog/ and on Instagram as @berndtofferings, accessed March 8, 2024.
46. Lopez, interview with author, March 4, 2024.
47. Lopez, interview with author, July 16, 2023.
48. That Parker destroyed many of Elvis's old clothes is lamented in an undated article on the Lansky Bros. website. The article documents how, early in his career, Elvis shopped at the store whose clientele was primarily Black. Ann Powers, senior curator of the Experience Music Project in Seattle, is cited, discussing how Elvis's clothing "flouted not merely the unwritten dress codes of segregation but migrated freely across the boundaries of sex." Said Bernard J. Lansky, "Elvis was working as a movie theater usher at Loews theater, and he used to go down to the churches around town and see what the people doing the gospel music wore. He liked the way they operated. He knew what was happening. He was sharp." The article goes on to lament that Elvis's attire from the 1950s had been lost to Parker's marketing scheme. Says Todd Morgan, then-media director at Graceland, "They put an envelope inside each [box set of Elvis flip sides] with a swatch. That's how a lot was lost. Who knows what was in his closet when they gathered that up?" https://lanskybros.com/blogs/news/hidden-for-years-at-graceland-his-clothes-have-left-the-building, accessed May 25, 2023.
49. El Vez, *Gospel Show in Madrid: Live at Sala Arena*, Last Bandit Films, 2007. All of the references in this section come from transcriptions and observations of the video.
50. He wears this for the opening segment of songs (shedding the jacket, undoing the tie, unbuttoning the shirt, and finally peeling off the suspenders over the course of the segment),

which includes "Where Could I Go But to the Lord" (listed as "Where Could I Turn But to the Lord" on the DVD set list), "I'll Fly Away," "Walk a Mile in my Shoes," "Huraches Azules," "Lily of the Valley" (which was then repeated as a vamp throughout the show), and Lysa María's Introduction.

51. Lopez [@mr.robertlopez], post, *Instagram*, January 21, 2023.
52. Given that this show was recorded in Spain, Lopez-as-El-Vez delivers this line first in English and then in Spanish.
53. "She's my sister, really. It's like Jack White and Meg. Only Brown" (my translation). Because this show was performed in Spain, Lopez-as-El-Vez performed most of his stage banter in (self-admittedly bad) Spanish and/or Spanglish. At one point he quips "Recuerde eso, Spanglish es la lengua a hablar con el Dios." ("Remember that Spanglish is the language to speak to God" [my translation]). Lopez recalls observing the editing process in Spain, "The guys were just cracking up because [...] my Spanish was so bad that I was saying even funnier stuff that if I had planned it." Lopez, interview with author, March 4, 2024.
54. They wear these costumes for "Immigration Time" and "Lordy Miss Lupe."
55. He wears this jumpsuit for one song only, "Rubbernecking."
56. "Is it [AIDS] a joke? What are you doing, man?" (my translation).
57. This includes "Oralé," "Lust for Christ," and "Arm of Obregon."
58. They wear black for "a moment of doubt" (my translation). They wear these outfits for a particularly powerful song, "I Just Wanna See His Face," which blends the Rolling Stones song with Bob Marley's, "Get Up Stand Up" and Elvis's "You Gave Me a Mountain," and ends with "Sweet Emotion," with plenty of other musical allusions smattered throughout.
59. He wears this for his final song before the encore, "J. C. Low-Rider Superstar," which combines "Jesus Christ Superstar," "C.C. Rider," "Baby I'm a Star," and "Paradise City."
60. The encore consists of the songs "Ask the Angels" and "Saved."
61. Though slightly rewritten here, this section first appeared as the chapter "Relic, Souvenir, or Just Hair? Exploring the Complexities of Objects as Actants and Things as Mementos in the Merchandise of El Vez, The Mexican Elvis," in *Performing Objects and Theatrical Things*, edited by Joanne Zerdy and Marlis Schweitzer (New York: Palgrave Macmillan, 2014), 174–84.
62. Lopez [@mr.robertlopez], post, *Instagram*, May 11, 2023.
63. I have assisted with merch many times at El Vez shows, and have anecdotally observed how eager (and sometimes outrageous, or shy, or emotional) fans are to meet El Vez, to interact with him, and to have him sign the merch they just purchased. I've even had fans glom onto me in surprising ways. For instance, after a show in Tempe in 2022, two new Latino fans held my hands and told me how meaningful it was to see El Vez perform and how much it meant to them as Latinos. When I made sure that Lopez-as-El-Vez signed their items, they were star-struck and extremely quiet with him, though they came back and talked with me some more.
64. Elizabeth Edwards and Janice Hart, "Introduction," in *Photographs Objects Histories: On the Materiality of Images,* edited by Elizabeth Edwards and Janice Hart (London: Routledge, 2004), 4.

65. Bill Brown, "Thing Theory," *Critical Inquiry* 28, no. 1 (Autumn 2001): 5.
66. Diana Coole and Samantha Frost, *New Materialisms: Ontology, Agency, Politics* (Durham, NC: Duke University Press, 2010), 7.
67. Industry resources stress the financial importance of merch as Direct-to-Fan (DTF) commerce and encourage musicians to offer items price points from $1 to $100. Jed Carlson estimates "more than 50% of our Artists' total revenue came from playing live shows and selling merch and music at those shows." Jed Carlson, "The 4 Reasons Fans Buy Your Products," *Music Think Tank*, April 27, 2010, accessed September 27, 2012, https://www.musicthinktank.com/blog/the-4-reasons-fans-buy-your-products.html.
68. Arjun Appadurai, "Introduction: Commodities and the Politics of Value," in *The Social Lives of Things: Commodities in Cultural Perspective*, edited by Arjun Appadurai (Cambridge: Cambridge University Press, 1986), 5.
69. Specialty items are a much-discussed merch category that offer "unique collectibles" and the "opportunity to speak with the artists, get engaged and walk away with a new album and/ or a t-shirt because of the pleasant experience," accessed September 27, 2012, https://www.musicthinktank.com/blog/merch-table-essentials-15-ways-for-musicians-to-increase-sal.html. Fans desire "Relationships," "An Experience," and "Something Unique," accessed September 27, 2012, https://www.musicthinktank.com/blog/what-are-music-fans-willing-to-pay-for.html. Musicians sell everything from dildos to drug-enhanced road trips.
70. Jane Bennett, *Vibrant Matter: A Political Ecology of Things* (Durham, NC: Duke University Press, 2010), xvi.
71. Bennett, *Vibrant Matter*, 3.
72. Including a sheet of El Vez stamps that Lopez created in 1993, which I discuss in Chapter 1. I thought these were long gone, but Lopez found an unknown stash when cleaning out his house in 2022, so I was able to secure this for my archive.
73. I also have Mr. Bob merch, which includes Lopez's used prescription bottles for anti-depressants filled with mints. As with the other merch I describe, these are very DIY. The RX# has been crossed off with Sharpie by an unsteady hand, which combines with details including his name and dosage to feel exceedingly intimate. In this instance, the unsteady human behind this merch was me. In 2019, years after having first written this section of the chapter, I helped Lopez by preparing these items for sale while he performed his sound check at the Casbah in San Diego.
74. As of the final revisions of this book, his website is largely dormant, though still a great research resource.
75. Including one of his T-shirts mislabeled as a Chuck Berry T-shirt and selling on ebay for $99.99. Lopez [@mr.robertlopez], post, *Instagram*, April 10, 2023. He also has posted images of his merch found in thrift stores and Goodwill carts.
76. Lopez proudly recounts tours in Europe where he would be greeted by elderly ladies, asking for autographs that they would later sell. He says, "I mean, there were certain points where if I got off the bus, there would be old ladies who would wait to get my autograph, but so they could resell them. And to me, that was romantic." Lopez, interview with author, May 22, 2018.

77. Susan Stewart, *On Longing: Narratives of the Miniature, the Gigantic, the Souvenir, the Collection* (Baltimore, MD: Johns Hopkins University Press, 1984), 136.
78. Stewart, *On Longing*, 136.
79. I bought these items to study, but as editor Joanne Zerdy noted during the revision process for the book in which this section was first published, perhaps equally pressing is my need to legitimate my scholarly interest in El Vez. With its emphasis on humor, spectacle, and fun, it is easy to overlook the subversive creativity and intellectual engagement in Lopez's art. In building an archive, I use these material objects to assert and validate his worthiness as an object of academic study.
80. Stewart, *On Longing*, 133.
81. Stewart, *On Longing*, 135.
82. A huge thank you goes to Michal Kobialka, Sonja Kuftinec, Tamara Underiner, and Margaret Werry for the community they built during my years of graduate study (and after) at the University of Minnesota. We had very fun parties!
83. However, I could also argue that the persona is the "real" interaction, and that the more personalized, scholarly relationship I have with Lopez now is the aberration.
84. Appadurai, *Social Lives of Things*, 31.
85. Stewart, *On Longing*, 136.
86. Christiane Holm, "Sentimental Cuts: Eighteenth-Century Mourning Jewelry with Hair," *Eighteenth-Century Studies* 38, no. 1 (2004): 140.
87. Holm, "Sentimental Cuts," 140.
88. Or at least these are the dates when the cards were originally designed by Lopez. They may have been printed and reprinted without having the dates updated. That the dates are unreliable somehow only adds to their El-Vez-ness.
89. All lyrics cited in this section were transcribed from the recording. El Vez, "The End of the CD," *God Save the King*.
90. Emphasizing the gap between the performed and the real even further, the show ended with the disco song, "To Be Real." Lopez, interview with author, March 4, 2024.

4

Like a Jukebox Exploded: Sound and Music in El Vez Performances

Still reeling from Donald J. Trump's shocking electoral win, a rowdy crowd packed the Casbah, a San Diego rock club, to see El Vez perform his 2016 Merry MeX-Mas show. Two days before Christmas, the show was a one-off, very much a hometown affair. Lopez grew up in nearby suburb Chula Vista; visiting for the holidays to see family and friends, he crafted his first post-election performance specifically for the venue. After the election, but before the inauguration—it was a nervous time, full of uncertainty and fear. There were tweets, conflicts of interest, the looming threat of wall-building and deportation plans, and a frightening cast of potential cabinet members and advisors parading through Trump Tower. But no one quite knew what a Trump presidency might be. Still untested, we wondered if (and feared that) it would be effective. Worse yet, the resistance had not yet taken a clear form. There had been impromptu protests, but most people (or was it just me?) were frantically Facebooking and reading think pieces, hoping to make sense of it all. Basking in the uncertainty, El Vez took the stage clad in a black patent leather bell-bottomed jumpsuit (fur-trimmed for the proper holiday effect) and proclaimed, "I am the Black Santa, for we live in troubled times."[1] His show heralded dark times ahead, a move that captured the anxiety of the moment. Yet, his performance was a gift; it engendered for the vocally anti-Trump crowd a space where they could gather together to dance, sweat, and sing along in a chorus of dissent.

This chapter delves into the sonic imaginings and the musical mash-ups of El Vez performances. In the previous chapter, I discussed how the visual spectacle of costumes and merch participates in meaning-making while also providing dramaturgical support to the narrative arc of the shows, contributing to the world-building of El Vez performances. Here, I want focus on how Lopez-as-El-Vez uses sound and music to perform subversion and to resist essentializing discourses in a variety of ways: through the accent he adopts, the humorous stage banter and audience interaction he employs, the lyrics he rewrites, and most importantly, the vast wealth of musical forms that he samples and merges within his shows. I begin with a consideration of Lopez's use of accent in the persona of El Vez, noting how the use of this performed voice poses questions about the way we hear race and ethnicity. Because Lopez's genius is evident in his ability to rewrite and refashion popular songs to evoke a subversive political stance, I then delve into a discussion of popular music, especially considering genre. Knowing that music is racially coded, Lopez purposefully blends punk, glam, soul, rap, rock, and more to disrupt essentialized understandings of sound and genre. Lopez unleashes a powerful sonic critique by destroying music's containing mechanisms. I discuss how his use of sound and music is crucial to his world-building. Through his innovative use of popular music, Lopez convenes a shared social space in which audience members not only can experience difference but also can try out different ways of being in community. The sound and music offers an entry point for diverse audience members, crafting what Josh Kun has dubbed audiotopias: the "almost places of cultural encounter that may not be physical places but nevertheless exist in their own auditory somewhere."[2] Finally, using my own experience at the 2016 Merry MeX-Mas show as reference, I will consider the way Lopez used language and sound to craft a "deliciously dark"[3] show that took the audience on a journey, allowing us to move from fear to grief and anger to rebellion and resistance. The result—so affirming in that disquieting political moment—was a performance that at once sustained those politically marginalized by Trump's election while also engendering through world-building a celebratory social space that was temporarily beyond the reach of Trumpian politics.

I'm Sure I Sound Funny When I Say My Spanglish: Hearing Voice and Accent

In embodying El Vez, Lopez uses his voice in performance in two distinct ways: speaking and singing. As obvious as this sounds, careful listening reveals the meaning-making in the different vocal choices he makes. Before I can get into what Lopez does, however, it is first necessary to consider the act of speaking and singing, the qualities of vocal performance through which we evaluate the voice—and the person attached to it—and the impact of the listener on this exchange. Indeed, this is what Nina Sun Eidsheim describes as the acousmatic question: "the foundational question asked in the act of listening to a human voice."[4] Jennifer Lynn Stoever similarly refers to this as the sonic color line: "both a hermeneutics of race and a marker of its im/material presence"[5] and its necessary companion the listening ear: "a historical aggregate of normative American listening practices [that] gives a name to listening's epistemological function as a modality of racial discernment."[6] Both scholars consider how we have been trained to hear race.

As Eidsheim makes clear in *The Race of Sound: Listening, Timbre and Vocality in African American Music*, several assumptions about the voice and its connection to the body that transmits it are embedded in the acousmatic question. We tend to think of sound—especially the voice—as an essential *thing* that is both "stable and knowable,"[7] rather than as a *process*, or what Eidsheim dubs a "thick event—[that entails] a multitude of intermingling phenomena set within a complex dynamic of power and deferral over who gets to assign the meaning"[8] of the voice and the perceived essence of the body from which it emanates. That is, "by drawing out the parallel between the multiplicity of the thick event and the multiplicity of a person,"[9] we believe that the voice allows us to identify a person—specifically, as her book title suggests, the race of a person—and that by identifying the race of the person, we can indeed *know* that person, often in a colonizing way. Eidsheim thus disavows the acousmatic question, and instead offers "three interrelated correctives that better capture what voice is and what we identify when we identify voice."[10] First is that the voice is not a singular thing, but rather it results from multiple bodily organs and physical processes involved in the production of sound, all of which are developed over the course of a lifetime and are culturally situated. Second is that vocal choices are shaped by one's position within one's collective or community, rather than by purely individual expression; social processes shape the way we use our voices. And third, and perhaps most important, is the interpretive power of the listener. Eidsheim stresses, "the voice does not arise solely from the vocalizer; it is created just as much within the process of listening."[11] Moreover, because it is the listener who actively produces meanings, listening is a political act.

Eidsheim makes clear that she seeks to take on what she describes as "the fiction of fidelity"[12] that often accompanies discussions of vocal performance, which in many ways hearkens back to the discussion of authenticity in Chapter 2. As I discussed, authenticity is often used to signify veracity, genuineness, and commitment. It can also be negatively evoked to enforce ideas of representational purity that can foreclose ethical exchange. Fidelity operates in a similar vein, as it seeks to locate a truth in the voice—a truth that Eidsheim rejects, declaring "Ultimately, I seek to disassemble any promise of 'accuracy.' I will go as far as to argue that its pursuit is a dead-end street."[13] The danger of fidelity, she suggests, is that in its desire to offer more nuanced and complex analyses, it often reinforces the myth of the voice—and particularly the characteristic of timbre—as an essential thing that is linked to the race of the performer. Instead, Eidsheim proposes a critical performance practice that uplifts the stylistic agency of the singer while also recognizing the interpretive power of the listener:

> Critical performance practice applies narrative analysis to objects, timbres, and discourse based on listeners' observations. It aims to tell the story not of whether a voice is authentic or maintains fidelity to a given idea, but of how a given vocalizer is associated with a particular category, culturally created group, or genre. In this

> way critical performance practice methodology can address performances carried out through listening.[14]

As I analyze the way Lopez-as-El-Vez uses sound and music in his performances, I draw on Eidsheim's approach by both marking the technique and style Lopez employs while also theorizing the meanings that audiences may take from his vocal choices.

In her book *The Sonic Color Line: Race and the Cultural Politics of Listening*, Stoever considers how sound functions as "An aural complement to and interlocutor of the gaze"[15] that reinforces racial privilege and prejudice by normalizing certain sounds and labeling others as noise. Not only does the sonic color line assert control over the soundscape of public space, but it also impacts individual, private lives by imposing upon them reductive, racialized aural stereotypes, linking certain sounds to specific bodies and deeming them "improper." Stoever notes that the sonic color line is especially useful in maintaining white supremacy in our ostensibly post-racial society, where many of the laws and policies that disproportionately harm BIPOC individuals are race-neutral:

> Reconsidering racialization as a sonic practice allows for a deeper understanding of why both race and racism persist, even as "color-blind" formations of race infuse federal law and political pundits insist America is a "post-racial" nation in the wake of Barack Obama's presidency. Although scholars of race have roundly challenged color blindness, it remains the United States' dominant ideology. *The Sonic Color Line* argues that American proponents of color blindness have been able to declare race invisible in the twenty-first century precisely because dominant listening practices grounded in antebellum slavery and shaped by segregation continue to render it audible.[16]

Sound is a powerful mode of enforcing racialized power structures. Yet, as Stoever makes clear, it can also be a mode of resistance to and subversion of those power structures—but it requires critical listening to hear these strains.

Both Eidsheim and Stoever point to timbre as a commonly (though erroneously) essentialized and racialized vocal trait. In her dissertation, Eidsheim interrogates the assumption "that the composite sound of a person's voice—the timbre—reveals something essential about the person's body, something that could not *but* be revealed through the timbre of the voice."[17] As she documents, there is in fact no physical difference to explain this phenomenon. Rather, "Because we believe in a racialized body, we believe in a racialized voice."[18] That is to say, we impose race onto what we hear. Even more striking, our beliefs about race will actually impact the process of hearing; Eidsheim cites several studies that document how our perceptions of a speaker (whether garnered through visual images or mere description) will actually impact what we think we hear. She notes, "If listeners are intellectually and perceptually comfortable with a historically and culturally contingent phenomenon (for example, that race matters and is evidenced in differing physiques and voices), they will be able to perceive it."[19] And because listeners will perceive this difference, it will be made manifest. Stoever similarly notes how the sonic color line acts as:

> a socially constructed boundary that racially codes sonic phenomena such as vocal timbre, accents, and musical tones. [...] White-constructed ideas about "sounding Other"—accents, dialects, "slang," and extraverbal utterances, as well as ambient sounds—have flattened the complex range of sound actually produced by people of color, marking the sonic color line's main contour.[20]

That is, perceived sonic truths are used to (re)produce racial ideologies and material conditions.

Carpenter similarly takes up the way we purport to hear race in the voice, noting that "despite the widely accepted recognition that race is a social construct, Americans still talk about what *sounds black* or *sounds white* in simplified racial terms."[21] Carpenter dissects the way we presume to hear race in terms of social, economic, and cultural capital. For instance, she notes how the use of Standard American English (SAE) is conflated with race and heard as "presumed aural whiteness." She further notes that "the value of SAE is imbued with a self-propagating notion of economic and cultural capital."[22] Yet, as she notes, other dialects and accents—for instance, African American Vernacular English (AAVE), or the easy mixture of English and Spanish into Spanglish—does carry currency within different communities. Carpenter also asserts that both style switching (the ability to switch between different styles of speech within the same language) and code switching (the ability to switch between different styles of speech as well as between distinct languages) are skills that mark an awareness of one's audience as well as the performative aspects of language and communication.

Della Gotta stresses the importance of sound in performance, especially in Latinx performance. In her book *Latinx Shakespeares: Staging U.S. Intracultural Theater*, she notes:

> the triangulation of power relationships result in an elevation of the aural. [...] the soundscape (language, accent, music, silences, noise, and sounds) is the key dramaturgical signifier used to convey Latinx culture. Spanish is often used to overcome the challenge of recognizing an "authentic" Latinx body onstage.[23]

Della Gotta purposefully puts the word authentic in quotes, in order to stress that there is no such thing. Because ethnic and racial categories are socially constructed, their definitions, meanings, and applications are unstable; and because individuals are complex and intersectional, there is no one authentic. As a starting point, Della Gotta offers that "Latinx refers to people in the United States who are from, or a product of, Spanish colonization and conquest of the Americas,"[24] but she deftly reveals how the term labors to encompass an exceedingly heterogeneous group of people of diverse racial, cultural, linguistic, economic, and geographical backgrounds. This, suggests Della Gotta, leads to the emphasis on aurality in Latinx performance:

> Any study of Latinx, the theater and beyond, requires an attunement to auditory signifiers of culture, especially Latinx who are either racially white or racially Black, as the aural distinction may be more prominent than the visual, or it may be the only outward difference at all.[25]

Finally, Della Gotta stresses the value of heteroglossic language play and code switching in Latinx performance. She notes:

> Movement between languages is part of the Latinx experience, often even for those who consider themselves monolingual English speakers. The inclusion of slang, verbal expressions, and the application of syntax from one language to the words of another are all forms of language play.[26]

More importantly, however, the movement in and between Spanish and English pushes back against the hierarchization of language and calls for English-only language purity, just as it reminds us that the United States (and the North American continent, indeed, all of the Americas) has always been multilingual.

Accent can be a potent sonic sign used to convey social placement. Similar to Della Gotta, Angela C. Pao acknowledges the importance of accent in locating character. Stressing that contemporary representational practices focus on race and racial authenticity, Pao considers how accent and dialect communicate more specific distinctions of ethnicity, nation, and social class. She notes, "the actor's physical appearance alone becomes inadequate as a marker and what is universally recognized as one of the most important defining features of an ethnic group—its language and speech—becomes the dominant material indicator of cultural identity."[27] This is especially true because, though race is often assumed to be visually readable, in fact the phenological traits through which we seek to read race are incredibly variable. Pao asserts that accent is a valuable signifier within performance; she states, "accents of all kinds (foreign, regional, class) function not on the mimetic plane (what is referred to) but on the semiotic place (the production of meaning)."[28] That is, sound *acts*, and accent can serve a dramaturgical purpose, performing identity and creating meaning.

Next to his sparkling wardrobe, El Vez's most distinguishing feature is his thick accent.[29] His stage banter, rapidly delivered in a high-pitched, accented English punctuated with Spanish, reinforces racial and national differences even as the content of his speech, replete with witty pop culture allusions and trenchant social and political commentary, reveals his intimate understanding of USAmerican society. Lopez in fact speaks and sings in a much lower pitch than El Vez, with the Standard American English dialect; he also tends to speak more slowly than does El Vez. Lopez has used this accent since he first began performing as El Vez; he easily slides into it as a trait when performing, and even outside of performance; for instance when discussing El Vez, he sometimes will speak in this performed voice. However, Lopez's reliance on the accent has diminished over his career. He notes, "The accent, it used to be the main concern. [...] I used to walk out the door with the accent on and not turn it off until I got to bed at the end of the day."[30] As he was establishing himself and the El Vez persona, the accent "used to be an anchor—an enjoyable anchor, an enjoyable frame—but somehow the action and the mood and the emotion became more of a driver than the accent."[31] That is, as Lopez embraced the power of El Vez as an artistic platform from which to speak, the ideas themselves became more meaningful than the accent alone. There is also a practical reason for Lopez's use of the accent. He states:

> The accent was also connected to the verbiage. [...] One of my things of being El Vez is I use my own dyslexia, and let it go free form, and that flips words, but it's also the idea of "Oh, he doesn't have control of his language, in flipping words and adjectives, and how you say with a gist of that."[32]

Thus, the accent provides a means of capitalizing on his own dyslexia, which often causes unexpected and playful linguistic inversions that open up new meanings and innovative ways of using language.

It should be said that the use of a performed accent raises ethical questions around representation, which perhaps have become heightened in recent years in the wake of the We See You White American Theatre movement. Heavy accents, such as that which Lopez adopts as El Vez, have long been used to reduce and contain racially marked characters in performance by stressing their Otherness. Victoria Sturtevant notes how anxieties surrounding "ethnic pollution" were reinforced through accent in the portrayals of racial Others, particularly immigrants, in early film and television where accent functioned as an example of "the kind of inert and fixed identity that defines the very concept of stereotype [...] there is no new ground to cover, no new personae to explore."[33] Indeed, for precisely this reason, Danny Hoch quite famously turned down the role of Ramon the pool boy on *Seinfeld* in 1995 when he was pressured to perform in a Spanish accent. Hoch crafted a monologue, "Danny's trip to L.A.," about this experience, in which he describes the pushback he received when he refused. Paraphrasing Jerry Seinfeld, Hoch reports being asked, "But I don't get it. Is it derogatory? I mean, aren't you an actor? Isn't that your craft? Isn't that what you do? You know, little accents?"[34] Seinfeld's response points out that accent and dialect are two among many vocal techniques used in performance. Yet, through Hoch's skillful retelling, it also hints at the way accent can be used to mock and deride: the "little accent" becomes all there is to Ramon, and Ramon and his "little accent" are the butt of the joke.[35] Hoch's response—"I play different characters"—marks the distinction in viewing Ramon as a full character, and in viewing him solely as a stereotype defined by his "little accent." Moreover, Hoch points to the dearth of complex Latinx representation combined with the industry's tolerance for (linguistic) brownface, noting,

> It's a big deal to me because there's too many friends of mine who are highly trained actors that are Cuban and Puerto Rican and Dominican, and all they get asked to do are one-dimensional roles and here I am, not even Latino, and you're asking me to play a clown and I can't.[36]

Ultimately, Hoch's monologue and his subsequent interviews and writings about the event grapple with the way power, privilege, and wealth intersect to limit the breadth and depth of Latinx representation. Similarly, Hari Kondabolu's 2017 documentary *The Problem with Apu* prompted discussion around Hank Azaria's performed accent and the ethics of a white man voicing characters of color; Azaria has since stepped away from the character, and, as of 2020, *The Simpsons* no longer has white actors voice characters of color.

Lopez's use of the performed accent is strategic in a number of important ways: it more clearly racializes his body so that he can engage in cultural critique surrounding the discriminatory representation of Latinx people as he sings, and it pushes back against notions that would restrict what kinds of voices should be amplified, given a microphone and a center stage platform from which to speak. The accent helps call attention to the materiality of Lopez's body to interrogate how we *see* race, just as it makes clear the way we believe that we can *hear* race and use it to determine social position, as Eidsheim, Stoever, and Carpenter discuss. This is especially important when we consider how the persona of El Vez relates to the characters in the songs, who often occupy the position of the marginalized, the undocumented, and the disenfranchised. The performed accent bridges the perceived distance between persona and character, allowing us to hear these stories brought to life through El Vez. Moreover, his use of Spanglish heightens the language play of the performance, revealing the linguistic innovation of the persona while also allowing for clever jokes and witticisms to emerge around and between the two languages of English and Spanish. Because Lopez willingly authors this linguistic performance and emphasizes irony and inauthenticity throughout, he thwarts its limitations. If a stereotype is meant to reduce, Lopez-as-El-Vez layers in complexity. Through his vocal choices and the topics he discusses, he interrogates the way such sonic representations are used to enforce political and cultural hierarchy, and he repositions the accented voice as the expert voice.[37]

Not only does the accent reinforce his racial identity, but also it works, as Dolores Inés Casillas posits, to project to his audience (especially its Latinx members) "sounds of belonging." Casillas notes how power and politics are encoded into the aural soundscape of the nation. Indeed, this fact seemed to take on new power during the 2016 MeX-Mas show following Trump's election. As was evident in the Trump campaign—and many times before in U.S. history—Latinx immigrants are easily and often scapegoated, labeled invaders and made the cause of all of neoliberalism's ills. In such a climate, both accented English and Spanish "evokes unwelcoming and at times hostile reactions, with racial, ethnic, and 'noisy' connotations"; moreover, these angry and potentially violent reactions are often positioned as patriotic.[38] While Casillas discusses the "distinct aural public sphere where citizenship is not a (quiet) formality tied to pen and paper, but a personal subject matter voiced publicly by callers and experienced collectively by listeners"[39] to Spanish-language radio, I suggest a similar, though differently localized, exchange occurs at El Vez performances. That is, the sound of El Vez's accented voice reinforces his alignment with immigrants, Latinx subjects, and their allies, as it also bolsters his unequivocal stance against nativist, white supremacist politics. By foregrounding a Latinx sensibility, the accent serves as a means to confront and criticize white heterosexual patriarchal capitalist supremacy as well as the ethnonationalism of Trump's "America First" foreign policy, which is rooted in exceptionalism and isolationism. Of course, audience members are likely not the immigrant workers that Casillas studies and Lopez often sings about—they are, first and foremost, rock fans with the ability and resources to come to the club. But as the performance unfolds, such voices are not only valued but also foregrounded and centered, applauded and adored.

Porque I'm El Vez, Come Mess Round with Me: Sampling Sources and Subverting Genre

Popular music exists as part of the aural backdrop to our lives, featured in commercials, movies, and television shows, and heard on the radio, streaming services, in retail environments, or out of passing cars. It's so true, it is its own cliche: Lopez, at the start of a conversation about what music means to him, actually joked that it is "the soundtrack to our lives," picking up the dusty aphorism and laughing at how trite, yet accurate, it is.[40] Truly, music makes us feel, makes us think, and makes us move. We invest a lot of meaning in our music choices (especially music we profess to love), and believe that they say something about us. Perhaps most importantly, popular music is a means through which we define ourselves individually and collectively. Thus, Lopez's use of popular music is strategic; it provides a familiar base on which he can build his art. Moreover, there are three important aspects of popular music that contribute to its power as Lopez's artistic medium: its ubiquity; its flexibility, coupled with its capacity to "ghost" meaning, especially in the way that he uses a form of live sampling or citation to invent potent remixes; and its invitation to participate. When considering these aspects alongside the way music and social identity interact, popular music's value to Lopez's world-building project becomes clear.

In his book *Performing Rites: On the Value of Popular Music*, Simon Frith grapples with the way that music is discerned and valued by both musicians and their audiences.[41] Players and listeners alike often use such vague terms as "good" and "bad" to describe music, and Frith asserts that these simple terms represent "aesthetic and ethical judgements [that] are tied together."[42] He notes:

> The marking off of some tracks and genres and artists as "good" and others as "bad" seems to be a necessary part of popular music pleasure and use; it is a way in which we establish our place in various music worlds and use music as a source of identity.[43]

That is, we engage with music in order to define ourselves. Popular music, and our debates and discussions about it, functions not only as a critical discourse linked to social grouping but also as an experience or process that produces our social selves. Frith writes that popular music:

> creates and constructs an experience—a musical experience, an aesthetic experience—that we can only make sense of by *taking on* both a subjective and a collective identity. The aesthetic, to put this another way, describes the quality of an experience (not the quality of an object); it means experiencing *ourselves* (not just the world) in a different way. My argument here, in short, rests on two premises: first, that identity is *mobile*, a process not a thing, a becoming not a being; second, that our experience of music—of music making and music listening—is best understood as an experience of *self-in-process*. Music, like identity, is both performance and story, describes the social in the individual and the individual in the social, the mind in the body and the body in the mind; identity, like music, is a matter of both ethics and aesthetics.[44]

We do not simply evaluate music and music performance as an art (or commercial) object. Rather—crucially—we use music in deeply personal ways. Through our encounters with music in different forms, suggests Frith, we come to imagine, understand, perform, and produce ourselves as both individuals and as members of a collective. Our participation in music—as musicians, as fans listening to recordings, or as audience members singing and dancing along with a live performance—at once allows us to "express ourselves, our own sense of rightness, and suborn ourselves, lose ourselves, in an act of participation."[45] To hearken back to Chapter 2, it provides an undoing and a becoming. Music itself holds the possibility of understanding both individuality and group relationships; experiencing music allows us to locate ourselves and our values within a collective. Finally, Frith stresses that "what's really at issue is a feeling. In the end, 'bad music' describes an emotional rather than an ideological judgement."[46] Music is something that we feel, literally and figuratively.

Like Frith, Kun similarly discusses the social value of popular music, linking our engagement with it to a form of democratic negotiation of the nation. In his book *Audiotopia: Music, Race, and America*, Kun asserts that popular music is "one of our most valuable sites for witnessing the performance of racial and ethnic difference against the grain of national citizenships that work to silence those differences."[47] Far from being a site in which difference is denied, erased, or forced to adopt "cultural consensus and racial univocality," Kun instead suggests that popular music "is the story of racial and ethnic difference; it is the story of both nation formation and de-formation, the audible soundtrack to a nation as it continually packs and unpacks itself."[48] That is, music is a site in which understanding of both nation and one's individual place within that nation can be negotiated and contested, and as such, it is endlessly robust and heterogeneous. There is always a back and forth, the assertion of (and appropriation by) the dominant, and subversion by the marginalized. And yet, as Kun asserts:

> we must never forget that popular music, like all forms of popular culture, is hybrid, synchronized, and the result of multiple convergences, compromises, overlaps, recodings and appropriations. As such, popular music does not simply produce difference; difference is not merely an effect of the popular. It *is* difference.[49]

That is, popular music necessarily reflects the diversity of USAmerica and its racial and cultural battles. If we listen carefully, popular music makes difference audible.

Of course, in considering how we define our individual, collective, and national identities through music, there is a difference between the music that we love and the music that we merely know. But the ubiquity of popular music adds to its value as fodder for Lopez's art. Frith offers a rather tongue-in-cheek definition of popular music when he writes, "Pop music could be defined as the music we listen to without meaning to; the songs we know without knowing how we know them."[50] There is something about the way that popular music seeps into our collective consciousness that Frith points to here, noting that it is exceedingly accessible to the public. We may come to know popular songs without ever having sought out the song or the performer. Indeed, this has apparently happened to Lopez, who writes of his use of the song "Jesus is Just Alright with Me" in The Gospel Show, "[This] is the 3rd time I've used The Doobie Brothers in an El Vez Show. I guess their music had lodged in my brain."[51] Moreover, popular music does not demand arcane knowledge of its audience, nor does it put up access barriers. It is produced commercially for profit, and is designed to appeal to a wide audience. This makes it an excellent connective point, on top of which Lopez is able to layer new meanings and ideas.

El Vez's shows are loaded with references and allusions, and this intertextuality performs important work, offering the repetition of cultural motifs with a signal difference; Lopez crafts new meanings through the interplay of the original he cites and his own remakings. In Chapter 1, I framed his citational work with the Gatesian concept of signifyin(g), through which minoritized subjects are able to offer double-voiced critiques of power. Without dropping the idea of signifyin(g) that is present in El Vez shows, I here want to layer in Hutcheon's discussion of parody, which she defines as "a form of repetition with ironic critical difference, marking difference"[52] What stands out in Hutcheon's conception is the importance of difference to the project; parody does not smooth everything into a unified whole, but rather "it is stylistic confrontation, a modern recoding which establishes difference at the heart of similarity."[53] Parody is intentional; it demands that an audience notice that difference, and then decode and contextualize it, rather than just assimilate it. As an obvious example, then, we are never expected to mistake El Vez for Elvis; we should always remain cognizant of the distance between the two.

This parodic intent continues in Lopez's use of a form of live musical sampling. Akin to sampling in remix culture, where portions of sound recordings are reworked into a separate recording to make something new,[54] Lopez embeds in his songs multiple musical samples and allusions, which the Memphis Mariachis perform live, in the real time of the concert; this is why El Vez gigs are so challenging for the musicians—they have to keep up with the references that Lopez layers in, often rapid-fire style. Throughout my descriptions of El Vez shows, I have noted the way Lopez slices musical phrases and references into his songs, and how he melds and mashes-up multiple pieces into one El Vez song: for instance, Pink Floyd at the start of "George Bush on the Guillotine," a Public Enemy allusion in "Say it Loud!," and the trio of songs that become his Virgen de Guadalupe set. Lawrence Lessig, quoting remix artist Victor Stone, reflects on the value of this creative act to consider how:

> [M]eaning [...] comes from the reference [...] Images and or sounds collected from real-world examples become "paint on a palette." And it is this "cultural reference"

> [...] that "has emotional meaning to people. ... When you hear four notes of the Beatles' 'Revolution,' it means something."[55]

Lopez's use of live musical sampling deepens his social and political critiques while also creating new meanings from a shared popular music library. Furthermore, Lessig stresses the way remix and sampling empower the audience, stating:

> It touches social life differently. It gives the audience something more. Or better, it asks something more of an audience. [...] It invites a response. In a culture in which it is common, its citizens develop a kind of knowledge that empowers as much as it informs or entertains.[56]

The sampling and Lopez's remix approach is key to the world-building of El Vez shows; it engages the audience as active decoders, prompting them to become attuned to difference and empowering them to track how new meanings are offered up through the shared sounds of popular music.

Perhaps unsurprisingly, the issue of authenticity rears its head in musical discussions, especially in order to stave off perceived cooptation or selling out. Yet, Frith asserts that such terms are misapplied, noting:

> [A] song's origin is really only of academic interest [...] Attempts to draw a clear distinction between authentic and inauthentic popular songs, whether using musicological or sociological criteria, are pointless. It's not where pop songs come from that matters, but where they get to.[57]

This is especially true for an artist like Lopez, who as El Vez embraces the malleability of popular music; it can travel, bringing with it the original context while also taking on new ideas. In a process akin to what Marvin Carlson defines as ghosting, which "presents the identical thing they have encountered before, although now in a somewhat different context,"[58] a song might carry with it both individual and collective meanings that then inform Lopez's meaning-making and world-building. And Frith's travel might also occur in the opposite direction. As Lopez notes:

> I know people who didn't know my musical references at all, and then by chance they'll hear it in real life. So my version is how they know that reference. And then they go look up that reference and look up that song and look up that artist, which is a whole other thing—if you like this, you might also like this—which is a good point of reference. It's a way to give musical history [...] When you hear a sample, then that's what that song is. Taking it on yourself to find out what that was I think can be very rewarding, and it gives you a delayed punchline.[59]

Our musical listening at an El Vez show might ghost other popular songs, or El Vez might ghost future encounters with music.

Finally, Frith also notes that a key element of popular music is our ability to perform along with it. Popular music:

> describes songs that we can and sometimes do perform as well as listen to. Much of this singing is collective [...] But we sing individually too [...] Indeed, I would add to the definition of pop as accessible music that it is also singable and performable music; it doesn't need the skills that classical or jazz or even rock musicians must acquire.[60]

This is especially true when experiencing live performance. Generally, rock clubs are loud and sweaty places where you are encouraged to sing and dance. Indeed, most artists, Lopez included, work moments of direct participation into their shows, thereby heightening the feeling of collectivity among the audience as well as its investment in the performance. For Lopez, this often involves having the audience sing along to familiar melodies, but using his rewritten lyrics, substituting "Aztlán" for "Graceland" or "Immigration Time" for "Suspicious Minds." These moments of participation are especially powerful in the way that they encourage the audience to enact different understandings of identity and nation—perhaps understandings that they do not actually uphold. For instance, in 2007, I witnessed a venue filled with undergraduates at Kansas State University sing along to "Viva La Raza." This was a free public performance in a conservative state; surely some students might object to the political content of El Vez shows—at least in other settings. But in the midst of the El Vez performance, they might also have sung along, carried away by the show. Similarly, Lopez reports that "I loved doing ['Say It Loud!'] in Holland and making all the white kids sing along."[61] What might it mean for KSU students to celebrate La Raza or Dutch kids to sing that they are Brown and Proud? I don't want to suggest that they would instantly be converted to a more progressive appreciation of a multicultural society. But if music, as Frith suggests, offers an experience of *self-in-process*, then their participation in moments like these might allow audience members to experience themselves in the world in a different way. This is why popular music is crucial to the world-building of El Vez shows. Indeed, I submit it is the primary and most potent mode of world-building that Lopez employs.

Additionally, the live musical sampling allows Lopez to insert new meanings into established songs while also disrupting and overturning music's containing mechanisms, offering a subtle commentary on race and racial divides through the music itself. One way that our musical listening is segmented is through genre. Franco Fabbri, among the first popular music scholars to discuss genre, defined it as "as set of musical events (real or possible) whose course is governed by a definite set of socially acceptable rules."[62] Thus, this initial definition of genre emphasizes how musical and social considerations are intertwined, and current thinking on genre continues to hold this dual focus. Genre in popular music serves multiple purposes, and different players (e.g., producers/marketers, performers, critics, listeners) use and understand it differently. As Frith notes, "The logic of labeling depends on what the label is for"[63]; thus, understandings of genre are multiple. Suggests Fabian Holt, "Genre is a fundamental structuring force in musical life. It has implications for how, where, and with whom people make and experience music."[64] Similarly, David Brackett notes, "musical genres participate in the circulation of social connotations that pass between musicians, fans, critics, music-industry magnates and employees."[65] Thus, genre is social, helping to define musical communities. It is also ideological, revolving around shared values or aesthetics, and mutual understandings about what music *should be* and what it *should do*.

As both Frith and Brackett note, genres are formed and expressed through language, and they become shorthand for musical, ideological, and social concerns. Though we tend to think of genre as reflecting something essential within the music itself—for example its instrumentation, rhythm, and sound, Brackett emphasizes that "genres and categories of music and people are neither true nor false, but rather ideological, in that they speak to a shared, tacit understanding about which differences are meaningful as well as how these differences are meaningful."[66] And because, as Brackett suggests, genre distinctions in the United States historically centered around race, class, and regional difference, genre has become racially marked; he writes, "In the United States in the early and mid-twentieth century, musical categories grew out of and contributed to a preoccupation with race, class, and geographical regions and how these might be articulated to technological developments and the imperatives of economics."[67] That is, genre is laden with assumptions about racial identity. Thus, the construction of racially marked musical genres insidiously reinforces the notion that musical expression is rooted in essentialized racial difference: "Black music" is inherently and indisputably different from "white music" or "Latin music." Racially coded musical genres suggest that we can hear race in the music.

El Vez's performances push against genre as a containing mechanism. Drawing on his vast musical knowledge, and reflecting his punk rock sensibility, Lopez purposefully blends glam, soul, rap, punk, rock, and more to reimagine relations between commonly held conceptions of cultural identity. These musical juxtapositions and layerings exemplify how, as Roshanak Kheshti posits in conversation with Daphne Brooks, "The sonic circulates at a vernacular level that has the potential to subvert the logics of language."[68] Through his use of live musical sampling and a remix aesthetic that effortlessly slides between genres in the course of a single song and over the length of the show,[69] Lopez confounds our own racialized listening. He also pokes fun at the idea that our racial identities might tyrannically constrict our musical tastes. In his song "En El Barrio," El Vez tracks the difficulties faced by "another Brown baby" born in the barrio. The song's unnamed subject runs into trouble when he joins a gang and steals a car—an endeavor he undertakes "Porque there's one thing that he can't stand / And that's to have to join a Mariachi Band."[70] Delivered with an almost deadpan sincerity, the song sets up a dire either/or situation, outlining the two pathways open to him: join a gang or become a Mariachi.[71] That one of the options is a forced musical career underlines the supposed links between race, ethnicity, and musical genre.

Without erasing different traditions and specificities, Lopez joins together disparate songs in surprising combinations to create a sonic landscape that defies differentiating boundaries. This has always been a part of his work as El Vez; he jokes that this is how his mind works, "referencing, referencing, referencing, because a reference is worth a thousand words."[72] Indeed, he notes that this is perhaps also linked to his dyslexia; he is especially adept at recognizing patterns and motifs in different songs, as well as in hearing how different songs might fit together. He explains that his mind:

> always go[es] to the references, be that a musical key, a chord progression, or how the words align [...] so a word or a line could be replaced, flipping it or turning it upside down, but still being in the same realm.[73]

Thus, his mash-ups make manifest the particular way that he hears music, just as they add to the meaning-making and world-building of the show in both content and form. He stresses that El Vez "wasn't supposed to be a straight show [...] it was always multiple things at once"; these references and mash-ups make "audio puns, visual puns, verbal puns, but with a frame of reference."[74]

Through his musical melding, Lopez creates what Iván Alejandro Ramos has dubbed "non-culturally locatable sound."[75] Ramos describes the importance of non-culturally locatable sound for Latinx subjects who "duly reject assimilation but also refuse to adopt the ancestral narratives of a 'native' culture that anti-assimilation discourse requires."[76] He suggests that sound becomes a conduit through which to inhabit a state of "negation, of unruliness, and of unbelonging,"[77] That is, sound and music can become "a mode of questioning what it is to be a proper political subject identified by national, ethnic, or cultural signifiers."[78] Moreover, Ramos suggests that "the sonic [can be] a tool to exist outside the space of identity."[79] That is, the sonic offers the possibility to push against tropes that would contain individuals, tropes that suggest identity is fixed and stable. (And yes, in this chapter, I have pointed to ways that El Vez shows offer sonic opportunities of both belonging and unbelonging. That his shows can do both makes clear the flexibility and scope of Lopez's world-building project.) Lopez builds his "non-culturally locatable sounds" from the familiar melodies of popular music. Habell-Pallán foregrounds how Lopez's transculturating through music enables "multiple layers of cultural hybridity and [promotes] complex instances of cross-cultural translation." She highlights how El Vez performances interrogate "traditional definitions of nationhood [...] and the criteria by which human rights and citizenship are granted to or withheld from subjects of the nation," using sound and music to pose questions. His shows ask the audience to consider how subjecthood is formed against a political backdrop.[80] And at the Casbah in 2016, Lopez's playing with popular music allowed the audience to grapple with Trump's election.

Hola and Welcome to My World: Creating Audiotopias

Though billed as a Christmas show, the Casbah performance was clearly built in response to the 2016 election. After a campaign that featured Mexicans are rapists, Build the Wall! chants, and Bad Hombres, to have El Vez swagger to center stage, call himself The Mexican Elvis, and sing out against Trump seemed a defiant gesture of unruliness and resistance around which the audience could rally. In this section, I offer a close read of the show to pinpoint how Lopez uses sound—through accent, stage banter, lyrical revision, and live musical sampling and remix reimaginings—to engage in world-building for and with the audience. As part of this, I offer my own emotional, intellectual, and physical responses in an autoethnographic account of the show. I will document how the first portion of the performance used lyrical rewrites and stage banter to voice sorrow and trepidation, often times in contrast to the upbeat tempo of the songs. This transitioned into an elegy of sorts, where El Vez covered songs by Leonard Cohen and David Bowie that honored and lamented the deaths of these artists while simultaneously drawing connections between those losses and the potential scaling back of civil liberties expected to happen under Trump. Building this emotion into a call for resistance against the Trump Administration and the sexism, white supremacy, anti-immigration, Islamaphobia, and homophobia his presidency was poised to represent, I switch my focus to discuss Lopez's strategic use of Blackness in his visual and aural storytelling. Finally, after a productively ambiguous finale, in which he enacted Trump's campaign promise to build a wall (of wrapped gifts), he returned to the stage to usher in revolution, using the noise, screams, and movements of punk rock to disrupt and contest Trump's looming authoritarianism.

Lopez carefully structures all of his shows, crafting a narrative arc to advance his ideas. As noted in the previous chapter, costuming supports the dramaturgical structure, with each costume selected to emphasize a theme or heighten a mood. This section explores how the music, lyrics, and banter contribute to the sonic dramaturgy to further clarify the meaning-making and aid in world-building. More than most rock performances, El Vez shows advance a theme and prompt affective emotional responses. Says Lopez:

> Show structure usually starts with a strong start for energy
> Huaraches is usually 2nd for "tradition" to give some "elvis"
> so I can go towards other things after the obligatory
>
> I usually put a "weight" in the middle
> meaning a slower?
>
> Pick up again from there
> Do a sexy
> before I round off with the "theme" I was alluding to.[81]

The Casbah set included fifteen songs, each paired with a loosely scripted monologue performed over musical vamps. These monologues, which are replete with jokes around a serious theme, conceptually bridge from the last song to introduce the next. They are often as long as the songs themselves. Lopez "consider[s] the set up to the song as a separate piece although many times it's just the same information as in the song."[82] That is, Lopez reinforces the ideas of the show, presenting them both through the persona of El Vez as expressed through the stage banter, as well as through the lyrics and sound of the songs themselves, thereby giving audience members multiple ways to process the themes and messages. Sonically, he will set the musical vamps in a different key, to "improve one's ear," bettering the chance that the audience is able to take in the information. He stresses, "since it's apart I don't want the set up to be in the same key as the song [...] To have set up and song in the same key would be a long time in that key [...] Hence the need to refresh."[83] Lopez thus considers the listening experience of the audience. The vamps themselves help drive the energy of the show, providing responsive musical backing to the monologues and seamlessly bridging the songs into one long revue-style show. Lopez's thinking about key also provides aural variety between the vamps and the songs that help maintain audience interest. My own experience of El Vez shows suggests that the vamps and the songs can either increase or resolve tension, depending on the key changes. Lopez skillfully employs music theory to help amplify his ideas.

Humor plays a large role in El Vez's monologues. Because Lopez sees entertainment as his main responsibility to his audience, frivolity and wit aid in that project, inviting people in through shared laughter. More importantly, Muñoz notes that humor serves as a "valuable pedagogical and political project" in disidentificatory performance.[84] Laughter acts as an intervention into the forces of marginalization and oppression; it can signal defiance, an unwillingness to internalize untruths. Humor and laughter allow for social critique. Lopez often describes El Vez as a sort of court-jester-like figure who, through joking, can speak the truth. Specifically referring to how he crafted his shows during Trump's presidency he adds, "dark times call for darker comedy."[85] In conceiving of the Casbah Merry MeX-Mas show, Lopez states, "2016, it was all so new and I wanted to point out longer over-reaching effects all involved in his [Trump's] workings."[86] Thus, the bulk of the stage banter focused on Trump's election, and most songs, though not all, contained live musical samples, musical mash-ups, and lyrical rewrites that in some way referenced politics. He called out the racist foundation of Trumpism and called attention to policy issues that were likely to change with the new administration. The arc of the show suggested that those who find themselves on the wrong side of the election cannot succumb to despair, but must instead remain vigilant against Trumpism by harnessing fear, rage, and grief and transforming these emotions into rebellion and resistance. While the subject matter might have been bleak, the music was not. Of the fifteen songs he played, six were "sad tunes," with two set in "minorish keys," while nine were "non sad tunes" (Figure 4.1).[87]

Lopez built the energy of the opening around the apprehension and anger following Trump's election. For instance, his rendition of "Blue Christmas" featured rewritten lyrics and pointed stage banter that, by using Nazi terminology to describe the incoming administration, made evident the ethnonationalism of Trumpism and the danger it poses, especially for racialized and minoritized subjects. Calling attention to his own body, he joked that, as a Chicano, he usually has a "Brown Christmas." However, Lopez-as-El-Vez continued, this year was different, "I'm blue because we now live in a red state." In the banter and the song, he plays on "blueness," situating it as both an emotional state and a political affiliation. The song, performed at more than double the time of the Elvis recording, also featured a relentless tempo that kept the energy up and the audience moving. Addressing the song directly to Trump, El Vez crooned that the holiday was ruined "Because of you" and went on to sing "When the Red commandos are calling / That's when the Blue memories start falling / ... / You'll be doing all right / With your Christmas that's Reich." What in Elvis was a mournful song about unrequited love became through El Vez a frenetic song of disdain—disdain for the man, and more importantly, disdain for his racist politics.

"Blue Christmas" transitioned into what Lopez-as-El-Vez referred to as "the sad part of the show" (or following the language of Lopez's email, the weight in the middle of his set), during which he lamented the election and the disturbing ethnonationalism that fueled Trump's victory. In the musical vamp before it,

NEEDLES IN CAMELS EYE
HURRACHES
God save the vamp
I WISH XMAS EVERY DAY
when the snowman vamp **BLUE XMAS**
there she goes vamp **MAMACITA DONDE**
shopping center vamp **DREYDEL**

WAITING FOR MIRACLE
pretty woman vamp
REBEL REBEL *vamp* **MOONAGE**
military beat vamp **STRANGE FRUIT**
run run run vamp **RUN RUN RUDOLF**
black keys vamp **LIL' DRUMMER BOY**

Carlos Moreno *vamp* **XMAS TIME IS HERE**
trouble vamp **SANTA CLAUS BROWN**

XMAS TIME-BELLS
end of the world vamp **BROWN XMAS**

FIGURE 4.1: The set list from the 2016 Merry MeX-Mas show at the Casbah. Courtesy of the author's collection.

Lopez-as-El-Vez suggested that Trump is taking the United States back— "like way back, to 1939 or so," again calling out the racist language used by Trump and predicting the way white supremacists and neo-Nazis would see his election as empowering. He painted a foreboding picture for the audience, reinforced sonically as he played a brief, slowed-down snippet of the song "Smile" on his melodica, adding that it is "the saddest instrument in the world—its name comes from melancholy" (Figure 4.2). He used the slower tempo and the timbre of the instrument to offer a brief dirge for our government. Inverting the lyrics made famous by Nat King Cole, El Vez sang that we should "Cry, if you love democracy."[88] The Lovely Elvettes begged him to end the song, pleading, "Make it stop!" while shedding performed tears.[89] "Don't worry," he responded, "it's only eight more years."

The show allowed other moments of emotional release, such as when Lopez-as-El-Vez brought up the deaths of several icons, which followed a chain of references to offer political commentary. "This has been some year," he pondered. "It was going so well until David Bowie died." Even this sad acknowledgment was tinged with humor—Bowie, one of Lopez's musical heroes, had died only ten days into the New Year. Pausing a moment to riff on the deaths of Bowie, Prince, and The Dark Prince (Leonard Cohen), he then launched into a new piece he had written specifically for this show, a very "Bowie-esque version"[90] of Cohen's "Waiting for a Miracle." Lopez suggests that the song works in several ways, noting how it "seems end of the worldy but also perhaps Xmasy as in the birth of Christ."[91] It also obliquely linked to the election through a process that the audience members could decode, exemplifying another truism that Kun asserts about popular music, that "A song is never just a song, but a connection, a ticket,

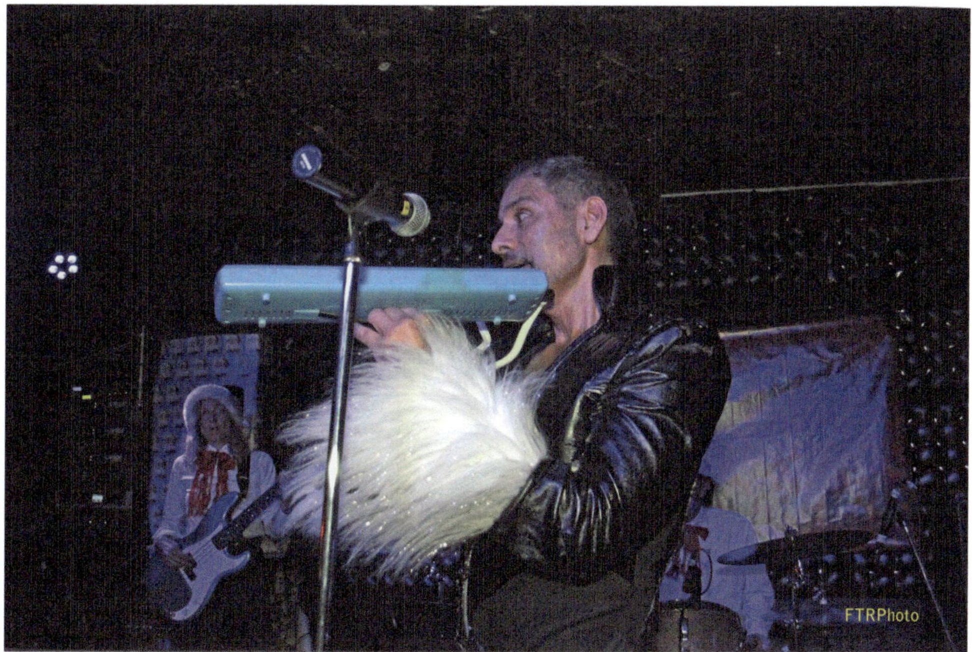

FIGURE 4.2: El Vez plays his melodica, the saddest instrument in the world, 2016. Photograph by FTR Photo.

a pass, an invitation, a node in a complex network."[92] Cohen had died just before Trump's surprising upset, though his death was not announced until a few days after. In an act of reverence and of grieving (both for the man and for the results of the election) on the Saturday after the election, Kate McKinnon sang his most famous hit "Hallelujah" as Hillary Clinton, a character she had played throughout the campaign, in a poignant *Saturday Night Live* cold open that immediately went viral.[93] Like McKinnon's emotional performance, the El Vez cover expressed despair, linking personal loss with electoral loss, and contemplating the very real consequences that could come from Trump's election:

Waiting for the miracle
There's nothing left to do
I haven't been this unhappy
Since George Bush Number Two

Nothing left to do
When you know that you've been taken
Nothing left to do
When you're begging for a crumb
Nothing left to do
When you've got to go on waiting
Waiting for the miracle to come.[94]

Sung with a mournful tone, it voiced the helplessness and hopelessness that many felt at the time. Indeed, the song wallows in that feeling. It proclaims that nothing but a miracle can right the wrong of Trump's election, but also makes clear that the miracle will never come.

Still, as Lopez is quick to point out, "Although something is sad or haunting, it still has to 'rock,'"[95] and the overall show has to move. Playing on the mention of Bowie in the stage banter and musical style, the song morphed into "Rebel Rebel," and the mood of the show shifted to defiance. Accordingly, Lopez-as-El-Vez re-emerged wearing a camouflage jumpsuit to call out Trump's bombast and how it might destabilize global geopolitics, singing "You got the UN in a whirl / 'cause they're not sure' bout the bombs that you hurl." He urged the audience to join him in rebellion, again referencing how Trumpian politics might provide cover for white nationalists and other ethnonational movements, "Hey babes, let's throw out the right / cause they're not sure of the flags you unfurl." The song, with its epic, droning guitar hook, culminated in El Vez and the Elvettes screaming, "Fascists! We hate thee so!" as the audience shouted along. The band then slid seamlessly into the "Now you do what they told you" section of Rage Against the Machine's "Killing in the Name,"[96] a song that condemns white supremacy, institutionalized racism, and police brutality. The moment was not only powerful, a dark presaging of what was to come under Trump, but also a call to rebel against injustice.

The thread of resistance continued throughout the next song of the show, in which all aspects of performance—costuming, banter, lyrics, sound—worked to convey a powerful message, one that visually and aurally called up Blackness and honored the work of Black activists. Returning to the stage dressed as a police officer, Lopez-as-El-Vez said frankly, "We now live in what they call a police state [...] And sometimes, a man with a gun is more than a man with a gun." The costuming choice was perhaps surprising; in wearing the uniform, Lopez-as-El-Vez seemed to embody the oppressor even as he offered a critique against police violence. This was resolved when he removed his hat to reveal devil horns beneath, and it reinforced the stage banter, which clearly alluded to the fact that, as agents of the government, the murder of Black people at the hands of the police amounted to state-sanctioned killings. Lopez-as-El-Vez went on to specifically praise the activism of Black Lives Matter. He then called for us all to "get in formation" as the Lovely Elvettes joined him onstage. They had changed into black jumpsuits and large hats, an homage to Beyoncé's iconic "Formation" video, and would mimic her lowered head, abrupt head nods, and defiant and sustained "fuck you" of her raised middle fingers throughout the song. Lopez revels in word play, and enjoys the way this statement both references Beyoncé and suggests that we need to remain vigilantly informed—"get information." In El Vez's usage, we must be informed about the workings of the Trump Administration, an idea he would return to in the finale (Figure 4.3a–d).

El Vez musically linked current police injustices to the long history of violence against Black people in the United States, covering an incredibly famous song to show its continued relevance today. Situating Donald J. Trump's election as the most recent, and most visible, manifestation of white supremacy, he proclaimed that we must take the country back from him. Amidst the cheers of the audience, his voice clearly intoned a slow, heartbreaking lyric: "Christmas Trees bear strange fruit." The original song, made famous by Billie Holiday, juxtaposes graphic descriptions of the lifeless bodies of lynching victims with images of Southern pastoral beauty; the El Vez version includes the additional complication of the winter holidays. The critique was heightened even more by the song's slow tempo; notes Lopez, "Moments made more sad in El Vez cases are slower and spaced, adding weight with the delivery and mood."[97] In fact, this was the slowest song of the entire show, which made it stand out in the lineup. The melody transformed into "St. James Infirmary," a song famously performed by Black artists Louis

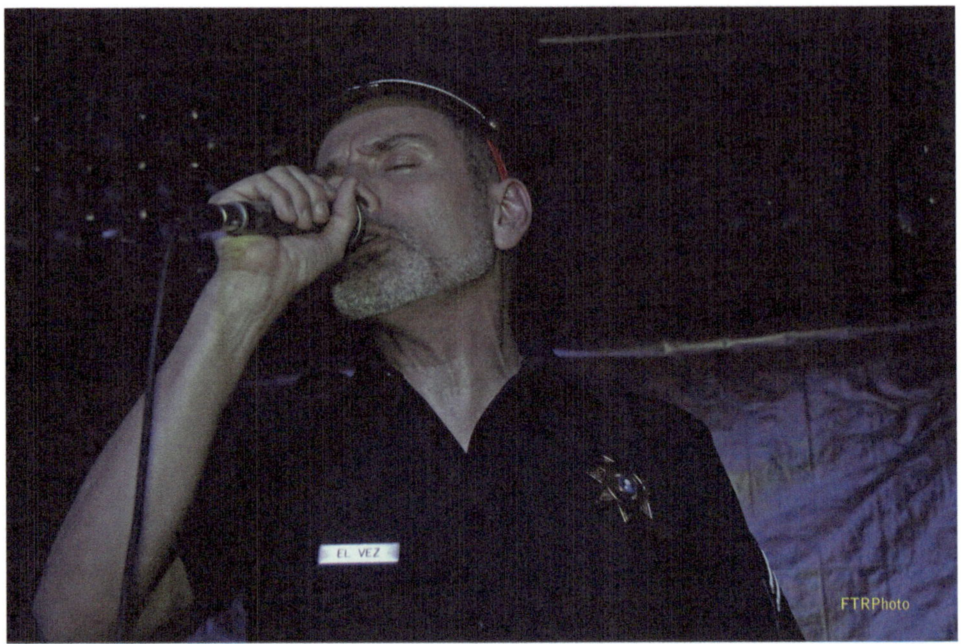

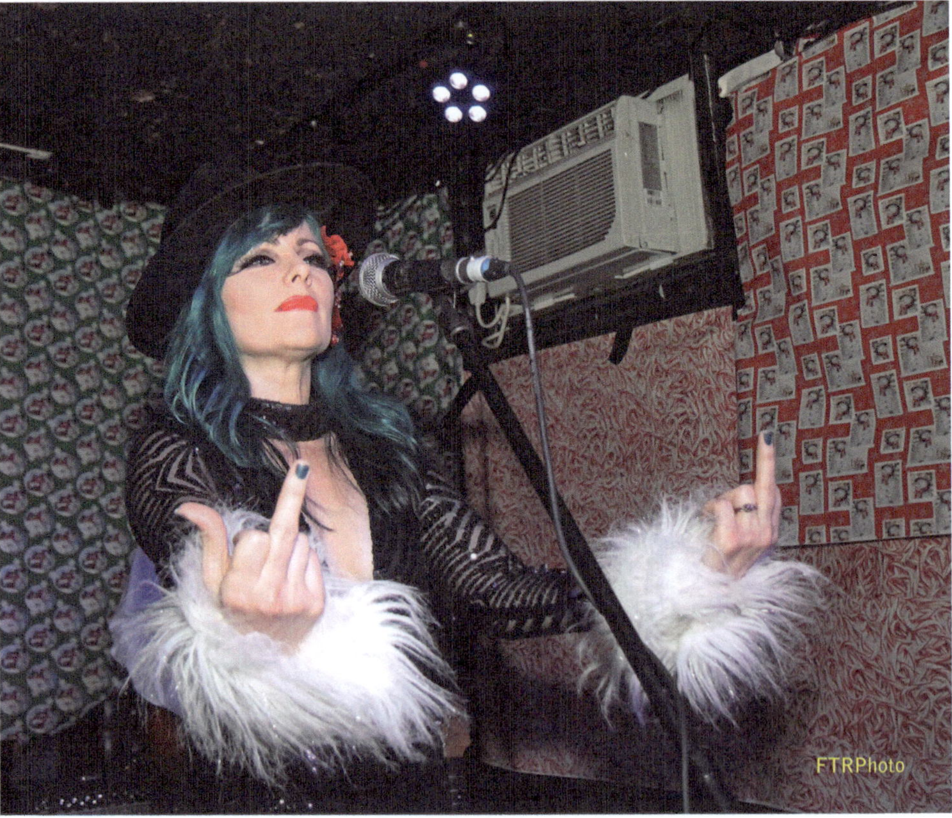

FIGURE 4.3a–d: (a) El Vez arrives on stage costumed as a police officer; (b–c) Lovely Elvettes Lisa María (Pinky Turzo) and Priscillita (Crissy Guerrero) in Beyoncé attire; (d) Officer El Vez's devil horns revealed, 2016. Photographs by FTR Photo.

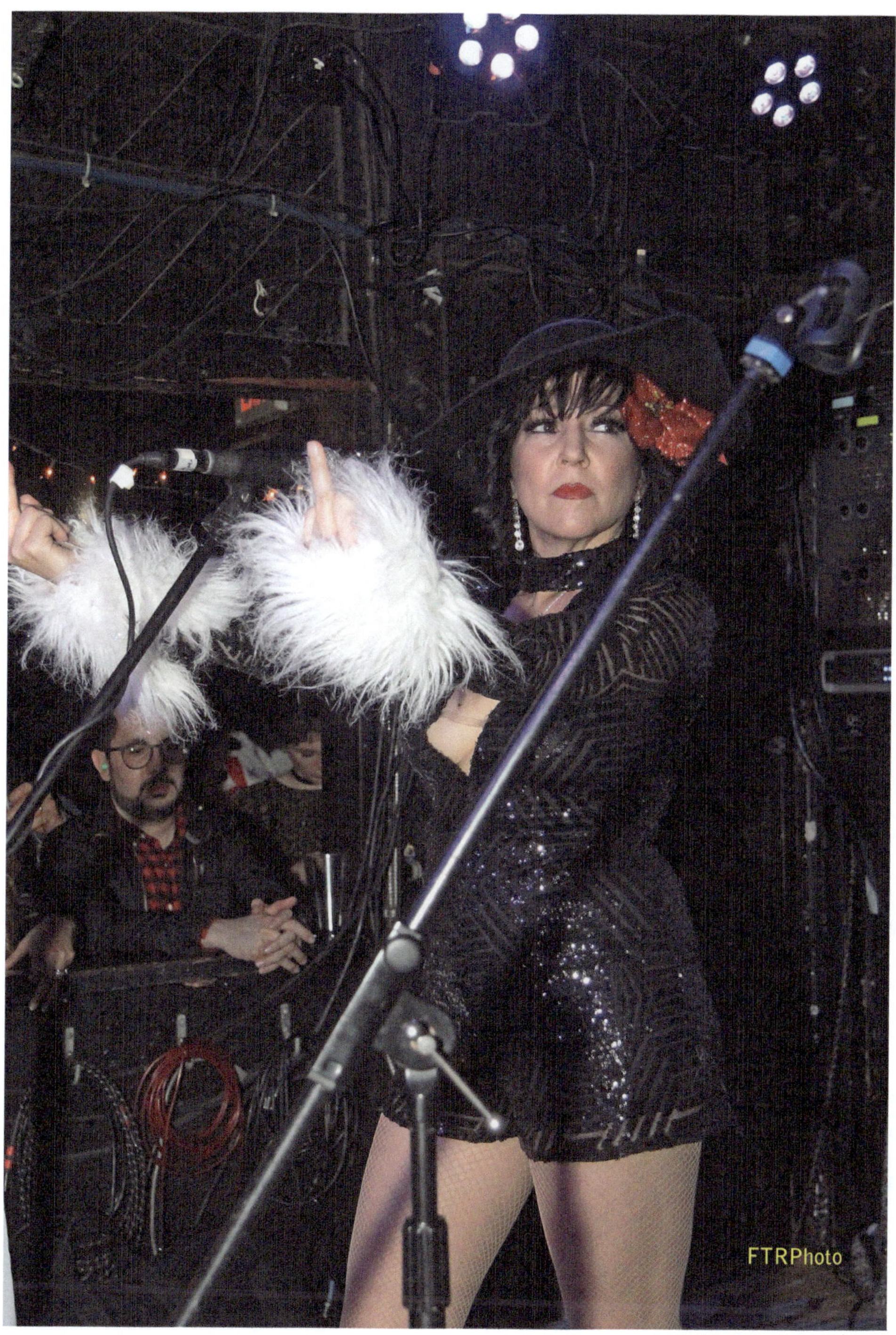

FIGURE 4.3a–d: (*Continued*)

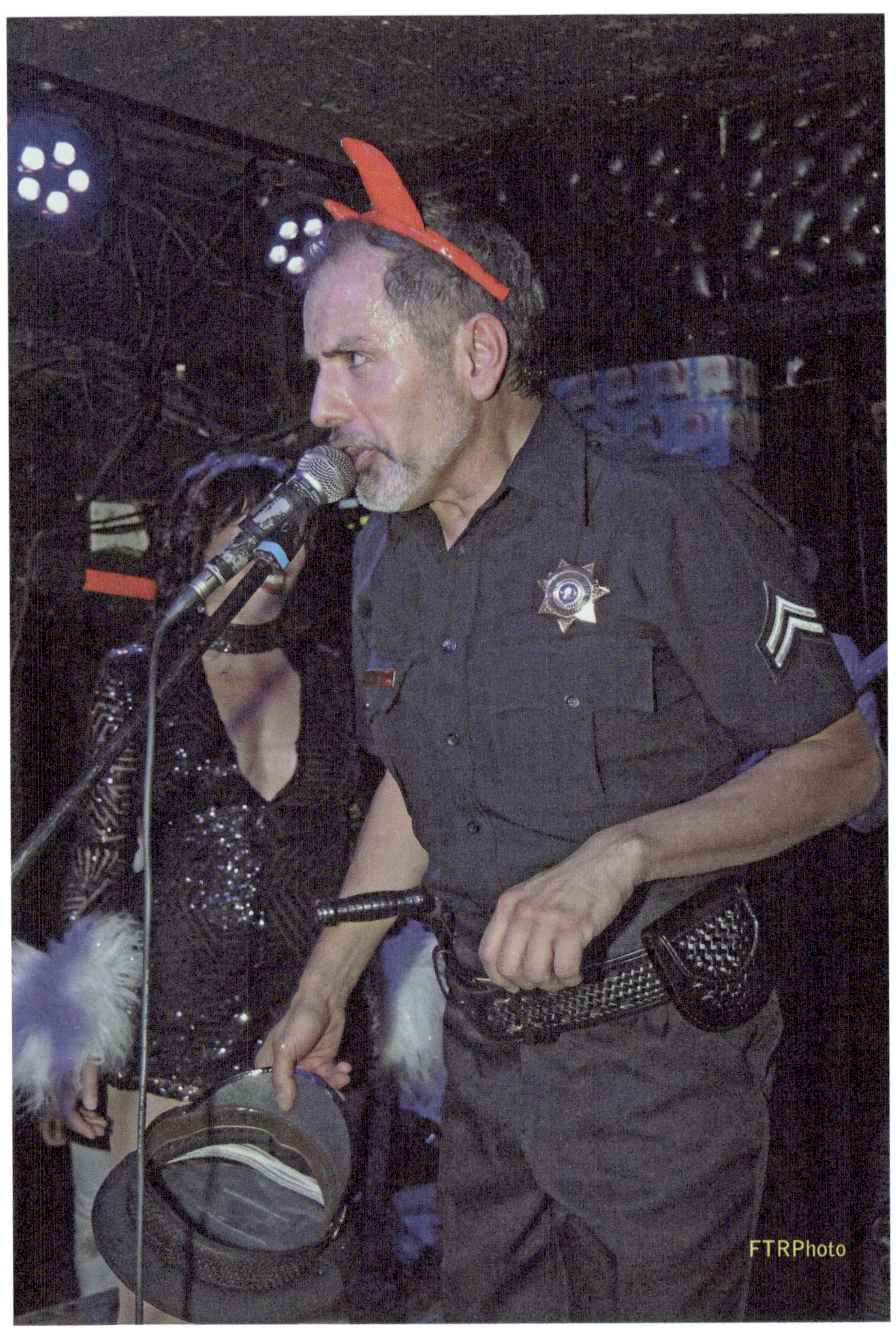

FIGURE 4.3a–d: (*Continued*)

Armstrong and Cab Calloway that sings of a young woman's death and foretells the narrator's own demise.[98] The rewritten El Vez lyrics tie together the tropes of lynching, impoverishment, and institutionalized racism, in a call for political action in response to Trump's election:

I went down to the demonstration
To get my fair share of abuse
There were signs reading "Not my President"
Signs saying "What's the use?"

Well you can't always get what you want, child
You can't always get what you need
But if you try some time, you might find
These are the days to let it bleed

My sister went to the Chelsea Drug Store
To get her prescription filled
She was waiting in line with Mr. Jimmy
He said Obamacare has been repealed

Well you can't always get what you want, child
You can't always get what you need
But if you try some time, you might find
These are the days to let it bleed.[99]

The first verse referenced the burgeoning protest movement that had erupted in nearly all major cities following the election, which in fact presaged the enormous turnout of the Women's March held the day after the inauguration. The second verse was more personal, referencing Lopez's diabetic sister, the high price of her insulin, and her fears of losing her insurance (raising the price even more) if Trump made good on his promise to repeal the Affordable Care Act (also known as Obamacare). The chorus was about artistic reclamation; by inserting the lyrics of "You Can't Always Get What You Want" into the melody of "St. James Infirmary," El Vez "took back" the Rolling Stones hit, which Trump played—without permission—during his campaign and following his presidential acceptance speech. Stressing that a Trump presidency was NOT what we the audience and we the nation wanted, the lyrics urged action.

In the finale of the show, outrage against the expected injustices of the Trump Administration took on an especially emotional color. With Lopez-as-El-Vez imploring the audience that "We cannot give up," the band launched into the vamp before the final song, a slowed-down version of R.E.M.'s iconic "It's the End of the World" while El Vez sang his rewritten lyrics:

> Not great, it starts with an earthquake
> Votes and snakes, and that Trump plane
> And all of us are so afraid.[100]

Stressing how important it is to stay informed and engaged, he warned that "You must know your enemies" as the Lovely Elvettes began to list off names of the Trump Team to the rhythm of the song: advisors including Steve Bannon, Newt Gingrich, and Rudy Guiliani; cabinet members such as Michael T. Flynn, John Bolton, Ben Carson, and Steve Mnuchin; and various other supporters like Sarah Palin and Tom Cotton.[101] The song closed with the words, "It's the end of the world as we know it, so make a sign," as the Elvettes held up placards reading "You Belong," "Still With Her," "Free Hugs," and "You Matter." This moment not only anticipated the massive protests that would rise up in resistance to Trump but also reasserted the importance of inclusivity and caring, despite his electoral victory.

As described in Chapter 2, Lopez often ends his Christmas shows with "Brown Christmas," opening with the Beach Boys, borrowing the melody of "White Christmas" and then layering in John Lennon's "Happy Xmas (War is Over)" to remind us that war is in fact ongoing. Lopez's rewritten lyrics to the song offer a lovely meditation about the importance of holiday gatherings and traditions within Latinx culture, "Where cousins and familia are tight / [...] /Holidays with La Raza are bright / and thank God your Christmases ain't white." Yet, while he sang of Christmases "just like the ones in Mexico," his stage hands[102] constructed a wall between the performers and the audience, enacting Trump's biggest campaign promise. Made of cheery, gift-wrapped boxes, the effect of El Vez's wall was disturbing nonetheless. The beauty of Mexico, family, and love was cut off, while the isolation and violence of war (militaristic and cultural) were pronounced. El Vez kept singing through a gap that remained, until, finally, as he sang, "A very Merry Christmas / And a Happy New Year / Let's hope it's a good one," the last "brick" was put in place and the song ended, its last line suspended and unuttered.[103] Order had been imposed.

It was a strikingly poignant moment for a rock show, one that—at least for me—prompted a strong affective response. What is notable about the emotion prompted by the El Vez performance, however, is that it did *not* rely on empathy as a methodology, as discussed in Chapter 2. When the Elvettes lifted their placards of protest, or when the stage hands completed the wall, audience members were not asked to identify with them, thereby gaining understanding. Rather, these moments were choreographed by Lopez to prompt an affective response through the interaction of the various performance elements: the stage banter, the rewritten lyrics, the music, the costumes and props. Instead of being asked to "feel with" the performers onstage, audience members instead were asked to confront their own emotions and beliefs as they decoded these performative moments. For me, these moments were ultimately fortifying; I saw my beliefs validated through the performance and was made to feel a part of a powerful, inclusive collective that would protest and resist injustice.

This affective response, I submit, offers yet another means around which world-building happens. El Vez's performances offer the possibility of interrogating identity by connecting to Otherness, not through empathy, but through an embodied practice. The physical process of listening—in which sound, with its own affective pull and sonic vibrations—contributes to this ability to confront one's self in Otherness. Kun notes that:

> music makes you immediately conscious of your identity precisely because something outside of you is entering your body [...] All musical listening is a form of confrontation, of encounter, of the meeting of worlds and meanings, when identity is made self-aware and is, therefore, menaced through its own interrogation.[104]

Moreover, typical song structure, which features unique verses and repeating chorus sections, allows for connection in difference. The repetition of the chorus provides a touchstone for the audience, a means for the individual to join in and dance and sing along as a member of a larger whole.

Lopez designs his shows to engender social space. Disidentificatory performances, like those of El Vez, have what Muñoz dubs a "worldmaking power"[105]; they allow for social configurations that serve as "the blueprint for minoritarian counterpublic spheres."[106] Similarly, sound can signal belonging; Lopez centers El Vez to create a counterpublic that promotes what Casillas refers to as a feeling of participatory parity. Or, conversely, it can signal a shared unbelonging, in which "feelings of existing outside the space of mainstream belonging could be embraced."[107] And listening to music—especially live music—creates space, what Kun dubs "audiotopias":

> music functions like a possible utopia for the listener, that music is experienced not only as sound that goes into our ears and vibrates through our bones but as a space that we can enter into, encounter, move around in, inhabit, be safe in, learn from.[108]

With a holiday performance centered around a Chicano trickster speaking accented Spanish and voicing anti-Trump political critiques, audience members were invited to revel in festive irreverence. The self-selecting site of a rowdy rock club temporarily became a social space of dissent. Indeed, this quite literally was an audiotopia "whose music is the space of racial difference, where racial difference is performed against the grain of a suffocating nationalism."[109] Within the Casbah, racial difference was celebrated and Trumpism rejected as the audience clapped and screamed for El Vez. While in other instances Lopez-as-El-Vez constructs audiotopias that offer a way in for those who might normally align against the progressive politics he espouses, this was not the goal of the Casbah performance. This performance did not offer outreach to political conservatives. Yet in my experience, it did more than simply preach to the converted. It affirmed progressive beliefs, ensured us of the justness of our ideals, and reminded us to fight the power. Trump's vision of white supremacist heteronormative patriarchy was roundly rejected and mocked. Not only could audience members spurn Trumpism, but they could also laugh at its big, ugly, orange face.[110]

This feeling was physicalized in the encore. After only a few moments of audience adoration, the Memphis Mariachis launched into a loud, blazing-fast punk version of "Feliz Navidad." Aided by the Lovely Elvettes, El Vez, now dressed in tight red patent-leather, tore apart the wall. They hurled the boxes into the audience, and an amazing bit of pogoing broke out. The dance is significant; it kinesthetically creates connection and community, hearkening back to the early days of punk and honoring the contributions of Chicanx artists to its development. Less violent than the hardcore, male-gendered slam dancing that would come to take over the mosh pit as L.A. punk morphed from a poor, queer, BIPOC art form to that of white middle-class males, the pogo, suggests Marlen Ríos-Hernández, was an embodiment of exuberance and fun that not only dissolved distances between performer and audience but also was "quite equitable across gender expressions and sexualities." She notes:

> Broader than a dance, the pogo signified a particular relationship between sound, community and a sense of belonging—a *home* for the outsider and their band of misfit friends, a home that created space for queer Chicanx/POC youth.[111]

This was what I felt in the closing moments of the Casbah show. As boxes flew in the air, people danced and jostled and laughed and howled. The sounds of punk rock, always about disruption, always about pleasure in difference, fueled the scene. It also highlighted Ramos' feeling of unbelonging, where the audience was able to physicalize "gestures of refusal" of Trumpian politics, practicing instead "disobedient listening [...] a deeply ethical act that can unveil social relations obscured by nationhood and limited racial paradigms."[112] The social space of the 2016 Merry MeX-Mas, created through world-building, ended in a frenzied dance pit, celebrating resistance to the

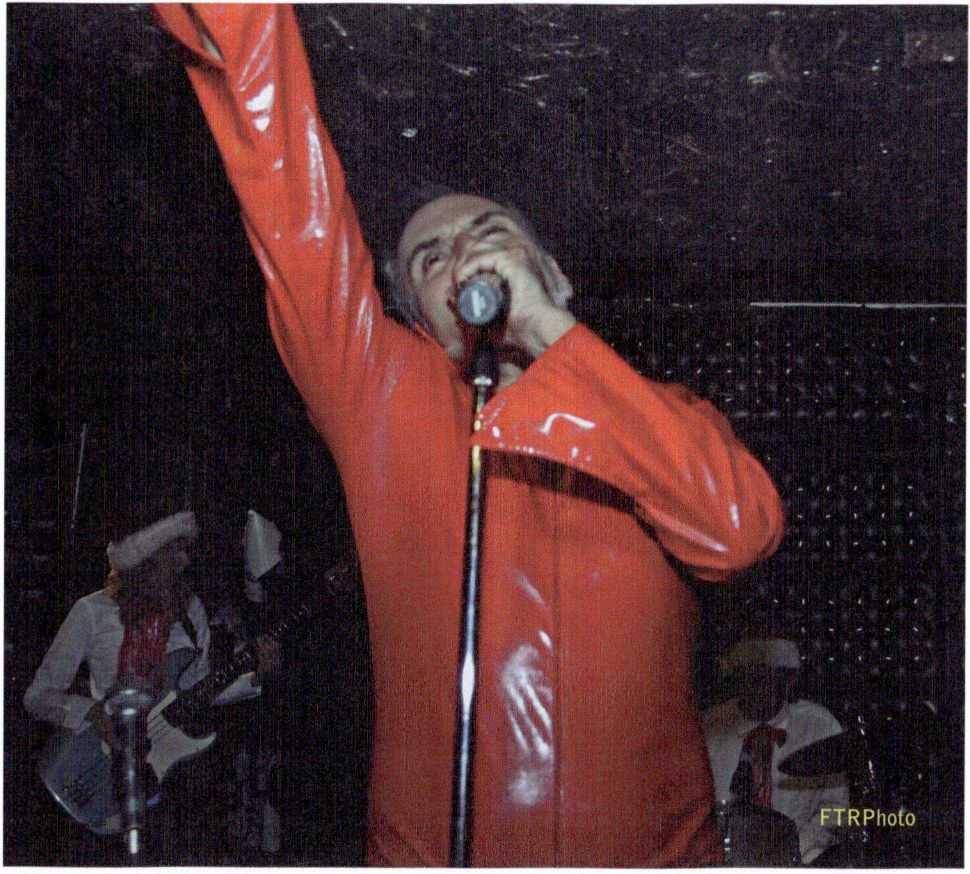

FIGURES 4.4a–b: (a) El Vez sings the encore with Mariachis Kim Serene and Slim Evans in the background; (b) Elvette Lisa María (Turzo) looks down at a box in disbelief, 2016. Photograph by FTR Photo.

dark political time ahead, sustaining the marginalized and their allies, and creating, momentarily, a chorus of dissent anchored by El Vez (Figure 4.4 a and b).

Music Just Happens To Be the Paint I Use: Feeling Different Ways of Being

Lopez crafts an incredible event that creates a dynamic social space through performance. Theatricalized rock performance allows Lopez to walk a distinct path of engagement, curating for his audience an imaginative emotional and physical

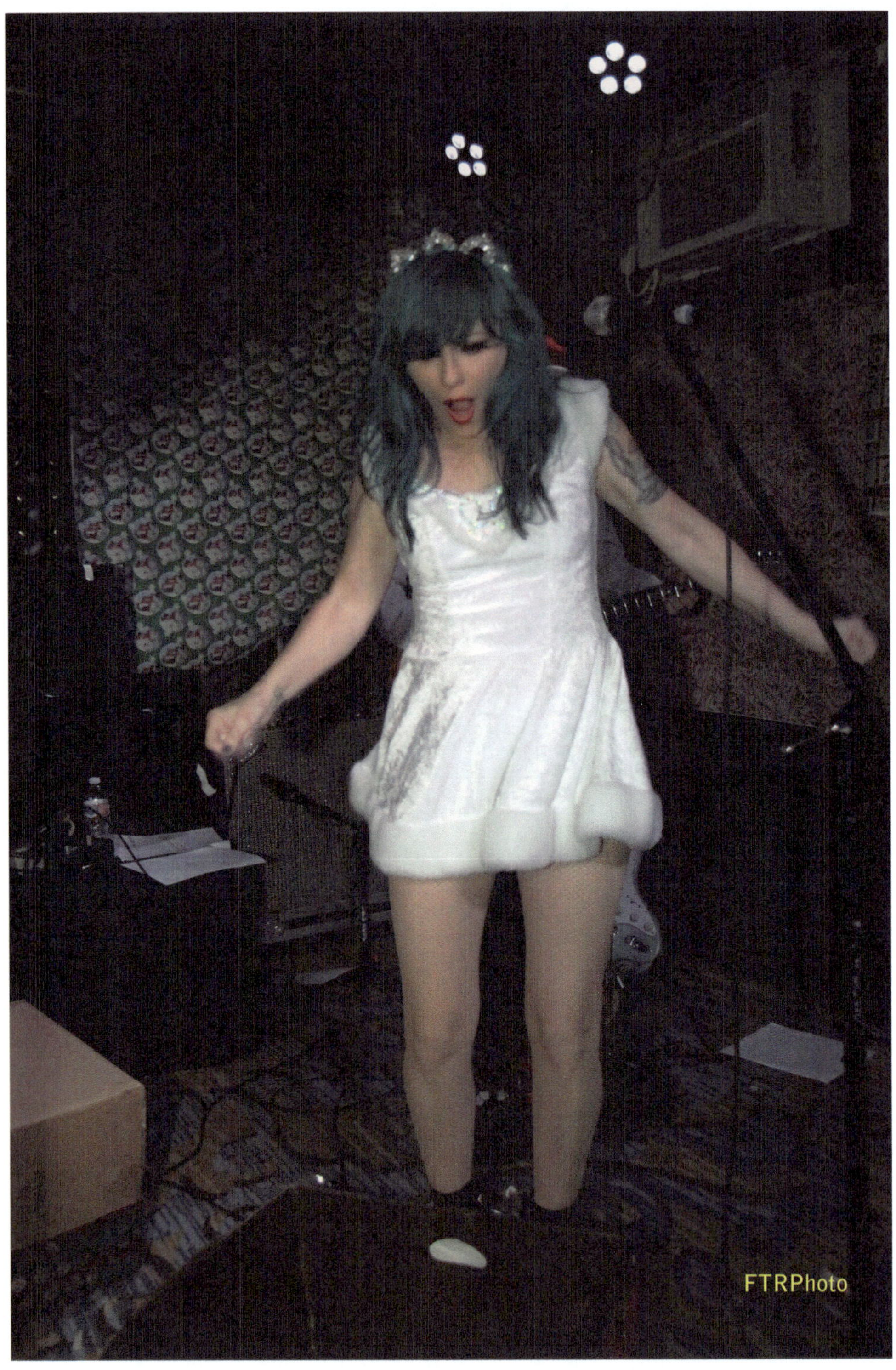

FIGURE 4.4a–b: (*Continued*)

experience. Though he uses theatrical elements such as persona, costuming, props, and merchandise to augment his shows, I believe the heavy lifting of his world-building comes through sound and music. Music was the starting point of his artistic practice, and therefore, "It does hold a special place." Lopez continues, "Music was the vernacular and the way I could express [my ideas], and then I took on other expressions—of dance clothes, the words, the commentary. But it started as music and that's what I do."[113]

Sound and music offer Lopez the ability to voice subversion and resist essentializing discourses in several key ways. His performed accent points to the way that we believe we can hear race, and the way that cultural, social, and economic capital is attached to and potentially determined by accent and dialect. His use of the accent is tactical, more clearly racializing his body to offer critiques of contemporary manifestations of racism, and it amplifies an inclusive perspective. As an Elvis impersonator, Lopez roots his art in popular culture and popular music, using its terrain to forge connections as he advocates for minoritized people. Popular music offers a worthy canvas for his art; it is a means through which we negotiate our individual, group, and national identities. Because Lopez uses already popular songs as his source material, even his new songs are old, carrying their original meanings alongside their El Vez revisions. He uses this familiar terrain to create powerful moments of emotional affect and physical response that engender audiotopias, shared "sonic and social spaces where disparate identity-formations, cultures *and* geographies historically kept and mapped separately are allowed to interact with each other."[114] As such, world-building in El Vez performances allows audiences to *feel* a different way of being, to exist within a rejuvenating social space of music and revelry.

NOTES

1. El Vez, Merry MeX-Mas, The Casbah, San Diego, December 23, 2016. All quotes from the show in this chapter are taken from the author's field notes.
2. Josh Kun, *Audiotopia: Music, Race, and America* (Berkeley, CA: University of California Press, 2005), 2–3.
3. As I fact-checked the references and musical samples in this chapter with Lopez, he commented on what a "deliciously dark" show he put together that year. Robert Lopez, personal interview, March 4, 2024.
4. Nina Sun Eidsheim, *The Race of Sound: Listening, Timbre and Vocality in African American Music* (Durham, NC: Duke University Press, 2019), 1.
5. Jennifer Lynn Stoever, *The Sonic Color Line: Race and the Cultural Politics of Listening* (New York: New York University Press, 2016), 10.
6. Stoever, *Sonic Color Line*, 13.
7. Eidsheim, *Race of Sound*, 3.

8. Eidsheim, *Race of Sound*, 10.
9. Eidsheim, *Race of Sound*, 5.
10. Eidsheim, *Race of Sound*, 9.
11. Eidsheim, *Race of Sound*, 11.
12. Eidsheim, *Race of Sound*, 23.
13. Eidsheim, *Race of Sound*, 21.
14. Eidsheim, *Race of Sound*, 29.
15. Stoever, *Sonic Color Line*, 13.
16. Stoever, *Sonic Color Line*, 27–28.
17. Nina Sun Eidsheim, "Voice as a Technology of Selfhood: Towards an Analysis of Racialized Timbre and Vocal Performance" (PhD Diss., University of California, San Diego, CA, 2008), 1, emphasis added.
18. Eidsheim, "Voice as a Technology of Selfhood," 115.
19. Eidsheim, "Voice as a Technology of Selfhood," 164.
20. Stoever, *Sonic Color Line*, 11.
21. Carpenter, *Coloring Whiteness*, 195, original emphasis.
22. Carpenter, *Coloring Whiteness*, 200.
23. Carla Della Gotta, *Latinx Shakespeares*, 22.
24. Della Gotta, *Latinx Shakespeares*, 1.
25. Della Gotta, *Latinx Shakespeares*, 61.
26. Della Gotta, *Latinx Shakespeares*, 63–64.
27. Angela C. Pao, "False Accents: Embodied Dialects and the Characterization of Ethnicity and Nationality," *Theatre Topics* 14, no. 1 (March 2004): 355.
28. Pao, "False Accents," 359.
29. The Lovely Elvettes also adopt a heavy accent when engaging in stage banter with El Vez.
30. Robert Lopez, interview with author, July 16, 2023.
31. Lopez, interview with author, July 16, 2023.
32. Lopez, interview with author, July 16, 2023.
33. Victoria Sturtevant, "Spitfire: Lupe Vélez and the Ambivalent Pleasures of Ethnic Masquerade," *The Velvet Light Trap* 55 (Spring 2005): 21.
34. Danny Hoch, *Jails, Hospitals & Hip Hop*, Loisaida Arts, 1998. Clip available at https://www.dailymotion.com/video/xq821, accessed July 5, 2023.
35. It also diminishes the labor of the actor, as if all it takes to perform well is a "little accent."
36. Peter Bogdanovich, "Seinfeld Battles Actor Danny Hoch…," *Observer*, March 9, 1998, accessed July 5, 2023, https://observer.com/1998/03/seinfeld-battles-actor-danny-hoch-party-of-jive-ally-mcshutupalready-a-decadent-sag-show/.
37. A particularly funny way that Lopez has used accent to subvert cultural hierarchies was in his performance of *Too Caliente to Handle* at Teatro ZinZanni in 2011. Performing alongside Christine Deaver as Tres y Cinco de Mayo, Deaver and Lopez at one point chided

another character by saying, "You're in America now. Speak Spanish!" Lopez, Robert, Christine Deaver, Ricardo Salinas, and Norm Langill, *Too Caliente To Handle*, Teatro ZinZanni, San Francisco, June 16, 2011.

38. Dolores Inés Casillas, *Sounds of Belonging: U.S. Spanish-language Radio and Public Advocacy* (New York: New York University Press, 2014), 6–7.
39. Casillas, *Sounds of Belonging*, 5–6.
40. Lopez, interview with author, July 16, 2023.
41. Frith carefully parses out the different ways that musicians, producers, and audiences (critical and not) value music. Musicians value creativity, collaboration, and professionalism (appropriate to the kind of music being made). Producers value connecting the music to its intended audience. Audiences bring social and psychological needs to their listening.
42. Simon Frith, *Performing Rites: On the Value of Popular Music* (Oxford: Oxford University Press, 1996), 72.
43. Frith, *Performing Rites*, 72.
44. Simon Frith, "Music and Identity," *Taking Popular Music Seriously: Selected Essays* (Hampshire: Ashgate Publishing Limited, 2007), 294, original emphasis.
45. Frith, "Music and Identity," 295.
46. Frith, *Performing Rites*, 72.
47. Kun, *Audiotopia,* 11.
48. Kun, *Audiotopia*, 19.
49. Kun, *Audiotopia*, 20, original emphasis.
50. Simon Frith, "Pop Music," in *Taking Popular Music Seriously: Selected Essays* (Hampshire: Ashgate Publishing Limited, 2007), 178. Here, he offers a slight differentiation between pop music as a genre versus other forms of popular music; yet the way he discusses pop music is useful to understanding Lopez's artistic approach, which blends together different popular forms (including, but not limited to, pop music).
51. Lopez, liner notes to *God Save the King*.
52. Linda Hutcheon, *A Theory of Parody: The Teachings of Twentieth Century Art Forms* (Urbana and Chicago, IL: University of Illinois Press, 2003), xii. It is important to note that Hutcheon eschews the idea that parody is meant to ridicule (though it certainly can). She stresses that parody is, first and foremost, a trans-contextualizing.
53. Hutcheon, *A Theory of Parody*, 8.
54. Hip hop was among the first musical genres to make extensive use of sampling; the art form was popularized by DJs Kool Herc, Grandmaster Flash, and Afrika Bambaataa.
55. Lawrence Lessig, *Remix: Making Art and Commerce Thrive in the Hybrid Economy* (New York: The Penguin Press, 2008), 74–75.
56. Lessig, *Remix*, 85.
57. Frith, "Pop Music," 180.
58. Marvin Carlson, *The Haunted Stage: The Theatre as Memory Machine* (Ann Arbor, MI: University of Michigan Press, 2001), 7.

59. Lopez, interview with author, July 16, 2023. I remarked that this has happened (and continues to happen) to me. Even after 20+ years of thinking about El Vez, I am still uncovering layers to his musical references.
60. Frith, "Pop Music," 180.
61. Lopez, liner notes to *God Save the King*.
62. Franco Fabbri, "A Theory of Musical Genres: Two Applications," in *Popular Music Perspectives*, edited by David Horn and Philip Tagg (Göteborg and Exeter: International Association for the Study of Popular Music, 1981), 52.
63. Frith, *Performing Rites*, 76.
64. Fabian Holt, *Genre in Popular Music* (Chicago, IL: University of Chicago Press, 2007), 2.
65. David Brackett, "Questions of Genre in Black Popular Music," *Black Music Research Journal* 25, no. 1/2 (Spring/Fall 2005): 75.
66. David Brackett, *Categorizing Sound: Genre and Twentieth-Century Popular Music* (Oakland, CA: University of California Press, 2016), 26.
67. Brackett, *Categorizing Sound*, 31.
68. Daphne Brooks and Roshanak Kheshti, "The Social Space of Sound," *Theatre Survey* 52, no. 2 (2011): 333.
69. As detailed in the introduction, El Vez songs include the melodies of several songs, brief "samples" of a few measures of other songs performed live by the Memphis Mariachis, as well as lyrical allusions to several more. I will describe several of these moments later in the chapter.
70. El Vez, "En El Barrio," *How Great Thou Art: The Greatest Hits of El Vez*, Sympathy for the Record Industry, 1994.
71. This of course mimics the heightened melodrama of the Elvis original, "In the Ghetto," which lays out a similar fate for its subject—who "buys a gun, steals a car / Tries to run but he don't get far" and winds up dead in the street. Elvis Presley, "In the Ghetto," RCA Victor, 1969.
72. Lopez, interview with author, July 16, 2023.
73. Lopez, interview with author, July 16, 2023.
74. Lopez, interview with author, July 16, 2023.
75. Iván Alejandro Ramos, "Sonic Negations: Sound, Affect, and Unbelonging Between Mexico and the United States" (PhD diss., University of California, Berkeley, CA, 2015), 2.
76. Ramos, "Sonic Negotiations," 15.
77. Ramos, "Sonic Negotiations," 2.
78. Ramos, "Sonic Negotiations," 3. It could be argued that Lopez, as a gay Chicano punk rocker, seeks through his musical practice to inhabit such unbelonging as Ramos discusses. For the purposes of this chapter, however, I am more interested in interrogating how he uses non-culturally translatable music as part of his sonic dramaturgy, to create meaning for the audience.
79. Ramos, "Sonic Negotiations," 5.

80. Habell-Pallán, *Loca Motion*, 184.
81. Lopez, email to author, April 25, 2019.
82. Lopez, email to author, April 25, 2019.
83. Lopez, email to author, April 25, 2019.
84. Muñoz, *Disidentifications*, xi.
85. Lopez, email to author, April 25, 2019.
86. Lopez, email to author, April 25, 2019.
87. Lopez, email to author, April 25, 2019.
88. He listed other things to cry for, though I was not fast enough to record them in my notes. They stuck to a common theme—equality, America, civil liberties, etc.
89. Lopez notes that an additional joke is that the Elvettes were actually pleading with him to stop his melodica playing because it's so bad. Lopez, email to author, April 25, 2019.
90. Lopez, interview with author, March 4, 2024.
91. Lopez, email to author, April 25, 2019.
92. Kun, *Audtiopia*, 3.
93. The video is available at https://www.youtube.com/watch?v=BG-_ZDrypec, accessed July 23, 2023.
94. Lopez, email to author, April 25, 2019.
95. Lopez, email to author, April 25, 2019.
96. This song also buttons back to David Bowie's "Moonage Daydream," which was performed by Pat Beers in full Ziggy Stardust attire to cover a costume change. The overall effect of this cameo appearance was a burst of hope, as if David Bowie had briefly been brought back to life. Lopez notes that another funny part of that song was that he melded in The Eagles' "Hotel California," as part of the guitar solo. Lopez, interview with author, March 4, 2024.
97. Lopez, email to author, April 25, 2019.
98. As a folk song of indeterminate origins, there are many different versions of the lyrics. Most suggest that the woman is a prostitute who has died of a venereal disease, and that the narrator—a drinker, a gambler, and a frequenter of her services—will soon die as well.
99. Lopez, email to author, November 16, 2016.
100. Lopez, email to author, October 4, 2017.
101. The turnover in this list of names is striking. Only a handful lasted throughout the Trump Administration, and a few, such as Bob Corker and Mitt Romney, have spoken out against him.
102. His stage hands were actually Pat and Lety Beers, musicians with whom Lopez often collaborates. As noted in a previous footnote, Pat Beers had already made an appearance earlier in the performance, following "Rebel Rebel," to cover the costume change from camo jumpsuit into the police uniform.
103. The stanza normally ends with the line "Without any fear."
104. Kun, *Audiotopia*, 13.

105. Muñoz, *Disidentifications*, ix.
106. Muñoz, *Disidentifications*, 5.
107. Ramos, *Unbelonging: Inauthentic Sounds in Mexican and Latinx Aesthetics* (New York: New York University Press, 2023), 5.
108. Kun, *Audiotopia*, 2. Muñoz also goes on to talk about utopias in ways that align with El Vez's project in his seminal *Cruising Utopia.*
109. Kun, 25–26.
110. Elsewhere I have written about Lopez's ability to invite in diverse crowds through his use of the popular to construct audiotopic "identificatory contact zones" (Kun, *Audiotopia*, 23). For instance, an article published in *Popular Entertainment Studies* (October 2017) suggests his EV4P performance at San Diego's Taco Fest offered the possibility for politically opposed parties to come together through his performance. The audiotopia of the 2016 Merry MeX-Mas show functioned differently, as I detail here and in my article published in *Theatre Annual* (2020).
111. Marlen Ríos-Hernández, "'Don't Be Afraid to Pogo!': Chicana Hollywood Punks Negotiate 'h/Home' after Hardcore Takes L.A.," *Sounding Out!*, September 25, 2017, original emphasis, accessed October 30, 2018, https://soundstudiesblog.com/2017/09/25/dont-be-afraid-to-pogo-chicana-hollywood-punks-negotiate-hhome-after-hardcore-takes-l-a/.
112. Ramos, *Unbelonging*, 4, 21.
113. Lopez, interview with author, July 16, 2023.
114. Kun, *Audiotopia*, 23, original emphasis.

The Future Is Unwritten, But I've Made Notes Already: A Conclusion, By Way of COVID and What Comes After

Forging an unlikely career as a Mexican Elvis was never going to be easy, but things got significantly harder in March 2020, with the arrival of the SARS-CoV-2 novel coronavirus, better known as COVID-19, in the United States. As the global pandemic quickly ramped up from dull background anxiety to nationwide lockdown, Lopez and I exchanged texts, swapping stories of event postponements that had begun to trickle in—for him, a performance at an academic conference that was to have kicked off his 2020 El Vez for Prez tour, and for me, in-person classes and an immersive version of *The Crucible* that was to have closed ASU's 2019–20 theatre season. He shared that he "did an impromptu show last night with Lenny Kaye of the Patti Smith band," adding, "Their show was the first of the cancellations."[1] In re-reading the thread of our exchange, I am struck by the cautious, yet escalating language we used around the lockdown: our events were *postponed*, my classes would be *modified* to be online for two weeks, but Patti Smith's tour was *cancelled*. Lopez described how theatre friends, musicians, and hospitality workers showed up at his performance, "all getting the word that they can't work for the next month." Indeed, the texts document our real-time processing of the grimness of the global pandemic and the economic pressure it would place on artists, performers, and service industry workers. What we perhaps suspected, but could not know at the time, was that this tiny "unannounced show in a basement club" would be his final live performance for almost 18 months. Reflecting on the mood of the evening, he said, "It was like a Titanic party," as everyone realized the cold fate that lay ahead. Lopez played guitar and sang, and then live performance fell silent.

In this conclusion, I will consider how the pandemic made undeniably clear the precarity under which so many performers live. To go back to Lopez's metaphor, artists are asked to provide culture as they entertain, and yet when disaster strikes, they are left to go down with the ship, nary a lifeboat in sight. I will first document the economic structure of the music industry, and discuss how it reflects the larger economy under neoliberalism. I will then turn to the way Lopez managed to stay afloat as the contingent nature of performance gave way to crisis, and he—like so many other artists—faced a near-complete loss of income. Like all of us, he was forced to pivot to virtual platforms, which for an independent artist is not sufficiently lucrative. In order to make ends meet, he started delivering pizza. I will then dissect his return to the stage in August 2021, in a show entitled *Stand & Deliver, Pizza!*, which, using his own experience as an extended punchline, allowed him to reflect on the inequities revealed by the pandemic as well as to imagine the art—and action—that may emerge from it, once again reminding his audience of the need to remake social structures, and to imagine and build the kinds of worlds that we want to live in.

I Got My Green Card, I Want My Gold Card: The Economics of the Music Industry

Alan B. Krueger, former Princeton economist, Assistant Secretary of the Treasury, and economic advisor to Presidents Clinton and Obama documents the peculiarities of the music industry in his book *Rockonomics: A Backstage Tour of What the Music Industry Can Teach Us About Economics and Life*. Music is an ever-present feature in our lives; USAmericans listen to an average of 3–4 hours of music daily. For as ubiquitous as music is, notes Krueger, "it is a surprisingly *small* industry, one that would go nearly unnoticed if music were not special in other respects"; indeed, it comprises less than 0.1% of the GDP and less than 0.2% of the workforce.[2] Not only is music a small industry, but it is also what Krueger calls a "superstar" industry, in which a small number of players attract the most attention and earn the most wealth. In a superstar industry, popularity grows geometrically, not linearly. This, explains Krueger, is a growth pattern known as a power law: "The popularity of the top performer is a multiple of the second-most-popular performer, which in turn is a multiple of the third-most-popular performer, and so on."[3] Thus, top performers vastly out-earn the majority of the field. For example, the top 5% of performers take in 85% of all concert revenues, and the share of concert revenues taken home by the top 1% has more than doubled from 26% in 1982 to 60% today, taking in more revenue than the bottom 99% combined.[4] In this, the music industry mirrors, in a slightly more extreme form, the distribution of wealth under neoliberalism; states Krueger, "the entire economy has veered toward a superstar, winner-take-all affair."[5]

Though there is a certain mythology that surrounds musicians, most working artists live decidedly unglamorous lives. Nearly half of the approximately 214,000 workers who identified as musicians in 2016 were self-employed, and the median income for this group was a startlingly low $20,000.[6] Krueger reports that musicians are, on the whole, "older and better educated than the workforce overall," with an average age of 45 years old. Only 4% did not finish high school, and 50% of musicians are graduates of four-year colleges.[7] Given these demographics, Krueger contemplates what motivates musicians to continue to dedicate their lives to their profession. As the data reflect, the majority of working artists are not naïve youngsters who dream of fame and riches. Rather, as mature adult professionals, musicians are not only clear-eyed about the economic precarity inherent to the industry but also committed to their art. Indeed, this might factor into the low wages most musicians earn. States Krueger:

> From an economic standpoint, the fact that there is an endless supply of people who are willing to create and perform music virtually for free because of its intrinsic appeal puts downward pressure on incomes in the industry for all but the superstars.[8]

That musicians are willing to trade financial stability for a creative life centered around performance may in fact contribute to the low earnings they can expect to make.[9]

When put into the context of the industry, Lopez has achieved a level of success far beyond what most musicians can expect. For a punk rock kid who first got onstage at age 16, he has maintained a remarkably accomplished and stable career. As he quips during Mr. Bob's Unhappy Hour, "I am a part of American culture—whether you like it or not."[10] Though his income has of course fluctuated, Lopez has maintained extended periods of high earnings.

The global pandemic threatened the livelihood of musicians across the industry, due to the surprising source of their income. As Krueger observes, "There is a fundamental disconnect at the heart of the music business today: the way artists earn most of their money differs dramatically from the way most fans enjoy the music artists create."[11] Though consumers primarily listen to music recordings—on the radio, on our devices, as the soundtrack to movies, television shows, and commercials, and in the ambient background of our daily lives—musicians, from the most humble singer-songwriter up to the top earners in the field, make the bulk of their money through live performance. Indeed, concert revenue will account for at least 80% of a musician's earnings.[12] For Lopez, this is especially true. While he has recorded several albums and singles, several of which are available to stream on different services, his music is quite niche and not in heavy rotation. His tours cater to old fans while also attracting new audiences, who often show up simply for the novelty of seeing a Mexican Elvis.[13] Moreover, as noted throughout this book, his shows are much more than just music. More theatrical than most rock performances, they combine over-the-top spectacle, outrageous costumes, musical mash-ups, and subversive content delivered through the playful persona of El Vez. All live performances seek to offer their audiences a unique, powerful experience. Yet, I have argued that it is truly through live performance that Lopez's art of El Vez comes alive, making it all the more important in his earnings breakdown. When live performance abruptly stopped in 2020, Lopez's income stream was all but completely cut off.

According to research compiled by the arts advocacy organization Americans for the Arts, the arts sector was among the most severely impacted by the pandemic, and it is recovering more slowly than other industries. 95% of artists lost creative income due to the pandemic, and 63% of artists experienced unemployment. 99% of producing and presenting organizations cancelled events.[14] Though the arts sector may be small in terms of the national economy, such statistics point to hundreds of thousands of lives disrupted. Like other artists, Lopez was able to pick up some virtual events—he was a featured guest in the Dreamocracy in America Zoom Series, he joined Puddles Pity Party[15] in a livestream event (and angered some Puddles fans by singing about immigration: said AnitaK, "Not happy with thie Elviz guy [...] Do not expect or want politics interjected into entertainment [...] really disappointing" and AngstotheClown added, "TRY DOING THE LEGAL WAY LIKE MILLIONS OF OTHERS." Puddles himself called it "work well done."[16]), and he did some short Zoom interviews and videos in the early days of the pandemic, when those were still fun. Yet, these were few and far between, and though they may have helped to satisfy an artistic itch, they did not bring in much income. Government relief checks and small grants helped to tide many artists over, but Lopez was not alone in having to pick up extra work in lieu of performance. Indeed, Lopez was better off than many artists because he had purchased a spacious home in Seattle, Washington, when his income was both high and steady. This investment proved to be fortuitous throughout the pandemic. Through Airbnb, he was able to rent out the bottom floor of his house, which included his Elvis bedroom and his downstairs living room, which was filled with El Vez memorabilia.[17] He hosted several long-term rentals, which ensured that he was able to meet his mortgage payment. It is striking to note that many musicians and artists—those who work in the original gig economy—relied on technology-assisted gig economies, such as Airbnb, to get by.[18] Even this, however, only provided the bare minimum. In April 2020, when it became clear that there would be no swift reopening, Lopez took a job at Zeek's pizza.

Stand & Deliver, Pizza!: *El Vez's First Post-COVID Show*

That a performer who has commanded the attention of audiences throughout the world would wind up delivering pizza during a pandemic reveals the precarity of an artist's life under neoliberalism. That Lopez would make his pizza delivery the punchline to one of his first performances back onstage says something about his approach to art and art-making (Figure 5.1). Rather than treating his unexpected change of fortune as a personal failure or embarrassment (as the logic of neoliberalism encourages), Lopez instead made it something to be acknowledged, debated, and addressed as we gradually emerged out of the pandemic. That is, he used this performance as a site of world-building, where we might recognize the injustice of our current social structures and imagine something different.

The show, performed at Seattle's Triple Door Theatre, was extremely ambitious. The Triple Door is a storied theatre in Seattle, and its unique history makes it particularly well suited to host El Vez. Built in the 1920s, it was a grand vaudeville venue that transitioned to film as tastes changed. By the 1960s, it had fallen from grace, so to speak, hosting XXX films and burlesque shows. It was renovated in the 1980s, and the ornate proscenium stage and ceiling fixtures remain intact.[19] This performance history seems to hit each of Lopez's values and inspiration: vaudeville, the gritty illicitness of porn, and the subversive community of burlesque. The lush red curtain was down as the audience entered, and the stage

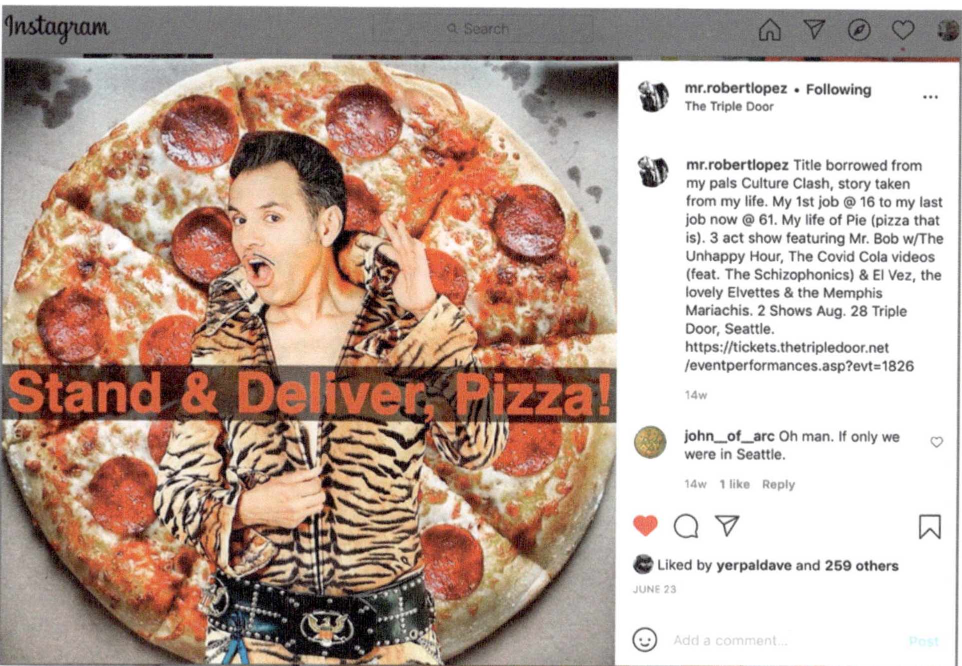

FIGURE C.1: Instagram post advertising *Stand & Deliver, Pizza!*, 2021. Courtesy of Robert Lopez's collection (also available on his Instagram).

was flanked by two giant pizzas placed on easels downstage left and right. *Stand & Deliver, Pizza!* threaded together three of Lopez's different projects: The Unhappy Hour with Mr. Bob, which served as the opener; Covid Cola, which functioned as an intermission; and El Vez, who headlined the show. Lopez interwove these different personae together in a single night's event, drawing together aspects of his own life to tap into political issues. Depression and mental health issues were one of the throughlines to the evening, and Lopez's multiple references to Adam Ant and David Bowie reinforced this.[20] Notes Lopez, "So me being Mr. Bob, it is an idea of schizophrenia, although they [Mr. Bob and El Vez] are both pieces of me, young and old [...] the negativity of the pandemic and working in pizza was Mr. Bob" while El Vez would face the pandemic with more positivity.[21] Each act also approached time differently: Mr. Bob reflected on the past, Covid Cola existed in the never-ending present of quarantine, and El Vez—ever the optimist—looked ahead to imagine what comes next.

Mr. Bob sings "New American standards delivered with world weary wit & warning"[22] (Figure 5.2). The Unhappy Hour features extended monologues that surround classic ballads such as "Happy Days are Here Again," "Rainy Days and Mondays," and "We Shall Overcome." Similar to the word play of El Vez, these lyrics are rewritten to (depressingly) comedic effect: "Unhappy Days are Here Again," "Rainy Days and Mondays, and Tuesdays, and Wednesdays, and Thursdays, and Fridays, and Saturdays, and Sundays Always Get Me Down," "We Are Overcome." The tempos are slightly slowed down, and the key at times adjusted to minor to create a melancholy mood. Conceived after his father's first stroke and his subsequent mental decline, and further complicated by the 2016 election and the rise of Trumpism, Lopez has characterized The Unhappy Hour as "the idea of becoming your parents [...] so there's the idea of arguing with him [his father], and wondering if I'm arguing with my future self."[23] The Unhappy Hour covers a dizzying amount of social issues: neoliberalist capitalism and the production of art, social media and its negative effects, healthcare and big pharma, gun violence, cannibalism and serial killings, and electoral politics. These issues are raised through deeply personal stories, including the recounting of Lopez's mother's morose drunken evenings, his father's hospitalization and decline into dementia, and his own struggles with depression and aging. Lopez also uses Mr. Bob to grapple with the trajectory of his own life, questioning what it is to make a living wearing gold lamé hotpants and acting as a "brown clown." Though he notes that El Vez is "a cross-cultural caped crusader for truth, justice, and the Mexican American way,"[24] the show pushes back against such heroics. Poignantly, he questions what impact he has had through his subversive art, when his own father voted for Donald Trump.

Opening *Stand & Deliver, Pizza!* with The Unhappy Hour allowed Lopez to use stories from his past to comment on the present via music and pizza. Backed

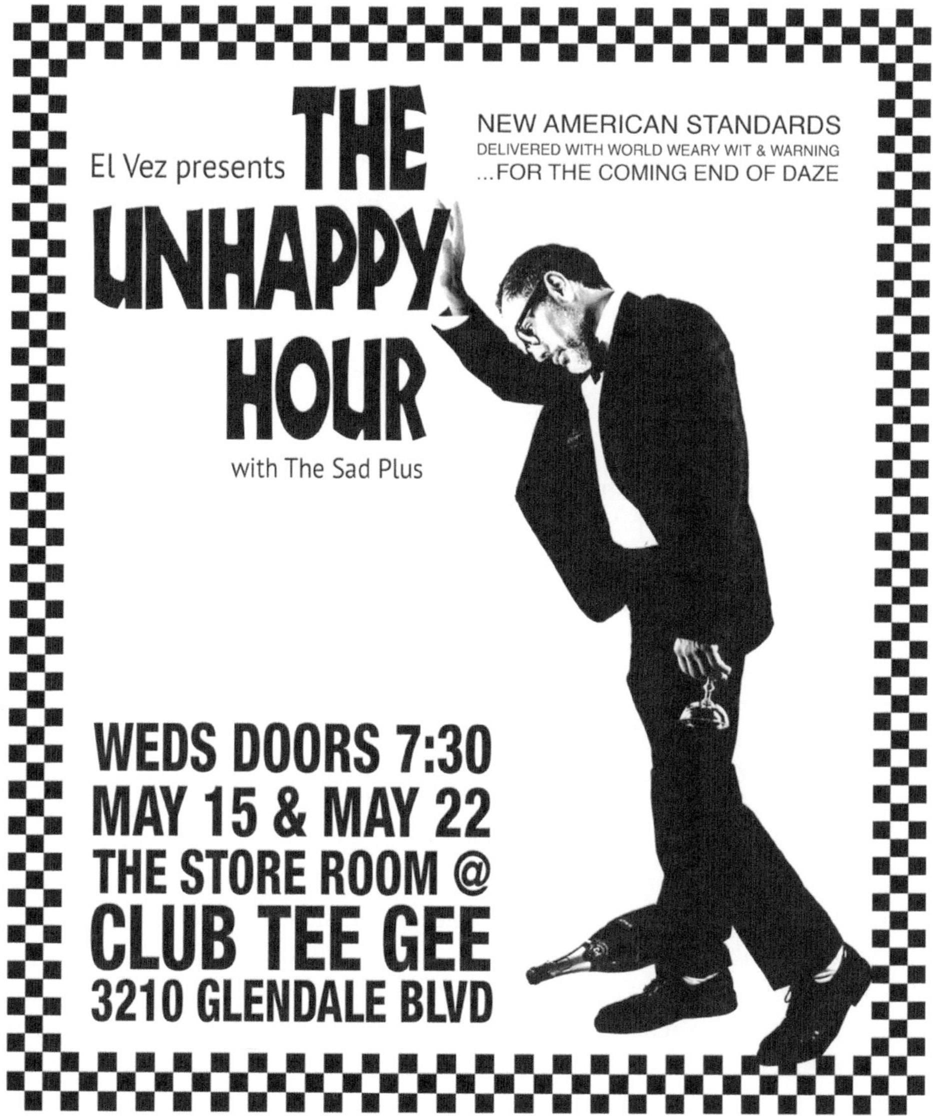

FIGURE C.2: Advertisement for a performance in Los Angeles of *The Unhappy Hour*, starring Mr. Bob, 2019. Photograph by Elliot Fisher. Courtesy of Robert Lopez's collection (also available on his Instagram).

by a pianist, and clad in a sharp blue suit and bow tie, he began by quipping that The Unhappy Hour was truncated because "El Vez is a slave driver and he has only given me twenty minutes." As discussed in Chapter 2, this funny bit of self-reference is another example of the way that Lopez separates artist from performance persona, suggesting that Mr. Bob is wholly separate from both El Vez and Robert Lopez. Yet at the same time, the monologues directly discuss his career as El Vez and the real incidents of his life, collapsing that distance. Because the monologues that surround the songs in The Unhappy Hour are so personal, the overall feeling of the performance is one of connection and intimacy. Interestingly, as Mr. Bob, Lopez primarily selects songs that predate his own entry into the music industry. He notes,

> And the music is from '71 to '78, which is my pre-punk days. So these songs are standards, but not like Gershwin standards. These are songs by artists like the Carpenters, or Gilbert O'Sullivan's "Alone Again," and are songs I consider standards of a later era.[25]

Foregrounding the fact that he had to take a pizza delivery job, Lopez-as-Mr.-Bob stated that, "We all got a pie to the face" with COVID. Referencing the tour that was postponed and then cancelled, he laments that he was supposed to run for President, but instead the pandemic "Took me back to square one," which was a "circle [...] a vicious circle of life," of pizza employment. It was his job when he was 16, and it was his job when he was 61. Lopez proceeded to mine his autobiography to capture through these stories the youthful feeling of possibility, sharing vignettes (all improbable but true) of living in GoGo's bassist Jane Wiedlin's old room at The Canterbury Apartments (L.A.'s punk rock mecca); learning that his manager at Straw Hat Pizza dabbled in drag; being propositioned by old men wanting to be his sugar daddy; and having a crush on a wholesome, straight, Midwestern boy. While recounting these stories, he described a rather run-down Hollywood of the late 1970s but romanticized through the eyes of a young man excited to be making his way in the world. These juxtapositions—a harsh and inhospitable world put in contrast with the energy and optimism of youth—helped to draw a contrast with his observations of the current moment, in which he was not only doing the same work but also seeing the same sort of economic depression and political angst. "Everything old is old again,"[26] said Lopez-as-Mr.-Bob, "and I am an essential worker. But am I?" The question lingers—which is more essential, pizza or art?[27] This helped him to paint a picture, in the final Unhappy songs, of an ever more dismal present, where that wide-eyed youthfulness is absent, both from himself and from his young co-workers. He sketched the current scene, describing being at work and watching huge trucks with multiple Trump bumper stickers drive by, while heat waves rock the town and protests and fires and COVID run rampant. He then added that his young co-workers each seem to work three jobs, trying to get ahead. "Where is the future?" he asked. As Mr. Bob, Lopez was able to dig into the human penchant for nostalgia that makes visible the way we idealize the past, but he did so in order to call attention to a present that is untenable and a future unimaginable.

As an intermission, Lopez shared videos from his quarantine project, Covid Cola. During the fall of 2020, Lopez's friends and artistic collaborators Lety and Pat Beers joined him at his home for a two-week residency, where they undertook "The Quarantine Songwriting Challenge." As Lopez, known in Covid Cola as Cold Pop, explains in the video intro, "We were holed up in Seattle for two weeks, and we wrote a song every day when I got home from delivering pizza. And we challenge you!"[28] The trio collectively penned short, fun pop tunes (hence the name), then donned outrageous costumes pulled from the El Vez closet and recorded short videos, which were edited by Pablo Prietto and shared, free of charge, on Instagram and YouTube (Figure 5.3). In originally describing the project to me, Lopez said they are "Funny, Pointy, Catchy, Make you laugh and say what a terrible world we live in and then want to dance!"[29] This description again speaks to the way music can impact its audience. Pop music especially is meant to be somewhat bounded by time: entertaining, of the moment, easily digestible, fun. As Lopez describes it, Covid Cola acknowledged the difficult reality of living through the pandemic, while also providing a momentary respite from it. Within the videos, Lopez again calls attention to his need to take a pizza delivery job; it is front and center in the introduction to each song. That the videos are framed with an acknowledgment of Lopez's necessary, yet unfulfilling labor alludes to another important function of pop music as a form of creative escape from the monotonous conditions of work. Marek Korczynski describes this as "multitonous musicking":

> Multitonous musicking involves a way of using music to be both with and against a monotonous social structure. It is a dialectical form of musical practice that is rooted in the concept of monotonous social structure. It is a form of musicking that allows the enactment of the social order within the monotonous while also allowing the expression of a spirit of resistance to that social order. In multitonous musicking people tend not to have a deep immersion of their senses in the music. Rather, music is used as a way of preventing the senses from being dominated by the monotonous.[30]

Though Korczynski's study focuses on listeners, documenting how factory workers use music during their shifts, I believe the concept doubly applies to the output of Covid Cola. The songs themselves are quite simple and fun, asking for minimal immersion or attention. And yet they also resist the monotonous, for audiences and artists alike. As Lopez describes them, they are short, catchy, and danceable, giving a viewer a brief break in the midst of the pandemic. Even more importantly, they allowed the artists to feed their own creativity. Crafting Covid Cola songs and videos provided a creative outlet within the endless present of quarantine, and

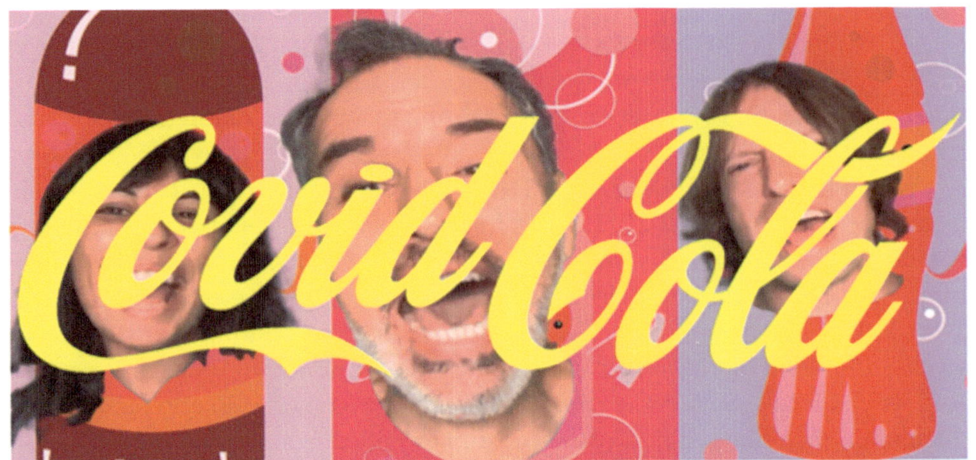

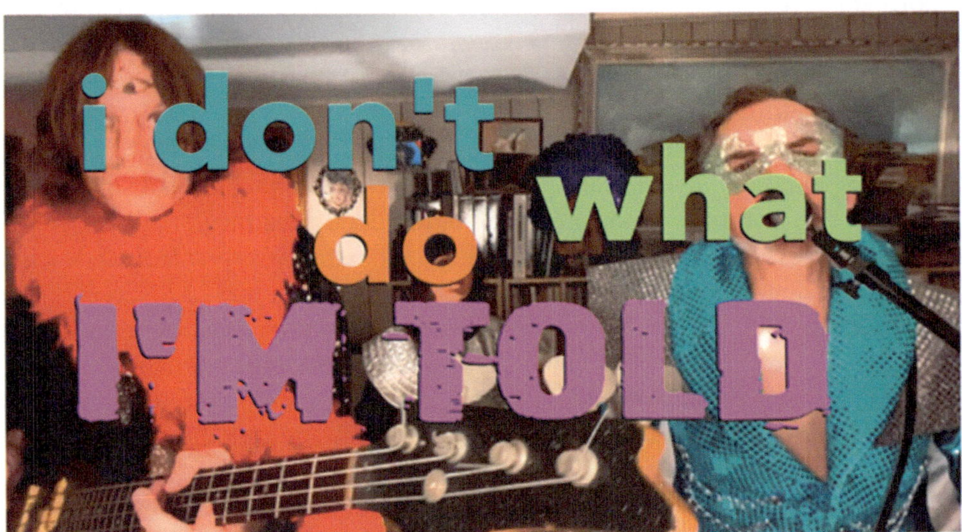

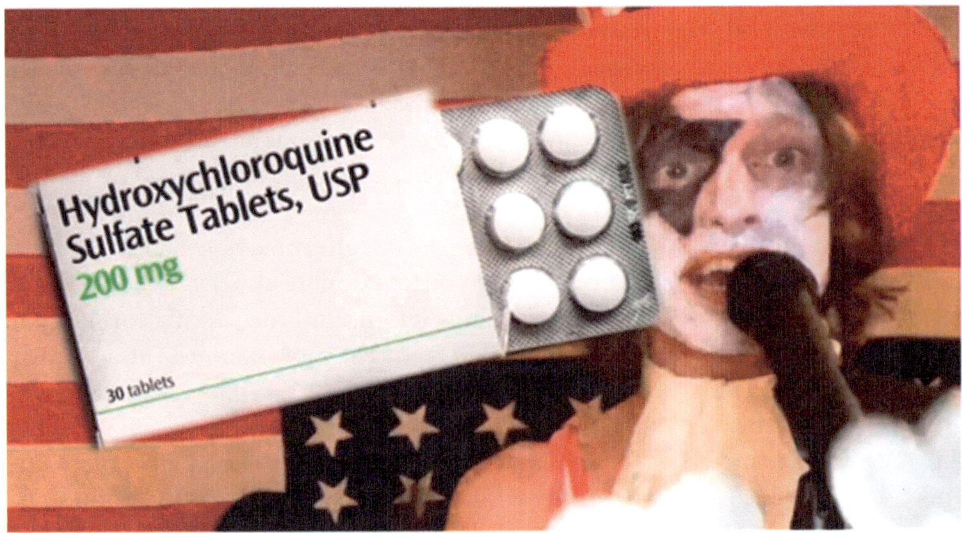

FIGURE C.3a–c: Covid Cola video stills, 2020. Filmed by Covid Cola and edited by Pablo Prietto. https://www.youtube.com/watch?v=y-p_0qb_Yr0 (accessed 31 July 2024 [link to bottom still video no longer available]).

a break from the economic pressures the pandemic amplified. Rather than serving as a money-making venture, the songwriting challenge balanced the numbing routine of a low-stakes service industry job with bursts of artistic play. And it was personally rewarding; said Lopez, "Makes me feel, the old man's still got it!"[31]

Covid Cola does offer thoughtful critiques through their music, even if the overall feel of the music is upbeat and cheery. Unsurprisingly, the songs themselves are highly topical, often addressing the politicization of COVID, the resistance to mask mandates, and the willingness to accept conspiracy theories and sham treatments over proven science. In fact, "Deep State," the final video aired at *Stand & Deliver, Pizza!,* was banned from YouTube for violating its cyberbullying policy, which prohibits "targeted harassment including, but not limited to, stalking, threats, bullying, and intimidation is not allowed on YouTube. Additionally, content that includes egregious insults based on personal attributes [...] is not allowed on YouTube."[32] Since the video lampoons conspiracy theorists and flat earthers, one wonders just who in the community YouTube is seeking to protect. Though unintended, the banning strikes me as a fitting conclusion to this initial portion of the project, capturing the spirit of creative critique the songs offered and marking the contentious social and political backdrop out of which it was born.

The main act of the night, of course, was El Vez, backed, as always, by the Lovely Elvettes and the Memphis Mariachis.[33] If Mr. Bob featured nostalgia-twinged insight gleaned through autobiography and vulnerability, and Covid Cola wrapped social critique in upbeat pop songs focused on the now, El Vez, the most established and long-standing act of the three, was also the most future-looking, suggesting through the lyrical rewrites, monologues, and theatricality that the pandemic has revealed social and economic issues that urgently need to be solved. El Vez was also the most developed act, both musically and theatrically, featuring an ambitious set list, multiple costume changes, props, and a bit of stage magic to emphasize the themes of the show. This performance exemplifies the meaning-making strategies and the world-building capacity present in Lopez's art. Using irony, inauthenticity, and theatricality, the performance revealed difficult truths about USAmerican society coming out of the pandemic. The costuming, which mirrored the costuming Elvis donned in his 1968 Comeback Special that relaunched his career after it had stagnated, reinforced the dramaturgical arc of the show. By wearing these iconic outfits, Lopez-as-El-Vez symbolically declared his own triumphant return to the stage and live performance. The costuming also asked the audience to imagine how a COVID comeback might reimagine society so that it works better for everyone. Finally, sound and music offered social and political critique, suggesting the work that lies ahead as we rebuild from the pandemic. As always, it created an audiotopia, forging a momentary community through which to envision a new way of being, a new world to create.

In keeping with the title, pizza was everywhere in the show, beginning with El Vez's entrance from the back of the house, clad in black patent leather, cheese pizza in hand. He handed out slices while singing, "I'm your pizza man, stop me as I'm passing by." The Lovely Elvettes entered the stage carrying Zeek's pizza boxes and wearing pizza tees and pizza box hats. The band, too, wore Zeek's T-shirts and hats (Figure 5.4). True to his blending of truth and fiction, nearly everything in fact came from Zeek's.[34] The Elvettes wore Lopez's actual work shirts (which he had made more aesthetically pleasing [for not only his own labor but also his own pleasure] by decorating the pizza with fun polka-dotted fabric), while the band wore work shirts and hats borrowed from Lopez's co-workers. Musically, the melody from "That's Amore" was threaded throughout several of the songs, an aural reference to the famous lyric, "When the moon hits your eye like a big pizza pie, that's amore." And, as one might guess, the word pizza was substituted into many lyrics as well, perhaps most notably in his version of "Tequila," where the audience joined in shouting out "Pizza!"

Though Lopez clearly poked fun at his employment throughout the entire evening—even featuring a pizza dough tosser (also from Zeek's) to cover a costume change and a surprise entrance from the house—he in fact used pizza to speak powerfully about labor issues and encourage political engagement. For instance, he referenced a highly visible lawsuit involving Zeek's Pizza. Seattle law requires restaurants that charge service and delivery charges to disclose on menus and receipts the percentage of the charge that is paid to employees. The logic of the law is that customers will assume this money goes to employees in lieu of tips; thus if an employer retains a portion of the charge, they must make this clear. Zeek's had violated this law, and workers had filed a class action suit against the company, seeking compensation for lost wages in the form of stolen tips.[35] Lopez-as-El-Vez joked that "Essential workers are keeping Seattle fed, so I hope you tipped well—so that Zeek's could take it away." This led to the title song, a cover of the Adam and the Ants hit "Stand and Deliver," in which he proclaimed:

I'm the essential worker
That you're too scared to mention
You spend your cash on the Door Dash
And apps in your collection
The devil took your very soul
But we, too, need protection
The way we work a life is took
So can you feel our tension
[…]

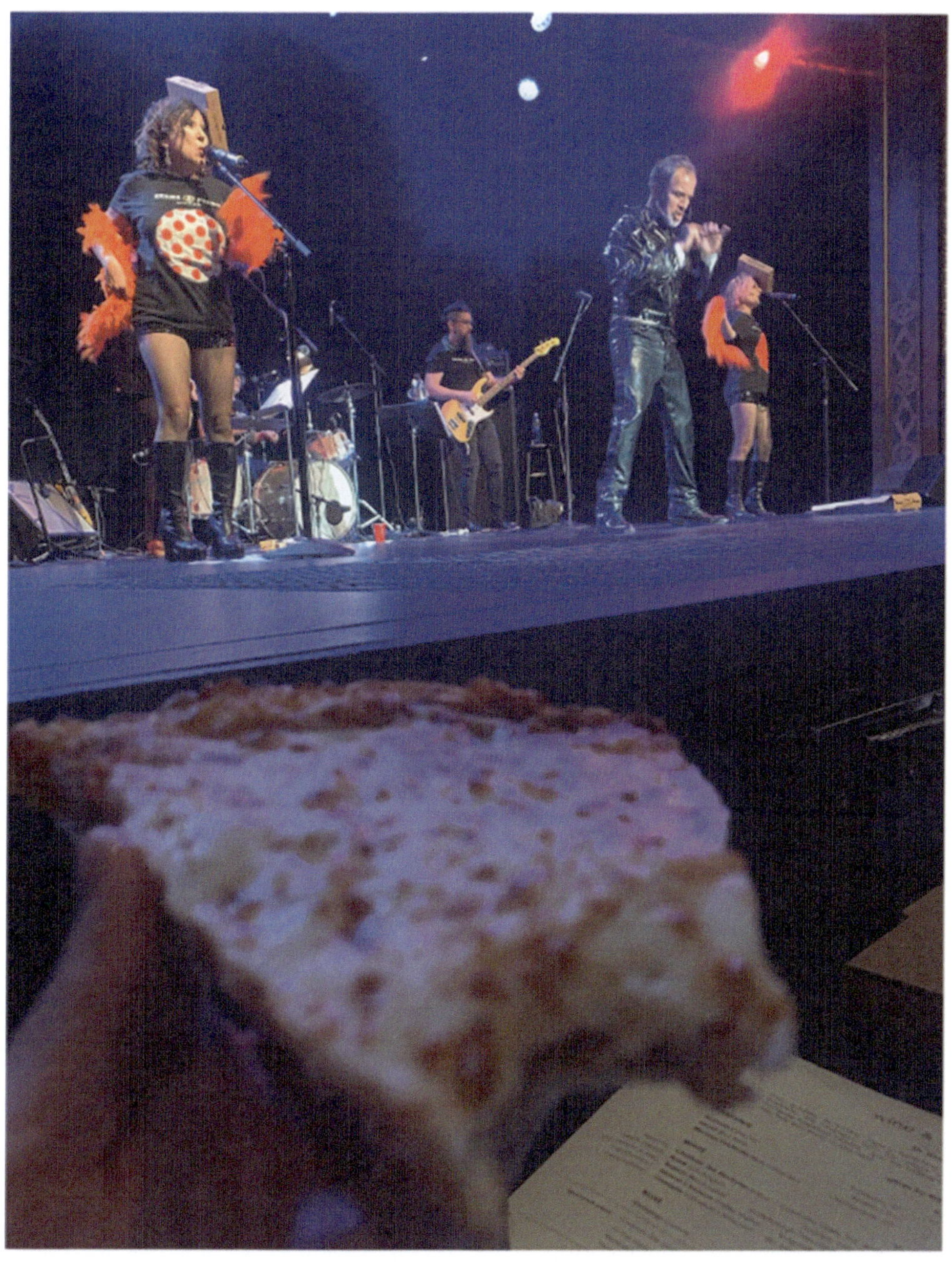

FIGURE C.4: An audience member enjoys a slice of pizza as El Vez sings, backed by the Lovely Elvettes (Guerrero and Turzo) wearing their pizza shirts and pizza box hats, 2021. Photograph by Rebekah Dawn Hall.

Minimum wage is robbery
Have I gotten your attention?
[We must fight]
In the Gig Labor economy
We don't get no back pension.

The rewritten lyrics offer a strong critique of how our convenience economy dehumanizes workers, erasing the labor of the people who are on the other side of gig economy apps, many of whom must work so much that their "life is took," while earning minimum wage with no protections, insurance, or retirement plans. And while blame should go primarily to companies like Door Dash, Uber, and the like who profit off of this undervalued labor and lobby hard to ensure precarity for their workers, we in fact are all complicit. He then married the topic of low wages for essential workers to our dysfunctional immigration system, alluding to the fact that the criminalization of undocumented workers is a tactic for keeping wages low for all. Expanding this out to reference the botched withdrawal from Afghanistan that had just occurred, he observed that we will have "a new wave of immigrants coming our way—and that's a good thing." This provided a transition into "Immigration Time," and "Mexicans in America" (his version of Kim Wilde's "Kids in America"). In such a move, Lopez-as-El-Vez bridged from the local to the national and global, making clear the connection between labor issues, immigration, and neoliberalist logics. Acknowledging that he has performed these El Vez standards for over 30 years, Lopez-as-El-Vez added, "Music does not always change the policy, but every time you hear Elvis you will hear my version, too," suggesting that art might subtly change minds. A giant Mexican flag unfurled, which remained in place for this section of the show.

Lopez-as-El-Vez offered a reflection on how the pandemic has impacted the local culture of our cities by naming the many independent businesses, restaurants, and venues that he would have taken the Elvettes to—had they not closed due to COVID. This motivated his discussion of engagement: the precarity of our economy, where only the wealthy get wealthier, is no longer tenable. While we may not know what comes next, suggested Lopez-as-El-Vez, it must include change, saying, "As Joe Strummer said, the future is unwritten, but I've made notes already." He launched into his cover of Elvis's "A Little Less Conversation," which he melds with George Michael's, "Freedom! '90." The lyrics to both songs stress the importance of taking action to actively build an equitable society.

A final bit of political commentary occurred as Lopez-as-El-Vez lauded a long string of artists: Aladdin Sane/David Bowie, Syd Barrett, Mr. Bob (another funny bit of self-reference), Brian Wilson, Mozart—"all those crazy motherfuckers who have inspired me." This monologue emphasized the value of art and the need for iconoclasts, yet as he spoke about the beauty of unorthodox artists and thinkers in our world, a police officer came on stage and forced El Vez to his knees. Seeing a Chicano man brought down before a cop—even within the fiction of the performance—was a potent reminder of the racial reckoning our nation witnessed in the Summer of 2020 and the continued work that must be done to address the ongoing threats of police violence and systemic racism. El Vez was escorted from the stage, and the pizza tosser mentioned earlier came out to entertain the audience. The audience reveled in watching the man throw and catch the dough. That we could be so quickly and easily distracted was an important performative comment. Of course, the arrest of El Vez was clearly authored and staged by Lopez, so no one could think he was in any sort of danger, and yet the moment spoke to the way that public attention so quickly moves on.

The pandemic has not been kind to artists. In an already precarious industry, the vast majority of live performers were left to fend for themselves. Indeed, it was not kind to many of us. Those who were able to work virtually found ourselves in perpetual, stressful labor; those who lost work and income experienced anxiety about how to make ends meet; and those who took on essential work had to take precautions against a virus we did not fully understand, often in workplaces where their safety was compromised. Yet, the superstar economy churned on. The rich got richer, income inequality grew, and the markets remained strong. And now, as we slowly come out of crisis mode, we run the risk of losing the one good that the pandemic revealed to us: that, as observed by Bruno Latour:

> [W]e have actually proven that it is possible, in a few weeks, to put an economic system on hold everywhere in the world and at the same time, a system we were told it was impossible to slow down or redirect.[36]

Having temporarily halted neoliberal capitalism, we should take the time to re-evaluate it. We must resist the return to the normal that was, instead calling out the injustice that seemed commonplace. More importantly, we must imagine what can be, as we stage our own comebacks.

To close the show, El Vez re-entered from the audience, reborn in his white '68 Comeback Special replica suit to sing his "Rock N Roll Suicide/If I Can Dream" medley. Both songs were show closers for the artists that made them famous; David Bowie ended his *The Rise and Fall of Ziggy Stardust and the Spider From Mars* album, live tour, and concert film with "Rock N Roll Suicide," and Elvis closed his Comeback Special with "If I Can Dream." Lopez has performed this piece many times, but it resonated especially well with the themes of *Stand & Deliver, Pizza!*. The Bowie song considers the trappings of celebrity and the passage of time, which fits nicely with the reflective arc of the evening; the Elvis song dreams of social justice and racial equity, which serves as a reminder of what we must imagine, and fight for, coming out of the pandemic. It calls out for us to create a new world, a world built out of this dream.

Let's make the dream real.

So There You Have It: You Are the King of All You Parlay

You would think, after some 84,000 words of writing about 20+ years of study, I would have exhausted all that there is to say about El Vez and Robert Lopez. You would be wrong. Instead, I am struck by all that I did not share: juicy quotes from hours of interviews; impactful moments from different performances; and more examples of the deep thinking that goes into his shows. There are so many stories from the road—of "lost" blue suitcases or black Beatle boots, busses stuck in the snow, flat tires to be changed without a jack (until a jack was improbably found in the middle of the desert), sprints through airports to catch international flights, and van doors flying open on the highway and Crissy's clothes spilling out. There's much more to say about the professionalism that he and the musicians he works with exhibit, and about his ability to read an audience and give them exactly what they need and want, to which Lopez countered:

> Or I give myself exactly what I need! Which might be what they need, or it might get one person angry, and that's all I needed. Which is back to that vaudevillian idea [...] come hell or high water, someone's going to get entertained! Even if it's just me!.[37]

I barely mentioned his many years working with Teatro ZinZanni in Seattle and San Francisco, where he not only performed consistently but also co-wrote *Caliente*, which featured all the TZ magic and fun, while also raising serious issues of corporate culture, labor exploitation, globalization, gentrification, and immigration. I did not go into detail about all the deals that might have been: the cartoon series *La Vida El Vez* that Klasky Csupo wanted to develop, depicting the life of El Vez, the Lovely Elvettes, and the Memphis Mariachis on tour; a different project for which Disney courted him (says Lopez, "I should have asked for free tickets!"); another project with Benny Medina that would have featured El Vez and Lopez's more intense Chicano poet persona Raúl Raúl in a Patty Duke-style identical cousins sitcom (which got him sent to acting classes and signed at Warner Brothers, with a hefty cash payout); a variety show project that would have put El Vez in the role similar to Carol Burnett, partnered with Culture Clash as his comedy ensemble; or a potential role as a taxi driver who sings "Hotel California" to Carrie Fisher in the opening scenes to *Postcards from the Edge*.[38] "But it's funny to talk about near-misses," says Lopez in thinking back on these different projects:

> And it's really funny to me, that I had so much buzz then, without even having a publicist—it was an organic buzz of being on TV enough that people knew there was this kooky character out there, and them coming to me.[39]

I very much did not mention the X-rated illustrations that a fan drew for/of him (a set of which he gifted me for my wedding), which depict—in explicit detail—wild sexual escapades between El Vez and the Elvettes (all of them! at once!). I didn't even mention that he has been a question on *Jeopardy!* or that he once sat in a hot tub with Iggy Pop, who wore his sunglasses the entire time. I did not talk about his long-standing relationship with burlesque performers, the Burlesque Hall of Fame (BHOF), and Tiki Oasis, communities that embrace feminism, queerness, and body positivity and empowerment for all people, regardless of age, race, nationality, religion, ability, appearance, gender, orientation, or socioeconomic status. I didn't mention the extensive network of friends and collaborators he has built, people who "are not the norm of society and thank god for that."[40] And I only touched on the many different bands and performances he is a part of such as The Little Richards, Bobby & the Pins, Covid Cola, and Mr. Bob. I also didn't mention that COVID continues to disrupt live performance and impact artists who make their living through the performing arts; it has affected his recent MeX-Mas tours, postponing the December 2021 dates to July 2022, then truncating that tour when COVID struck again, and then rearing up once more in 2023.

But that is the nature of inquiry, and of knowing, and of not knowing yet. And it is also the nature of art. There is always more to explore, always more to consider. I do hope that this book, through its focus on Lopez's performance of El Vez, allows readers to think about the intersection of entertainment, social and political critique, spectacle, and music as a site of world-building. I hope it has also helped to further secure Lopez's place in the performance archive. Most importantly, I hope it allows us to question some of the assumptions we might make about performance, especially in the ways we think about the use of empathy and authenticity versus irony and inauthenticity, and realism over theatricality; and to think through the ways that costumes reveal different bodies-in-process and how this can enhance meaning; and to consider all that is carried in our listening, and the new worlds that music can take us to. For those familiar with El Vez, I hope this book affirms your fandom, and perhaps allows you to see even more of the details and the thinking that make his shows so incredible. And for those of you who have not yet seen El Vez—I hope that you do so soon.

NOTES

1. Robert Lopez, text to author, March 12, 2020. All subsequent texts cited in this paragraph are from this exchange.
2. Alan B. Krueger, *Rockonomics: A Backstage Tour of What the Music Industry Can Teach Us About Economics and Life* (New York: Currency, 2019), 27, original emphasis.
3. Krueger adds, "Scientists have documented power laws in all kinds of outcomes, from the frequency of use of various words to the size of cities and the number of hurricanes a year," 13.
4. Krueger, *Rockonomics*, 84.
5. Krueger, *Rockonomics*, 14.
6. Krueger, *Rockonomics*, 52. Of course, since musicians are self-employed, it is in their interest to deduct as many business expenses as possible and minimize their income, which may partially account for the low median earnings. Yet, it is undeniable that independent artists assume great risk in many aspects of their career.
7. Krueger, *Rockonomics*, 53.
8. Krueger, *Rockonomics*, 58.
9. Krueger notes that even the superstars of music are less well-paid than superstars in other fields, earning less than the median pay for top CEOs and professional athletes. Their pay pales in comparison to leaders in the especially lucrative financial industry, such as at hedge fund and private equity companies.
10. This is a set line in the loose script Lopez has crafted for this performance persona (more on that later). He used the line in *Stand & Deliver, Pizza!*, Triple Door, Seattle, WA, August 28, 2021.
11. Krueger, *Rockonomics*, 10.
12. Krueger determines this figure by analyzing the incomes of the top 48 musicians who toured in 2017. Because these artists' recordings account for the bulk of industry-wide music revenue, it is safe to say that the record sales of someone less popular than a Taylor Swift, Beyoncé, Billy Joel, Paul McCartney, or U2 will likely make only minimal income from recordings and an even higher percentage of income through live performance.
13. Indeed, as I have noted in other articles and chapters, the first time I saw El Vez perform, I went as a joke, expecting him to be an earnest (and probably terrible) impersonator. In all of the shows I have attended, there always seems to be first-time attendees present.
14. Randy Cohen, "COVID-19 Pandemic's Impact on the Arts: Research Update," May 12, 2022, accessed July 19, 2022, https://www.americansforthearts.org/node/103614. The one-page report summary notes that unemployed rates were higher for BIPOC artists (69% versus 60%), who also lost a larger share of their income (61% versus 56%).
15. Puddles Pity Party is the baritone-singing, 6'8" Pagliacci-style clown created by Michael Geier. During the pandemic, he hosted eleven episodes of his "Sequestered Show" comedy series.
16. Lopez, text to author, August 15, 2020.

17. His Airbnb profile hearkens, "Elvis would have slept here," and guests frequently comment on the unique artistry of his home. https://www.airbnb.com/rooms/2474569?source_impression_id=p3_1633213440_1A81725k1dFdxmlq&guests=1&adults=1, accessed October 1, 2021. In May 2020, he did have a guest—one who was booked for six months—skip out without paying, and he has since had some other tenant issues, but for the most part, renting his home has provided a steady means of covering his bills.
18. Kreuger makes this point in *Rockonomics*, noting that the term gig was coined by jazz musicians in the 1920s, but has expanded to cover an entire sector of workers today. He notes, "Musicians have long been at the vanguard of the gig economy, facing many of the same problems that gig workers face today: obtaining health insurance, saving for the future, paying down debt, planning for taxes, and recordkeeping," 55.
19. History summarized from the Triple Door website, https://www.thetripledoor.net/about, accessed October 2, 2021.
20. Adam Ant has rather publicly addressed the mental health issues caused by his bipolar disorder, and Bowie, whose brother Terry Burns suffered from schizophrenia and ultimately committed suicide, wrote many songs considering mental health issues, and was reportedly afraid that he might also succumb to mental illness and hoped that his art-making would help to stave it off.
21. Lopez, interview with author, March 4, 2024.
22. From a publicity image posted to Lopez's Instagram on May 14, 2019.
23. Bobby Weirdo, "Robert Lopez on the Unhappy Hour, El Vez, the Early Diverse Days of L.A. Punk, and more," Weirdo Music Forever, December 28, 2016, accessed October 2, 2021, https://www.weirdomusicforever.com/weird-news-and-interviews/2016/12/26/robert-lopez-on-the-unhappy-hour-el-vez-the-early-days-of-la-punk-and-more.
24. Lopez, *Stand & Deliver, Pizza!*. All quotes are from the entire evening's performance and taken from the author's field notes.
25. Bobby Weirdo, "Robert Lopez on the Unhappy Hour."
26. As noted in Chapter 1, Lopez plays with this line a lot in performance, and says it differently at times, to different effect.
27. When I shared a draft of this chapter at the ASTR 2021 conference, Jennifer A. Kokai responded meaningfully to this question, noting that perhaps both were essential, criticizing the neoliberalist logics that would have us choose between them, and more importantly between the people who labor in these professions.
28. Several of the Covid Cola videos are available on YouTube, on Pablo Prietto's channel. The band continues to write new songs and perform together.
29. Lopez, text to author, September 14, 2020.
30. Marek Korczynski, *Songs of the Factory: Pop Music, Culture, and Resistance* (Ithaca, NY: Cornell University Press, 2015), 11.
31. Lopez, text to author, September 14, 2020.
32. YouTube policy cited by Lopez in text to author, May 13, 2021.

33. For this show, Lopez played with Seattle-based musicians Tom Kellock (piano), Jeremy Lightfoot (bass), Maxwell Eddison (guitar), and Pete Capponi (drums). Though the band had rehearsed leading up to the show, it was their first time actually playing an El Vez show. As noted elsewhere in the book, the Memphis Mariachis play revue-style, underscoring Lopez throughout as he frames the concepts he explores through his stage banter, as well as performing live mash-ups or samples, slicing together multiple songs under Lopez's direction. The performance definitely challenged the band. Fortunately, they were anchored by veteran Elvettes Guerrero and Turzo, who flew in from L.A. for the performance.
34. The cheese pizza was the exception—it was purchased from a nearby Dominos immediately before the show.
35. Zeek's had faced a similarly lawsuit in 2019, and paid out $285,000 to 257 drivers then. The most recent case also went in the workers' favor; Zeek's paid out $409,000 to 224 current and former drivers. See coverage in the *Seattle Times*, accessed July 27, 2023, https://www.seattletimes.com/business/zeeks-pizza-chain-to-pay-409000-after-alleged-service-charge-violation/, https://www.seattletimes.com/business/local-business/zeeks-pizza-chain-underpaid-delivery-drivers-lawsuit-says/.
36. Bruno Latour cited in Rick Mitchell, "Epic Cruelty: On Post-Pandemic Performance," *NTQ* 37, no. 2 (May, 2021): 122.
37. Lopez, interview with author, March 4, 2024.
38. Lopez, interview with author, March 4, 2024.
39. Lopez, interview with author, March 4, 2024.
40. Lopez actually sang these words to the tune of "My Way" in the closing BHOF ceremony in Las Vegas, June 7, 2015.

Everything Old: An Afterword

Should I do this? Should I address the white elephant in the room?

—El Vez, Merry MeX-Mas Especial, December 2024[1]

On November 5, 2024, Donald J. Trump was re-elected to the office of the President of the United States. Despite his low approval ratings upon leaving office, his connection to the January 6 insurrection, and the fact that he is now a convicted felon and an adjudicated sexual abuser, Trump made gains in every state and nearly every county. For the first time in twenty years, the Republican candidate won both the electoral college vote and the popular vote,[2] making Trump the second president to serve two nonconsecutive terms (the first was Grover Cleveland in 1884 and 1892). In an election where partisanship was high, margins were narrow, and both sides framed the outcome as a monumental test of democracy, this result was either celebrated or reviled by roughly half the electorate.

The strange months between the election and the inauguration of a new presidency—especially one that sees a shift in the ruling party—are perhaps always filled with some uncertainty, but Trump's unprecedented election in 2016 carried with it a profound feeling of trepidation. As I describe in Chapter 4, the 2016 El Vez MeX-Mas show harnessed this anxiety, affirming the fear that some people experienced while also bolstering a commitment to resistance. The 2024 election results felt different. For one, though the Trump re-election still defies many norms and expectations, it carries with it an air of familiarity, and perhaps of weariness. Once again, Trump, full of grievance and divisive rhetoric and short on policy, triumphed over an extremely well-qualified woman; once again, his bombast beat out the studious preparation of his opponent. These are not unchartered waters; we have been here before.

The 2024 Merry Mex-Mas Especial featured a different configuration from other more recent holiday stagings. Instead of touring with the Lovely Elvettes and the Memphis Mariachis, El Vez instead toured with the rockabilly trio The Centuries[3] (although Elvettes Crissy Guerrero and Pinky Turzo made cameo appearances as "two mystery girls" who ripped off El Vez's Santa Suit during "Huaraches Azules" and later returned to the stage to dance to the song "Elvette"[4] at the Los Angeles show). Lopez-as-El-Vez raised the white elephant comment approximately two-thirds of the way through the performance, bringing together dual meanings by referencing the white elephant gift exchange game popular at holiday parties and an uncomfortable topic that nobody wants to talk about, while marking the racial politics that animate Trump's stance. But rather than delve into that discomfort by offering a critique of Trump, he instead jumped back into the music, leaving the white elephant unspoken. In fact, he never directly addressed Trump at all.

This is not to suggest that the show did not bring in political critique. Indeed, from the very start, Lopez pushed against rigid understandings of customs and traditions. Before entering the space, a recording of Tchaikovsky's "Dance of the Sugar Plum Fairy" played, only to be interrupted by a "Bruja Chant," a spooky-sounding track of female voices chanting in Spanish, conjuring the hidden secrets of the "diosas antiguas."[5] This opening sound cue alluded to the way Christian traditions have been layered on top of ancient pagan practices, and European culture imposed upon Indigenous knowledges in the Americas. Lopez-as-El-Vez furthered the irreverence in his own introduction, noting that his show would "evoke the spirit of Satan–oops!–I mean Santa." The topics he addressed throughout the show were wide-ranging: Lopez-as-El-Vez offered wisecracking commentary on consumerism and fast fashion, pointing out how his pants from Forever 21 "ripped really, really bad, but they were really, really cheap"; colonization, noting how La Virgen de Guadalupe helped bring Christianity to the Aztecs, "which ruined everything ... but that's a different song"; and music streaming services–"I thought it was just for peeing."

His most sustained critique, however, was embedded in his own area of expertise: music. Early in the show, he stated his surprise that in Mexico, where he now lives, he is sometimes proclaimed to be the King of Rockabilly. Lopez-as-El-Vez assured the audience that this categorization is wrong; in fact, he continued, "I came to destroy rockabilly. I came to inject [Elvis's] rockabilly with the other January 8 birthday – David Bowie!" He promised to infuse the sex and power of glam into the sex and power of rockabilly. Lopez-as-El-Vez would follow these two threads– rockabilly and sex – throughout the performance, using both as touchstones that he could refer back to and depart from. Through his banter, he situated rockabilly as a culture that uses the past to enliven the present, but Lopez-as-El-Vez demanded that the past be scrutinized when necessary. For instance, in his introduction to the blues song "Milk Cow Blues" by Kokomo Arnold, which Elvis recorded in a rockabilly style and retitled "Milkcow Blues Boogie," he noted that the original song was sexist, equating women with cows to be milked. Lopez-as-El-Vez then presented–and instantly refuted–a typical excuse for the bad behavior of the past, saying, "It was a different time. But that doesn't make it right."

His version, he proclaimed, would transform the sexist into the sexy, the first step of which is to acknowledge the misogyny that was (and is) there. Though subtle, this critique served to remind the audience to stand vigilant against the erasure or excusing of past harms and injustices.

Though sex is always a factor in El Vez shows, his commentary felt especially impactful in the wake of the election. The Trump platform, Project 2025, and the America First Policy Institute agenda, all of which might guide the incoming administration, emphasize conservative, Christian values and the importance of the traditional family while vilifying the "wokeness" of feminism and LGBTQ+ protections.[6] These policy platforms threaten to further scale back the rights and protections of women and of the LGBTQ+ community. Speaking from my own positionality, women feel especially imperiled. Misogynist trolls circulated the "Your body. My choice. Forever." rallying cry on social media following the election–a direct threat.[7] Even more troubling, multiple cabinet nominees have been accused of sexual misconduct,[8] as has Trump. Quinta Jurecic, writing in *The Atlantic*, has dubbed it the #MeToo Cabinet, noting that "this particular slate of picks represents a remarkable commitment to moral ugliness."[9] In response, many women are expressing support for the 4B movement, which disavows heterosexual dating, sex, marriage, and childbearing. Writes E. Tammy Kim:

> The conditions under which 4B started to trend in the U.S. are both the same and uniquely dismal. It's the 2017 pussy-hat moment all over again, only worse. Donald Trump's reëlection has made women understandably fearful about their protection from discrimination, their ability to get an abortion, their physical safety.[10]

Though trending topics on social media do not necessarily equate to real-world action, they do signal shared anxieties. And they reveal how gender identity and expression, sexual orientation, and sex itself has become highly politicized.

The El Vez show dared to reclaim sex, "putting the X back in Xmas." Lopez-as-El-Vez continually referenced sexual pleasure, placing his own body on display and emphasizing that "Christmas is the sexiest time of the year."[11] He extended sexual desirability to those often deemed outside of it, dedicating the song "Black Magic Woman" to older women, to "all the mamas who know their sexuality."[12] And he reflected this desirability back on himself, saying, "At 65 years-old, I can be proud of my sexuality." This condoning of sexual enjoyment, informed by the perspective of an aging gay artist, served as a reminder of the power of taking pleasure, not just in sex, but in everything El Vez had to offer: music, wit, irreverence, and community. Coming together in jubilant celebration may in fact be a radical act that denies fuel to fear and hatred. It offers another way of being, a model for how to deflate Trumpism, through the simple practice of experiencing joy.

Lopez-as-El-Vez returned to the topic of rockabilly, and his own punk rock sensibility, in his final monologue, while also obliquely engaging with the white elephant. Speaking over a vamp of "Christmastime Is Here," he offered the closing thoughts to his Especial, recalling the good times he had had on the road and issuing thanks to the band and to the audience before saying:

> 2025 is unknown territory. Many Latinos I know will not be here. And more that I don't know will be asked to leave. [...] I said I wanted to kill rockabilly, but we can keep the beauty. What I mean is that I want to kill the things of the past, the racism, the sexism, the misogyny, and the discrimination, so that we can go forward. And that was what punk rock was doing. Punk rock destroys to make something new, something better.

Time in the monologue is in motion. There is a folding backward, to both rockabilly and punk, but not to locate and fix a mythical past. Rather, Lopez-as-El-Vez looks back to look forward; he uses his punk past to see a better future. In this, I am reminded once again of Muñoz, and his writings on utopia, queerness, and punk rock:

> Utopia is not prescriptive; it renders potential blueprints of a world not quite here, a horizon of possibility, not a fixed schema. It is productive to think about utopia as flux, a temporal disorganization, as a moment when the here and the now is transcended by a then and a there that could be and indeed should be.[13]

The monologue harnesses Muñoz's temporal flux; it uses the here and now to point to then and theres both past and future, offering both as correctives, as visions of what should be. Deftly moving from political engagement around expected deportations in 2025 to a nuanced engagement with rockabilly's value today, the monologue makes visible the propensity to elide the wrongs of the past in our embrace of it, just as it displays a willingness to preserve what in the past is beautiful and enjoyable. Lopez-as-El-Vez then positioned himself where he has always been: not as rockabilly, not even as an Elvis impersonator, but as a punk rocker, informed by punk's willingness to tear down what doesn't work and instead build something that does. Rooted in the present of performance, he reminded us, "Christmas is a time of love. Keep that feeling all year round." And he closed with a fitting encore: three punk rock songs, each building a new future.

NOTES

1. El Vez and The Centuries, Merry MeX-Mas Especial, Lodge Room, Los Angeles, CA, December 20, 2024, and The Casbah, San Diego, December 21, 2024. All citations in

this afterword are from the author's field notes. Lopez-as-El-Vez raised the white elephant comment in Los Angeles, but not in San Diego.

2. Analysis shows that, even with these gains and with a 312–266 electoral vote win, the national popular vote was within 1.5 percentage points, an exceedingly close margin. Geoffrey Skelley, "America's Swing to the Right Was Wide, If Not Always Deep," ABCNews.com, December 10, 2024, accessed December 21, 2024, https://abcnews.go.com/538/americas-swing-2024-wide-deep/story?id=116639076.
3. The Centuries feature Bert Avalos on guitar, Zander Griffith on stand-up and electric bass, and Dylan Patterson on drums. Lopez had previously partnered with them for a May 2024 El Vez show in Las Vegas surrounding the Punk Rock Bowling music festival, and for a reincarnation of the band Trailer Park Casanovas for an August 2024 performance in San Diego at Tiki Oasis.
4. "Elvette" is based on the song "Claudette," written by Roy Orbison early in his career and first made popular by the Everly Brothers in 1958.
5. The recording was from the Spanish-dubbed version of the WB TV show *Charmed*.
6. These documents also advocate for mass deportations, the elimination of DEI initiatives, a crackdown on protests, voter restrictions, reliance on fossil fuels, and tax cuts for the wealthy, among other things. There is much to critique, but here I am limiting my focus to the discussion of sex that Lopez raised.
7. White-supremacist Nicholas Fuentes tweeted this to X following Trump's election, and it quickly spread on social media. The post is discussed in many articles, including the two cited below.
8. These include Pete Hegseth, Robert F. Kennedy, Jr., Linda McMahon, Elon Musk, and Matt Gaetz (withdrawn). Such credible accusations would have been disqualifying in the past.
9. Quinta Jurecic, "The #MeToo Cabinet," *The Atlantic*, November 22, 2024, accessed December 22, 2024, https://www.theatlantic.com/ideas/archive/2024/11/trump-cabinet-sexual-assault-allegations/680773/.
10. E. Tammy Kim, "The Rise of 4B in the Wake of Donald Trump's Reelection," *The New Yorker*, November 23, 2024, accessed January 8, 2025, https://www.newyorker.com/news/the-lede/the-rise-of-4b-in-the-wake-of-donald-trumps-reelection.
11. He offered as evidence "the wrapping and unwrapping of presents, the yule log," all delivered in a provocative tone to emphasize the double entendre.
12. He changed the lyrics to sing, "I'm in love with Santa's woman," changing the way we might look at Mrs. Claus.
13. José Esteban Muñoz, *Cruising Utopia, 10th Anniversary Edition: The Then and There of Queer Futurity*, (New York: New York University Press, 2019), 97.

Bibliography

Adams, Tony E., Carolyn Ellis, and Stacy Holman Jones. "Autoethnography." In *The International Encyclopedia of Communication Research Methods*, edited by Jorg Matthes, Christine S. Davis, and Robert F. Potter, 1–11. Wiley Online Library, 2017. https://doi.org/10.1002/9781118901731.iecrm0011.

Amidei, Aly Renee Amidei. "Where'd I Put My Character? The Costume as Character Body and Essential Costuming for the Ensemble Actor." *Theatre Symposium* 26, no. 1 (2018): 49–57.

Anderson, Patrick. "I Feel for You." In *Neoliberalism and Global Theatres: Performance Permutations*, edited by Lara D. Nielson and Patricia Ybarra, 81–96. New York: Palgrave Macmillan, 2012.

Appadurai, Arjun Appadurai. "Introduction: Commodities and the Politics of Value." In *The Social Lives of Things: Commodities in Cultural Perspective*, edited by Arjun Appadurai, 3–63. Cambridge, MA: Cambridge University Press, 1986.

Auslander, Philip. *Liveness: Performance in a Mediatized Culture*. London: Routledge, 1999.

Auslander, Philip. *Performing Glam Rock: Gender and Theatricality in Popular Music*. Ann Arbor, MI: Univesity of Michigan Press, 2006.

Auslander, Philip. *In Concert: Performing Musical Persona*. Ann Arbor, MI: University of Michigan Press, 2021.

Bag, Alice Bag. "Work that Hoe: Tilling the Soil of Punk Feminism." *Women & Performance: A Journal of Feminist History* 22, no. 2–3 (December 2012): 233–38.

Behar, Ruth. *The Vulnerable Observer: Anthropology That Breaks Your Heart*. Boston, MA: Beacon Press, 1996.

Bennett, Jane. *Vibrant Matter: A Political Ecology of Things*. Durham, NC: Duke University Press, 2010.

Bogdanovich, Peter. "Seinfeld Battles Actor Danny Hoch…" *New York Observer*, March 9, 1998. Accessed May 25, 2021. https://observer.com/1998/03/seinfeld-battles-actor-danny-hoch-party-of-jive-ally-mcshutupalready-a-decadent-sag-show/.

Brackett, David. "Questions of Genre in Black Popular Music." *Black Music Research Journal* 25, no.1/2 (Spring/Fall 2005): 73–92.

Brackett, David. *Categorizing Sound: Genre and Twentieth-Century Popular Music*. Oakland, CA: University of California Press, 2016.

Brooks, Daphne and Roshanak Kheshti. "The Social Space of Sound." *Theatre Survey* 52, no. 2 (2011): 329–34.

Brown, Bill. "Thing Theory." *Critical Inquiry* 28, no. 1 (Autumn 2001): 1–22.

Brown, Patricia Leigh. "A Decade after Elvis: Faithful at the Shrine." *New York Times*, A1+, August 14, 1987. Accessed May 25, 2021. https://www.nytimes.com/1987/08/14/us/a-decade-after-elvis-faithful-at-the-shrine.html.

Brown, Wendy. *Undoing the Demos: Neoliberalism's Stealth Revolution*. New York: Zone Books, 2015.

Cabral, Javier. "Why Do Mexican Americans Love Morrissey So Much?" *The Washington Post*, October 8, 2014. Accessed July 23, 2018. https://www.washingtonpost.com/posteverything/wp/2014/10/08/why-do-mexican-americans-love-morrissey-so-much/.

Calafell, Bernadette Marie. "My Love/Hate Relationship with El Vez." *Latina/o Communications Studies*, 71–86. New York: Peter Lang, 2003.

Carlson, Marvin. *The Haunted Stage: The Theatre as Memory Machine*. Ann Arbor, MI: University of Michigan Press, 2001.

Carpenter, Faedra Chatard. *Coloring Whiteness: Acts of Critique in Black Performance*. Ann Arbor, MI: University of Michigan Press, 2014.

Casillas, Dolores Inés. *Sounds of Belonging: U.S. Spanish-language Radio and Public Advocacy*. New York: New York University Press, 2014.

Chalmers, Jessica Chalmers. "Marina Abramović and the Re-performance of Authenticity." *Journal of Dramatic Theory and Criticism* 22, no. 2 (Spring 2008), 23–40.

Coole, Diana and Samantha Frost. *New Materialisms: Ontology, Agency, Politics*. Durham, NC: Duke University Press, 2010.

Cummings, Lindsay B. *Empathy as Dialogue in Theatre and Performance*. London: Palgrave Macmillan, 2016.

Day, Amber. *Satire and Dissent: Interventions in Contemporary Political Debate*. Bloomington, IN: Indiana University Press, 2011.

Deevoy, Adrian. "Chuck D: I Smack Myself Twice in the Face and I'm Good to Go." *The Guardian*, March 26, 2014. Accessed September 18, 2014. https://www.theguardian.com/music/2014/mar/26/chuck-dinterview-public-enemy-fight-the-power.

Della Gotta, Carla. *Latinx Shakespeares: Staging U.S. Intracultural Theatre*. Ann Arbor, MI: University of Michigan Press, 2023.

Devin, Lee. "Conceiving the Forms: Play Analysis for Production Dramaturgy." In *Dramaturgy in American Theater: A Source Book*, edited by Susan Joans, Geoff Proehl, and Michael Lupu, 209–19. Fort Worth, TX: Harcourt Brace College Publishers, 1997.

Dolan, Jill. *Utopia in Performance: Finding Hope at the Theater*. Ann Arbor, MI: University of Michigan Press, 2005.

Duncombe, Stephen Duncombe. *Notes from Underground: Zines and the Politics of Alternative Culture*. London: Verso, 1997.

Edmondson, Laura. "Of Sugarcoating and Hope." *TDR: The Drama Review* 51, no. 2 (Summer 2007): 7–10.

Edwards, Elizabeth and Janice Hart. *Photographs Objects Histories: On the Materiality of Images*. London: Routledge, 2004.

Eidsheim, Nina Sun. "Voice as a Technology of Selfhood: Towards an Analysis of Racialized Timbre and Vocal Performance." PhD diss., University of California, San Diego, CA, 2008.

Eidsheim, Nina Sun. *The Race of Sound: Listening, Timbre and Vocality in African American Music*. Durham, NC: Duke University Press, 2019.

El Vez. *Graciasland*. Sympathy for the Record Industry, 1994.

El Vez. *How Great Thou Art*. Sympathy for the Record Industry, 1994.

El Vez. *G.I. Ay, Ay! Blues: Soundtrack for the Coming Revolution*. Big Pop, 1996.

El Vez. "*Say It Loud!*" Music video directed by Pablo Prietto, 1997.

El Vez. *Son of a Lad from Spain?* Sympathy for the Record Industry, 1999.

El Vez. *Sno-Way José*. Graciasland Records, 2002.

El Vez. *Endless Revolution: G.I. Ay Ay Blues Service Re-Issue*. Graciasland Records, 2004.

El Vez. *The Gospel Show in Madrid*. Last Bandit Films, 2008.

El Vez. *God Save the King: 25 Years of El Vez*. Munster Records, 2013.

Evans, Sophie Jane. "Smiths Singer was Quizzed by Scotland Yard over Controversial Thatcher Song Margaret on the Guillotine." *The Daily Mail*, October 18, 2013. Accessed April 23, 2018. https://www.dailymail.co.uk/news/article-2465742/Smiths-singer-Morrissey-quizzed-Scotland-Yard-controversial-Thatcher-song-Margaret-Guillotine.html.

Fabbri, Franco. "A Theory of Musical Genres: Two Applications." In *Popular Music Perspectives*, edited by David Horn and Philip Tagg, 52–81. Göteborg and Exeter: International Association for the Study of Popular Music, 1981.

Fraser, Benson P. and William J. Brown. "Media, Celebrities, and Social Influence: Identification with Elvis Presley." *Mass Communication & Society* 5, no. 2 (2002): 183–206.

Frith, Simon. *Performing Rites: On the Value of Popular Music*. Cambridge, MA: Harvard University Press, 1996.

Frith, Simon. "Pop Music" (2001). In *Taking Popular Music Seriously: Selected Essays*, 167–82. Hampshire: Ashgate Publishing Limited, 2007.

Frith, Simon. "Music and Identity" (1996). In *Taking Popular Music Seriously: Selected Essays*, 293–312. Hampshire: Ashgate Publishing Limited, 2007.

Gates, Henry Louis. *The Signifying Monkey: A Theory of African-American Criticism*. Oxford: Oxford University Press, 1988.

George-Graves, Nadine. "An Environment of Cascading Consequences." In *Theatre, Performance, and Change*, edited by Stephani E. Woodson and Tamara Underiner, 99–109. Cham: Palgrave Macmillan, 2018.

Goldstein, Patrick. "POP EYE." *Los Angeles Times*, January 29, 1989, 86K (via ProQuest Historical Newspapers, ASU library).

Gordon, Robert. *Memphis Rent Party: The Blues, Rock & Soul in Music's Hometown.* New York: Bloomsbury, 2018.

Grim, Ryan Grim and Alexander Zaitchik. "George W. Bush Gave Us Donald Trump. Now He Wants to Be Forgiven," *The Huffington Post*, March 18, 2018. Accessed May 9, 2018. https://www.huffpost.com/entry/george-w-bush-trump-forget-history_n_58c6e69ee4b0598c66989c6e.

Grossberg, Lawrence. *We Gotta Get Out of this Place: Popular Conservatism and Postmodern Culture.* New York: Routledge, 1992.

Habell-Pallán, Michelle. *Loca Motion: The Travels of Chicana and Latina Popular Culture.* New York: New York University Press, 2005.

Haraway, Donna J. "Situated Knowledges: The Science Question in Feminism and the Privilege of Partial Perspective." *Feminist Studies* 14, no. 3 (Autumn 1988): 575–99.

Heim, Caroline Heim, "Participant Observation in Practice and Techniques for Overcoming Research Insecurity: A Case Study at the Deutsches Theater." In *Impacting Theatre Audiences: Method for Studying Change*, edited by Dani Snyder-Young and Matt Omasta, 26–38. London: Routledge, 2022.

Heyneman, Peter. "BYT Interview: El Vez!" BrightestYoungThings, December 3, 2009. Accessed June 4, 2021. https://brightestYoungThings.com/el-vez.

Hirschfield Davis, Julie. "Trump Calls Some Unauthorized Immigrants 'Animals.'" *New York Times*, May 16, 2018. Accessed May 17, 2018. https://www.nytimes.com/2018/05/16/us/politics/trump-undocumented-immigrants-animals.html.

Hoch, Danny. *Jails, Hospitals & Hip Hop*. Loisaida Arts, 1998.

Holm, Christiane. "Sentimental Cuts: Eighteenth-Century Mourning Jewelry with Hair." *Eighteenth-Century Studies* 38, no. 1 (2004): 139–43.

Holt, Fabian. *Genre in Popular Music.* Chicago, IL: University of Chicago Press, 2007.

Hutcheon, Linda. *Irony's Edge: The Theory and Politics of Irony*. London: Routledge, 1994.

Hutcheon, Linda. *A Theory of Parody: The Teachings of Twentieth Century Art Forms*. Urbana and Chicago, IL: University of Illinois Press, 2003.

Jenkins, Henry. *Textual Poachers: Television Fans and Participatory Culture*. New York: Routledge, 2012.

Johnson, E. Patrick. *Appropriating Blackness: Performance and the Politics of Authenticity*. Durham, NC: Duke University Press, 2003.

Jones, Sarah. "Donald Trump is the New George W. Bush." *The New Republic*, March 15, 2018. Accessed May 9, 2018. https://newrepublic.com/article/147477/donald-trump-new-george-w-bush.

Jurecic, Quinta. "The #MeToo Cabinet." *The Atlantic*, November 22, 2024. Accessed December 22, 2024. https://www.theatlantic.com/ideas/archive/2024/11/trump-cabinet-sexual-assault-allegations/680773/.

Kondo, Dorinne. *Worldmaking: Race, Performance, and the Work of Creativity*. Durham, NC: Duke University Press, 2018.

Kim, E. Tammy. "The Rise of 4B in the Wake of Donald Trump's Reelection." *The New Yorker*, November 23, 2024. Accessed January 8, 2025. https://www.newyorker.com/news/the-lede/the-rise-of-4b-in-the-wake-of-donald-trumps-reelection.

Korczynski, Marek. *Songs of the Factory: Pop Music, Culture, and Resistance*. Ithaca, NY: Cornell University Press, 2015.

Krier, Beth Ann. "El Vez: Colorful Impersonator Gets a Big *Ole*." *The Los Angeles Times*, May 12, 1989, D1+ (via ProQuest Historical Newspapers, ASU library).

Krueger, Alan B. *Rockonomics: A Backstage Tour of What the Music Industry Can Teach Us About Economics and Life*. New York: Currency, 2019.

Kun, Josh. *Audtiotopia: Music, Race, and America*. Berkeley, CA: University of California Press, 2005.

Kutner, Brad. "El Vez Is Like a Jukebox Exploding in Your Face." RVAmag.com. August 15, 2013. Accessed September 27, 2013. https://rvamag.com/music/el-vez-is-like-a-jukebox-exploding-in-your-face.html.

Larson, Susan. "Rock and Revolution: An Interview with El Vez, The Mexican Elvis." *Arizona Journal of Hispanic Cultural Studies* 1 (1997): 141–52.

Lessig, Lawrence. *Remix: Making Art and Commerce Thrive in the Hybrid Economy*. New York: The Penguin Press, 2008.

Lopez, Robert. "Punk-Rock Teenage Heaven." In *Under the Big Black Sun*, edited by John Doe with Tom DeSavia and Friends, 95–109. Boston, MA: Da Capo Press, 2016.

Lynch, Signy. "The Gaze Turned Inward: A Reflexive Autoethnographic Approach to Theatre Research." In *Impacting Theatre Audiences: Method for Studying Change*, edited by Dani Snyder-Young and Matt Omasta, 88–99. London: Routledge, 2022.

Mageary, Joe. "'Rise Above/We're Gonna Rise Above': A Qualitative Inquiry into the Use of Hardcore Punk Culture as Context for the Development of Preferred Identities." PhD diss., California Institute of Integral Studies, San Francisco, CA, 2012.

Magelssen, Scott. "Why Do They Think This Is Okay?: Critiquing Performance as a Means for Change." In *Theatre, Performance, and Change*, edited by Stephani E. Woodson and Tamara Underiner, 223–33. Cham: Palgrave Macmillan, 2018.

Martinelli, Dario. *Authenticity, Performance and Other Double-Edged Words*. Helsinki: Unweb Publications, 2010.

Mitchell, Rick. "Epic Cruelty: On Post-Pandemic Performance." *NTQ* 37, no. 2 (May 2021), 119–36.

Monks, Aiofe. *The Actor in Costume*. London: Palgrave Macmillan, 2010.

Moore, Allan. "Authenticity as Authentication." *Popular Music* 21, no. 2 (2002): 209–23.

Moore, Ryan and Michael Roberts. "Do-It-Yourself Mobilization: Punk and Social Movements." *Mobilization: An International Journal* 14, no. 3 (September 2009): 273–91.

Morrissey. "Morrissey: Thatcher Was a Terror without an Atom of Humanity." *The Daily Beast*, April 8, 2013. Accessed April 23, 2018. https://www.thedailybeast.com/morrissey-thatcher-was-a-terror-without-an-atom-of-humanity.

Muñoz, José Esteban. *Curising Utopia: 10th Anniversary Edition: The Then and There of Queer Futurity*. New York: New York University Press, 2019.

Muñoz, José Esteban. *Disidentifications: Queers of Color and the Performance of Politics*. Minneapolis, MN: University of Minnesota Press, 1999.

Music Connection. "Los Angeles Declares Morrissey Day." November 8, 2017. Accessed July 23, 2018. https://www.musicconnection.com/los-angeles-morrissey-day/.

Naylor, Brian. "Read Trump's Jan. 6 Speech, a Key Part of Impeachment Trial." *NPR*, February 10, 2021. Accessed September 3, 2023. https://www.npr.org/2021/02/10/966396848/read-trumps-jan-6-speech-a-key-part-of-impeachment-trial.

Needham, Alex. "Q & A: Morrissey." *The Face*, November 1999. Accessed July 23, 2018. https://www.morrissey-solo.com/news/1999/620.shtml.

Negus, Keith and Pete Astor. "Authenticity, Empathy, and the Creative Imagination." *Rock Music Studies* 9, no. 2 (2022): 157–73.

Noboa y Rivera, Raf. "Morrissey and Mexico Fit Together Like Hand in Glove. Is That Really So Strange?" *The Guardian*, March 7, 2016. Accessed July 23, 2018. https://www.theguardian.com/commentisfree/2016/mar/07/morrissey-popularity-mexicans-smiths-chicanos-california.

O'Neal, Sam. *Elvis Inc.: The Fall and Rise of the Presley Empire*. Rocklin, CA: Prima Publishing, 1996.

Orr, Shelley. "Critical Proximity: A Case for Using the First Person as a Production Dramaturg." *Theatre Topics* 24, no. 3 (2014): 239–47.

Pao, Angela C. "False Accents: Embodied Dialects and the Characterization of Ethnicity and Nationality." *Theatre Topics* 14, no. 1 (March 2004): 353–72.

Proehl, Geoff. *Toward a Dramaturgical Sensibility: Landscape and Journey*. Madison, NJ: Fairleigh Dickinson University Press, 2008.

Purdum, Todd S. "The Nation: Focus Groups? To Bush, the Crowd Was a Blur." *New York Times*, February 23, 2003. Accessed April 17, 2018. https://www.nytimes.com/2003/02/23/weekinreview/the-nation-focus-groups-to-bush-the-crowd-was-a-blur.html.

Ramos, Iván Alejandro. "Sonic Negations: Sound, Affect, and Unbelonging Between Mexico and the United States." PhD diss., University of California, Berkeley, CA, 2015.

Ramos, Iván Alejandro. *Unbelonging: Inauthentic Sounds in Mexican and Latinx Aesthetics*. New York: New York University Press, 2023.

Rathje, Steve, Leor Hackel, and Jamil Zaki. "Op-Ed: Why Theater Makes Us Better People. Bring it Back." *Los Angeles Times*, May 2, 2021. Accessed June 22, 2022. https://www.latimes.com/opinion/story/2021-05-02/theater-empathy-live-performance-psychology#:~:text=Why%20does%20live%20theater%20have,behaviors%20were%20changed%20by%20it.

Reed-Danahay, Deborah. *Auto/Ethnography: Rewriting the Self and the Social*. Oxford: Berg, 1997.

Rodman, Gilbert D. *Elvis After Elvis: The Posthumous Career of a Living Legend*. London: Routledge, 1996.

Ronayne, Kathleen and Michael Kunzelman, "Trump to Far-Right Extremists: 'Stand Back and Stand By.'" *APNews*, September 30, 2020. Accessed March 23, 2024. https://apnews.com/article/election-2020-joe-biden-race-and-ethnicity-donald-trump-chris-wallace-0b32339da25fbc9e8b7c7c7066a1db0f.

Rubin, Rachel. "Interview with El Vez." *Journal of Popular Music Studies* 16, no. 2 (August 2004): 213–20.

Saldívar, José David. *Border Matters: Remapping American Cultural Studies*. Berkeley, CA: Univerisiy of California Press, 1997.

Saldívar, José David. "In Search of the 'Mexican Elvis': Border Matters, 'Americanicity,' and Post-State-Centric Thinking." *MFS Modern Fiction Studies* 49, no. 1 (Spring 2003): 84–100.

Schulze, Daniel Schulze. *Authenticity in Contemporary Theatre and Performance: Make It Real*. London: Bloomsbury, 2017.

Skelley, Geoffry. "America's Swing to the Right Was Wide, If Not Always Deep," ABCNews.com, December 10, 2024. Accessed December 21, 2024. https://abcnews.go.com/538/americasswing-2024-wide-deep/story?id=116639076.

Snyder-Young, Dani. "Despite Artists' Intentions, Emancipated Spectatorship Reinforces Audience Members' Existing Attitudes and Beliefs." In *Theatre, Performance, and Change*, edited by Stephani E. Woodson and Tamara Underiner , 295–301. Cham: Palgrave Macmillan, 2018.

Sommer, Doris. *Proceed with Caution, When Engaged by Minority Writing in the Americas*. Cambridge, MA: Harvard University Press, 1999.

Spigel, Lynn. "Communicating with the Dead: Elvis as Medium." *Camera Obscura* 8, no. 2 (1990): 176–205.

Stewart, Susan. *On Longing: Narratives of the Miniature, the Gigantic, the Souvenir, the Collection*. Baltimore, MD: Johns Hopkins University Press, 1984.

Stoever, Jennifer Lynn. *The Sonic Color Line: Race and the Cultural Politics of Listening*. New York: New York University Press, 2016.

Sturtevant, Victoria. "Spitfire: Lupe Vélez and the Ambivalent Pleasures of Ethnic Masquerade." *The Velvet Light Trap* 55 (Spring 2005): 19–32.

Suskind, Ron. "Faith, Certainty, and the Presidency of George W. Bush." *New York Times Magazine*, October 17, 2004. Accessed April 17, 2018. https://www.nytimes.com/2004/10/17/magazine/faith-certainty-and-the-presidency-of-george-w-bush.html.

Taylor, Diana. *The Archive and the Repertoire: Performing Cultural Memory in the Americas*. Durham, NC: Duke University Press, 2007.

Trinh, Jean. "Soap Plant & WACKO Turns 50: A Look Back at Its Underground Art Scene and Legendary Parties." *KCET Online*, June 8, 2021. Accessed July 16, 2021. https://www.pbssocal.org/shows/artbound/soap-plant-wacko-turns-50-a-look-back-at-its-underground-art-scene-and-legendary-parties.

Ventura, Patricia. *Neoliberal Culture: Living with American Neoliberalism*. Surrey: Ashgate/Taylor & Francis, 2012.

Weirdo, Bobby. "Robert Lopez on the Unhappy Hour, El Vez, the Early Diverse Days of L.A. Punk, and More." Weirdo Music Forever, December 28, 2016. Accessed October 2, 2021. https://www.weirdomusicforever.com/weird-news-and-interviews/2016/12/26/robert-lopez-on-the-unhappy-hour-el-vez-the-early-days-of-la-punk-and-more.

West, Cornel. "The New Cultural Politics of Difference." *October* 53 (1990): 93–109.

Wynter, Leon E. *American Skin: Pop Culture, Big Business, and the End of White Culture*. New York: Crown Publishers, 2002.

Ybarra, Patricia. *Latinx Theatre in the Times of Neoliberalism*. Chicago, IL: Northwestern University Press, 2018.

Zaragoza, Alex. "In Honor of LA Declaring Nov. 10 Morrissey Day, Here's Why Mexicans Love Moz So Damn Much." *Mitú*, November 10, 2017. Accessed July 23, 2018. https://wearemitu.com/street-culture/why-mexicans-love-morrissey/.

Zibart, Eve. "Echoes of Elvis in Memphis." *Washington Post*, B1+, August 14, 1987 (via ProQuest Historical Newspapers, ASU library).

Index

Endnotes are indicated only where the information would not be readily found from the page and are given as page and note number e.g. 150n.31